The Bloomsbury Introduction to Creative Writing

The Bloomsbury Introduction to Creative Writing

Tara Mokhtari

Bloomsbury Academic
An imprint of Bloomsbury Publishing Plc

B L O O M S B U R Y
LONDON • NEW DELHI • NEW YORK • SYDNEY

Bloomsbury Academic
An imprint of Bloomsbury Publishing Plc

50 Bedford Square	1385 Broadway
London	New York
WC1B 3DP	NY 10018
UK	USA

www.bloomsbury.com

**BLOOMSBURY and the Diana logo are trademarks of
Bloomsbury Publishing Plc**

First published in 2015
Reprinted by Bloomsbury Academic 2015

© Tara Mokhtari, 2015

Tara Mokhtari has asserted her right under the Copyright, Designs and
Patents Act, 1988, to be identified as Author of this work.

British Library Cataloguing-in-Publication Data
A catalogue record for this book is available from the British Library.

ISBN: HB: 978-1-4725-7844-0
PB: 978-1-4725-7843-3
ePDF: 978-1-4725-7846-4
ePub: 978-1-4725-7845-7

Library of Congress Cataloging-in-Publication Data
A catalog record for this book is available from the Library of Congress.

Typeset by Fakenham Prepress Solutions, Fakenham, Norfolk NR21 8NN
Printed and bound in Great Britain

Contents

Acknowledgments

The best teachers are a product of the best teachers, and mine included the magnanimous Antoni Jach, Lisa Dethridge, Francesca Rendle-Short, Tony Brown, and Richard Manning.

For their ongoing nurturance of a supportive and collaborative teaching environment which motivated the writing of this book, I thank my Australian colleagues, Michael Hyde, Tom Clark, Ian Syson, John Weldon, and Eloise Brook.

Introduction

On writing

Almost everybody writes. Each day millions of people are writing emails, shopping lists, text messages, memos, diary reminders, and social media interactions. We write notes for other people, notes to ourselves, we write reports and papers for work and school, we write names and phone numbers down on the back of our hands or on napkins, and we write in journals for catharsis. Some of us get other people to write permanent words onto our bodies with ink and needles. We write to communicate, to avoid certain types of communication, to express ourselves, to advocate for others, to be read and not to be read. Very few people who write are writers by profession, but writing permeates our daily lives.

A person becomes a writer because she or he perpetually has *something to say* in a way which is essential to her or his identity and existence. I mention this fundamental (albeit dicey) point here at the beginning of this practical guide to creative writing because the yearning to say something to the world and to be heard is the one thing which cannot be taught in a text book or in a lecture theater. The act of writing a novel or a play or a film to be published or produced—physically filling the empty page with words in ink—is invariably the last phase of the writing process. Before the words come the ideas, obsessions, preoccupations, and thought processes. Then there is the natural impulse to share all those things indiscriminately with anyone who will listen. These are the reasons to become a writer: the ideas and the urge to be heard.

It isn't sufficient to want to be a writer merely for the romance of it, for the ego, for the fame, for the money: mostly because only a very small number of writers achieve the kind of career which affords them any or all of these delicious benefits. Any bona fide writer of books or films or poems will gladly sit down over a whiskey and regale you with yarns of the years or decades of rejections and personal and professional setbacks she endured before having her first volume published or her first film made.

This is not at all to say that having ambitions for becoming a writer are futile; it's just that such ambitions need to come from a very vital part of your being in order to sustain you through what is inevitably a slow-growing and exigent career.

In November of 2012, articles began to emerge about debut novelist Julian Tepper who met his literary hero Philip Roth at a New York deli. Tepper approached Roth who offered this advice:

> Really, it's an awful field … Just torture. Awful. You write and write and you have to throw almost all of it away because it's not any good. I would say just stop now. You don't want to do this to yourself. That's my advice to you.[1]

What is the meaning of this: a prominent writer discouraging his deli protégé from fulfilling his dreams of becoming a writer? The articles published in various newspapers and journals about this apparently outrageous exchange exposed Roth's brazenness to have originated from a place of compassion.

If viewed in a prudential light (as Jane Austen might say), it would be negligent for an influential writer to give a sugary carbonated response when asked for general career advice by a rookie. Beware the famous author who claims that the writer's career is a happy walk in the park. That writer is probably one of three writers in the history of the world who had a stroke of luck so brilliant that she made billions from her first book and is under no pressure from her publishers to do anything more than slouch around basking in her success until such time as she feels like writing something new.

Roth is not the first writer to offer advice in the form of an earnest warning-off. In his poem "So you want to be a writer," Charles Bukowski examines the innumerable factors which hinder good writing, and implores the reader to become a writer only if the compulsion to write is truly immutable:

> if it doesn't come bursting out of you
> in spite of everything,
> don't do it.
> unless it comes unasked out of your
> heart and your mind and your mouth
> and your gut,
> don't do it.[2]

---

[1] Alison Flood, "Philip Roth tells young writer 'don't do this to yourself'," in *The Guardian online edition* (UK: November 16, 2012) [accessed July 1, 2013].
[2] Charles Bukowski, "So you want to be a writer," in *Sifting through the madness for the Word, the line, the way* (New York: HarperCollins, 2009), p. 3.

What is this "it" Bukowski refers to throughout this stanza and over and over again in the remainder of the poem? "It" is the work; the ideas incarnate as words and phrases and metaphors and juicy portrayals of people and place and events and hearts and guts in a piece of prose or poetry. Bukowski's writer is some kind of irrepressible monster from whom "it" spits forth with little regard for politeness or process.

These might seem like discouraging lines of poetry to quote at the beginning of a book about learning how to write, but they should be relatable for students who naturally feel they are already writers. If you want to be a writer it needs to be because you have an irrepressible urge to explore different themes, stories, imaginations, and the complex weirdnesses of being.

In one way it might be fair to say that you either are a writer or you're not, harsh though that may sound. This is not to say that either Bukowski or the author of this book is rejecting the notion of writing as hard work for even the most committed writer. It is hard work—perhaps not all the time, but most of the time. There are many would-be writers the world over who never realized their potential because they didn't take their desire to write seriously and dedicate years of structured and independent study to improving their natural talent. University programs and practical guides like this one are helpful not only because they offer tools and skills you are unlikely to acquire on your own but also because they challenge you to experiment with different creative writing practices, and they force you to write every day. It is also worth considering that the true writer is the one who persists and reaps satisfaction from the work itself rather than the external validation the work might earn, say, from a teacher, publisher, or a literature award judging panel.

It is for reasons around the idea that one either is or is not naturally a writer that debates emerge about the value of university creative writing courses. If a student can't be taught the most important thing about writing—that is, insatiable curiosity and its expressions thereof—why then, in an age when education has become a commodity, offer university degrees which fail to promise a practical career path?

Well, aside from the fact that writers should be nurtured within the academy as much as they should be nurtured within society, it could be argued that writing should be offered in universities if for no other reason than because it is a highly transferrable skill. Every industry relies on strong writers in one way or another. You might not end up being a renowned novelist, but then, you might! You also might work in fields such as media or editing and publishing, applying the skills you developed at university through dedicated study. You might pursue a different career path and use your experiences as material to gradually develop a freelance career in writing. All of these possibilities begin here, with an introduction to a range of different creative writing genres.

Most importantly, though, learning how to shape your ideas into well-crafted pieces of writing is essentially learning how to think critically and creatively at the same time. To imagine all the intricate details of a story is one part of the creative process. To arrange the story's presentation on the page through the manipulation of language, selecting certain words and phrases over others, evoking imagery, cognition, and emotion through grammar, syntax, and literary choices—this process is necessarily as critical as it is creative. And yet, incredibly, all of these things mostly happen simultaneously and almost unconsciously when we sit down to pen a short story or a poem. Any good writing teacher will tell you that learning how to write is tantamount to learning how to think. This point forms the foundation for each of the discussions and exercises in this book.

The key theme of this practical writing guide is the relationship between knowledge derived from experience and the pursuit of writing. The emphasis therefore is on ways into new writings which draw from real life, sensory stimuli, observation, research, guided contemplations, and, of course, your fertile imagination.

By diligently applying these modes of knowing to the conceptualization and production of creative writing, you will begin to see opportunities for new writing in the everyday. You will train your creative brain to see inspiration and material each time you leave the house and go out into the world. In this way you are cultivating your innate writer self; you are feeding your Bukowskiesque writing monster and promoting its hungry, hungry appetite.

So, chances are you are either already a writer, or you are taking this course in creative writing because you are under the illusion that it will be an easy way to earn extra credit for the degree in which you are enrolled. If you come under the former category, you might be wondering how this book is going to help you become a better writer, and that question will be answered shortly. If you come under the latter category, you are very, very wrong. That isn't to say that you won't get a lot out of combining your focal studies with a writing course, only that it won't be an easy task adapting to the highly practical nature of a writing course where you are expected to walk into class, leave the week's baggage at the door and develop characters, plots, settings, themes, and write creatively in a limited time frame, and then immediately afterwards share your work with your peers and your instructor. That entails a whole lot of not falling asleep!

There are some strategies outlined later in this introduction which will help you prepare for the demands of this type of practical creative writing workshop class, but the key is to go into each workshop exercise with a bit of mustered courage and an open (and busy) mind.

The exercises in this book will force you to try new ways of employing the techniques which are essential to the genres of self-writing, fiction, screenwriting, performance writing, poetry composition, writing for digital media, and critique and exegetical writing. All of the exercises provide you with a guided writing scenario or stimulus to inspire you, but you will need to color them with your own imaginations and experiences. You will have to tap into your innate writer self quite quickly in order to embark on each writing exercise with commitment in an effort to make the most out of your workshops. Some of the exercises will inspire you straight away; you'll read them and know immediately what you would like to write about. Other exercises may cause you to draw a total blank, and that's alright, too.

The exercises in Chapter 1: Writing and Knowledge will prepare you for those moments when you come to a new task and can't think of a topic to write about. By the time you make your way through each chapter, you will have engaged in several productive and unusual ways into new pieces of creative writing, and workshopped your ideas and first drafts with your classmates using methods which are designed to illuminate the strengths and weaknesses of your work.

On knowing

The culmination of everything that has happened to you, everything you remember, every *Sherlock Holmes* book you read as a teenager, every news story you watched on the television, every piece of music you ever loved, every poster you pinned to your bedroom wall, every first time, everything that anyone ever told you which you keep locked away in memory stores, every smell and scene from your hometown, the whole lot of it is what forms your knowledge. All of these things are potential starting points for new and original works of literature. More than all of that, though, is the knowledge you derive from the composition of creative writings. New knowledge begins to materialize through the ways you bend your memories and imagine new possibilities in worlds separate from the one you live in.

Simultaneously, the discovery of the process of turning existing knowledge into new knowledge through the written word bears more knowledge still.

A reconciliation of the often contradictory relationship between literary theory and creative writing practice forms the basis for many of the exercises in this book, especially in the chapters on Self-writing, Fiction, and Poetry. Whereas literary theory seeks to evaluate the existing literary text through a variety of modes which are concerned with social and linguistic factors such as historicism, hermeneutics and interpretations through close reading, feminism, critical race theory, and poetics, the creative writing scholar is challenged with the task of articulating the techniques she employed in the process of composition before the text came into being. These techniques include narrative voice, tense, choice of language and sentence structures, the use of dialogue in the exposition of character and plot, and the thematic goals of the creative text.

What this means, in essence, is that the creative writing scholar will depend on existing critical theory to develop rationales for her creative process from a practice-led viewpoint rather than from the viewpoint of a reader who has only the text itself from which to determine the writer's intent. The exercises in this book include introductions to a few basic critical theories alongside practical creative writing techniques, so that you will be able to identify when you are applying what theory in your creative practice. Then, in the last chapter, you will develop strategies for demonstrating the ways in which your creative writing implements existing theory in a critique or an exegesis. The idea here is to introduce creative writing scholarship as an addendum to developing your practical writing skills.

In recent years, criticisms have emerged about the value of terminal Masters programs in Creative Writing in America. Increasingly we are seeing a new demand for the academic rigor and rewards of the far less common Creative Writing PhD program which is prevalent in Australia and consists of a complete creative manuscript and an accompanying scholarly dissertation. In order to prepare undergraduate students like you for potential graduate programs like the Creative Writing PhD, faculties are beginning to introduce scholarly components to their writing subjects. The last chapter in this book on Critique and Exegesis will introduce you to the types of academic writing you might be expected to do as part of your creative writing studies.

Literary theory and the creative practice of "writing what you know"

The exercises in the chapters on Writing and Knowledge and Self-writing ask you to use your everyday life experiences for inspiration for creative writing. This notion in itself indirectly contradicts critical theories on the connection between real life and literature.

In Tzvetan Todorov's examination of Northrop Frye's theory for a system of genres, he posits that:

> The literary text does not enter into a referential relation with the "world", as the sentences of everyday speech often do; it is not "representative" of anything but itself ... Thus the literary text participates in tautology: it signifies itself: "the poetic symbol means primarily itself in relation to the poem."[3]

What are the implications of this idea of literature as something which is independent from everyday utterances? If we are not writing to represent anything other than writing, what is the value in drawing from our experiential and synthetic knowledge to create a literary text? The lesson here is not towards writing practice, but towards an understanding of what the end product of our writing practice should achieve.

Writing a short story, even one which is inspired by real life, is a process of demarcation, beginning with the everyday, and resulting in what is known as "art." This requires the writer to observe life in terms of everyday poetics—the subtle ironies, symbols, metaphors, and everything else which gives deeper and imaginative meaning to the mundane—and then to translate those observations into writing which engages the reader in ways in which the everyday fails to engage us. We sometimes talk about the way a book provides us with escapism from everyday life, even when the book is literary nonfiction or realist in genre. We generally don't get the same effect through everyday conversations in which we are working to comprehend what is being told to us, applying it to our knowledge, and responding to it verbally, pragmatically, and instantly.

In a more direct sense, Frye's allusion to the value of the poetic symbol as meaning 'primarily itself in relation to the poem' is essential to one basic

---

[3] Tzvetan Todorov, "Literary Genres," in *Twentieth-Century Literary Theory: An Introductory Anthology*, Vassilis Lambropoulos and David Neal Miller (eds) (Albany: State University of New York Press, 1987), p. 195.

convention of writing fiction of any genre (but which is usually talked about in relation to science fiction and fantasy genres); this is the importance of creating a believable world which does not necessarily adhere to the conventions of everyday reality, but which is self-sufficient and allows the reader to achieve *suspension of disbelief*. We draw from everyday reality, but we create a new and coherent reality which is confined to the word portrayed within our creative writing project. Once again, this differs from everyday speech which is dependent on the conventions of everyday reality in order to make sense.

In a practical capacity, the exercises in this book ask you to draw from different parts of what constitutes your knowledge, and to pay attention to the poetic details of those different parts to craft short, engaging pieces of creative writing. This means structuring your stories and using literary and poetic techniques to expose your themes, plots, and characters—rather than merely retelling experiences just as you would in conversation with a friend (although you'll do some of that, too).

Knowledge and fiction; truth and lies

It is important to remember that the process of fictionalization is crucial to all our creative writings, even those derived from life experience. Knowledge, as we will discover in the first chapter, is a combination of the truths which are formed through sensory experiences, the things we are told by family, friends, and media, the music and art and films we enjoy, emotional upheavals, and a whole gamut of other factors. All of these things (and more) will contribute to the creative writing you do in this course. But all of these things are necessarily personal parts of us which are merely the starting point for our writing.

By imposing your imagination onto your knowledge, using language, you are engaging in a process of fictionalization which is essential to most of the exercises in this book, and to much of the creative writing you will do in the future.

So, what is the difference between creative writing and lying? Plato rejected poets from his Republic on the grounds that "all poetical imitations are ruinous to the understanding of the hearers, and that the knowledge of their true nature is the only antidote to them,"[4] meaning that literature lies—

---

[4] Plato, *The Republic*, trans. Benjamin Jowlett (Adelaide: ebooks@adelaide, 2012) [accessed July 12, 2013].

it is misleading in its imitations of reality—and, in so doing, it is damaging to its readers. Aristotle's cautious response to this idea is that:

> the instinct of imitation is implanted in man from childhood, one difference between him and other animals being that he is the most imitative of living creatures, and through imitation learns his earliest lessons; and no less universal is the pleasure felt in things imitated ... Imitation, then, is one instinct of our nature ...[5]

Whereas Plato believes in the destructive nature of literature as a fictionalized imitation of life, a concept we embrace in our everyday existence (i.e. that fallacies are destructive), Aristotle flags the importance of imitation to the human experience. We know this from the novels we have read; we are fully aware that they are fiction and yet they have changed our lives in one way or another. We still have things to learn from the texts which we accept as fiction.

The differentiation between imitation in life and imitation of life in literature is what gives the creative writer ultimate freedom in her use of language to craft literary works. To come from a basis of knowledge of the everyday (combined with knowledge of existing literature), and then to create a new world in a piece of writing which is a variation on real life, is a practicable skill. This way of imaginatively representing life through language—as opposed to a faithful representation—is central to many of the exercises in this book. Whereas knowledge is the origin of the writing you will produce here, the way you will manipulate your knowledge through language to create something new will in turn give you new perspectives on your way of thinking.

Tips on attacking the practical exercises

Don't over-think it, don't talk about it

All writers are thinkers. Many writers are introverted, perfectionist, anxious, depressive ... There are countless reasons why, when faced with a writing task and 20 minutes in which to complete it and show it to her peers, the

---

[5] Aristotle, *Poetics*, trans. H. S. Butcher (Adelaide: ebooks@adelaide, 2012) [accessed July 12, 2013].

writer is well within her rights to freak out a little bit—especially when experimenting with unfamiliar forms and genres. Another consideration is that of confidence. In life we are social beings who obtain a sense of validation for our ideas and pursuits from the external world: we seek feedback from our bosses on the job we're doing and we take a friend clothes shopping with us to get their opinion on what looks good. As early career writers, without the benefit of the experience of sharing our drafting process with other writers and editors, it can be intimidating to suddenly be forced into reading aloud something which we scratched out in 20 minutes under pressure.

A common first reaction to exercises like the ones in this book is to consult with your friend or classmate: "What are you writing about? What do you reckon I should do?" Here's the thing about doing that: Don't! Your friend is probably feeling a little confronted by the task at hand, too. How should he know what you should or shouldn't write about? Besides that, these exercises are meant to challenge your usual writing process and give you a breadth of new starting points from which to explore your own unique experiences and concepts. If you attempt an exercise in this book and end up with something which is completely different from what your peers have written—then you're probably doing it right.

So, when you come to a new exercise and you have understood the premise and the instructions, take a minute to relax into what is being asked of you and how you can use the requirements of the exercise to tell the story you want to tell. If you find that you are drawing a blank, revisit the exercises in the first chapter, which are designed to help you organize your thoughts into tangible material which you can use for future writings. If you get through the exercise description and you have an immediate gut reaction to it (as in, it inspires an idea straight away), and you feel ready to start writing: Do it!

If all seems lost, and you have been staring at that blank page for more than five minutes, and the exercises you did in Chapter 1 are failing you, then go for a five-minute walk. Don't get a drink or smoke a cigarette or talk to anybody, just walk for five minutes with the exercise in mind and come back to your blank page fresh, oxygenated and with some new perspective, and then use your remaining time to give the exercise your best shot.

Frame your ideas appropriately according to the demands of the Exercise

The amount of time you allocate to each exercise will vary according to the type and number of steps outlined. In general, an exercise which requires you to come up with one short piece of writing should not take longer than 15 to 20 minutes of combined conceptualizing, planning, and writing time. Most exercises also probably won't span over more than one to two pages of hand-written work.

These limitations of time and space have certain implications for the kind of story you can effectively tell. An idea you have for a novel or a feature-length film, for example, is probably not going to be right for exploring in its entirety within the confines of 20 minutes and two pages. It is highly unlikely that you could fit a character's entire life story into a piece of writing of such a short length, either (although, arguably, not impossible if you're being wildly creative about it).

Likewise, it would be very difficult to do justice to extremely serious and complex themes such as sexual abuse, racism, or war, with only 20 minutes' combined thinking and composing time. That is not to say you should avoid these sorts of big ideas altogether, but it may help to keep the topics you explore in these exercises relatively simple, at least until you get the hang of the process. Figure out how to frame your stories so that they reveal enough to satisfy your readers without overwhelming them with too much information in too short a space of time. This means thinking carefully about where your stories really begin and end. For example, if you want to write about the disintegration of a complicated relationship, rather than starting when the two characters meet and working your way through to the break-up, just pick the one major turning point event where things changed forever between the two characters and write about that. Allow the surrounding context and details of the characters' relationship to emerge suggestively through your description of the now. The origins of the relationship's downfall can be exposed in bits and pieces through that single coherent event.

If you are grappling with a really difficult issue like sexual abuse, it can be useful to focus on one tangible part of the issue. For example, if you want to write about somebody being attacked, you could focus on the moment while the abuse is taking place when the protagonist enters self-preservation mode and stops physically fighting off the attacker in the hope that the trauma will end sooner. This is a way of exploring one essential fragment of a much larger issue in a way that avoids posturing, preaching, or just flat out telling the reader how something like that feels. Instead, you are able to expose something very overwhelming in a way which puts the reader in the protagonist's shoes for a moment. It still won't be an easy read, nor should it be, but it will allow you to touch on something important in a short word length without trivializing the experience or the issues surrounding it.

Give each genre a chance, even if it's not really your bag

Each of the chapters in this book deals with a different literary genre. Although there are traditions and practices which are unique to each genre, some of them also share certain conventions. For example, characterization techniques are relevant to fiction-writing, self-writing, and scriptwriting. Beyond the obvious ways in which different literary genres are linked, there are certain skills you will learn which are unique to one genre, but which will strengthen your techniques in other genres.

In the chapter on screenwriting, you will learn how to write action for screen, which is usually a challenge for writers of fiction prose because it demands a commitment to physical present tense description without elaborate internal dialogue. Some fiction writers find this style restrictive and clinical at first. You are forced to think visually and show your characters' innermost feelings and motivations through their physical behaviors. Despite being tricky and probably an unnatural way to write for many people, if you can master this technique, you can apply it to your exposition in fiction prose as a way of getting out of your characters' heads and into their real worlds, to make for a more compelling read. Likewise, the economy of language which you will practice in the chapter on Poetry will help you in your editing of other genres by getting you to think about how to choose the right words to communicate your intended meaning, and ways in which you can evoke a striking image and associated emotion and tone through succinct language. In the chapter on self-writing you will learn new ways of drawing inspiration from your life experience in all of your creative writing practice.

The chapter dedicated to critique and exegesis is intended to help you in your academic treatment of creative writing. Although exegetical writing is not creative writing per se, this chapter will act as a companion to your scholarly practice-led research and writing which is progressively more integral to any undergraduate and graduate creative writing program of study. You might be tempted to ask: Why do I need to write essays alongside my creative work? Shouldn't the work speak for itself? It is true that your creative work should speak for itself, but it is also important for the author to be able to critically analyze and discuss the creative choices she or he has made in the composition of the work in relation to both creative writing and literary scholarship and the work of other creative writers who have either directly or indirectly influenced the work.

While it is important not to think excessively on these things while you are in the process of writing creatively, it is equally as important to be able to look at your writing after it is finished and understand what it is you have done and to be able to talk about all of its intricate parts—not only in creative writing academia but also in the "real world" of publishing and editing. Writers are not always confident speakers, and they are also not always able to naturally talk about their work in an objective way. Learning how to research and write exegeses on your creative writing is the most comprehensive way of learning how to talk about your work to other people in a way which contextualizes and elucidates its finer points for others to understand. This skill is going to be crucial, not only to your further creative writing studies and your contribution to creative writing scholarship but also to pitching your writing to publishers and agents and having meaningful and productive collaborations with editors.

The reality of being a professional writer is that, over the course of your career, you will have the opportunity to write across many different genres. Think about all your favorite novelists; invariably all of them have also written poetry or plays or articles or films or nonfiction. I began my writing career in theater, first as an independent co-operative theater company founder and then as a commissioned playwright. Then I changed my focus to poetry and completed postgraduate studies in Creative Writing. I wrote a music documentary for television in 2006. Then I became a reviewer, translations editor, and I had articles and papers published. Eventually I had my first book of poetry published and then I co-edited a book of essays. Later I started working on a novel. This is the life of a writer! The more genres you can comfortably work within, the more opportunities you have to work.

So, even when you come to a genre which has previously never appealed to you, consider that, at the very least, the new skills you will master in that genre will almost certainly positively affect your other writings, and, at the very most, you may find an unexpected new passion.

Read! For goodness' sake!

What you will find as you move through the exercises in each chapter is that there are only a few short examples included in this book from existing literature. A snippet of one or two paragraphs from something written by the great George Orwell is nowhere near enough to understand the value of the full text. It is, however, just enough to exemplify how you might interpret the exercise for which the example is provided. It is up to you to locate the books, poems, and articles that grab you and read them in full.

Some of the tasks in the following chapters are reading assignments. However, they are reading assignments of an unusual kind because they do not assume to tell you what you should read. Instead you will be given some guidelines and asked to research and select your own readings. This is intentional. The design here is to give you some autonomy in the development of your unique voice as a writer, to dig deeper for inspiration where you intuit you are most likely to find it, and hopefully also to reinvigorate your enthusiasm for reading. You are told what to read enough in literature classes, and necessarily so; there is no need to force too many specific books on you in a creative writing course provided you are reading something. Anything. Really. Go on. Try it.

Be prepared to share

The exercises in this book suggest that you collaborate in study groups with your peers to get feedback on your drafts. As early career writers, you may tend to have limited opportunities and even less desire to show your work to other people—we all write stories and poems which are relegated to the bottom drawer of our desks to gather dust for all time. Occasionally we write something for school that is assessed by a teacher. Occasionally we write something for a friend or a lover. Once in a while we might feel like showing a new story to our parents or siblings to get their feedback. These writings we pen in our teenage years and young adulthoods are essential to both our personal development and also to cultivating our passion for words. Sometimes in the process we strike gold and write something truly beautiful, even if nobody else ever sees it.

But, here's the thing: ultimately, writers write to be read. Yes. Otherwise, why would we bother taking the time to finesse the craft of verbalizing our thoughts and ideas and arranging them on a page? Why not just have the great idea and let it evaporate in the heat of the rest of our day? Or mention it to a colleague over lunch to avoid an awkward silence? Why go to all the trouble of writing it down if nobody will read it?

Most of the exercises in this book have workshop components that require you to share your writing with your peers. In many cases this will entail giving your freshly penned, rougher-than-rough drafts to near-perfect strangers and having them discuss your work. Shock! Horror!

Some students will revel in the opportunity to have instant readers, other will hope a black hole will open up in the floor directly below their desk and suck them into oblivion before they are forced to hand their writing over to the scrutiny of others. If you are in the former group, it is important to evenly distribute your enthusiasm for the workshopping process between sharing your own work and listening and responding to the work of your classmates. If you are in the latter group, try not to panic. Bear in mind that your class-mates are all in the same boat—everyone has had the same amount of time in which to complete their writing exercise, everyone is new at this process, everyone is nervous about showing their work to others, and everyone is working towards a common goal: to use the exercises to develop new creative writing skills. At no other time in your writing career will you be in a position of total equality with the people who are reading your work. In the future, the first people to read your work will inevitably have a degree of power over your career: publishers, editors, agents, publicists, assessors, examiners, etc. Now is the moment to practice giving your work away after it is written, because you are in a safe place. Your peers are not going to judge you for your work because they have been under the same pressure you've been under.

If all this reassurance and reason is not enough to persuade you to participate actively in the workshop process—well then, you just might have to go against your instincts and simply make yourself do it a few times until you feel more comfortable about it. It might be painstaking and frightening, but it will be worth the initial discomfort ultimately to learn how to allow your writing to be read.

The exercises depend on the workshop components for the work you produce to be fully realized and ready for further drafting. Take the feedback you receive from your peers seriously, but choose the comments which are the most constructive to inform subsequent rewrites of the piece. It may be useful to think of specific questions about your writing to ask readers of the first draft, before beginning each workshop session, as a way of directing the kind of feedback you receive. You should also note down the responses you receive from your workshop group so you can revisit them later if you need to.

Finally, keep all of your work ...

... Even the work you are dissatisfied with. There could be opportunities in the future to rework the exercises and turn them into complete stories, scripts, essays, or poems. Alternatively, you might rewrite and polish several of the pieces you come up with through these exercises and begin to collate a comprehensive writing folio which you could use later for job or study applications.

1

Writing and Knowledge

The exercises in this chapter are designed to help you organize your ideas into tangible material for new writings. You can use the products of these exercises to help you come up with ideas for the work you do in future chapters.

Everything is potential material for the writer. Students are often advised in writing classes to "write what you know," but what does this actually entail?

According to Immanuel Kant, knowledge is derived from experience—both empirical and synthetic.[1] This essentially means that the ways in which we ascribe experience to knowledge is partly about first-hand sensory experiences, and partly about applying our judgments (which arguably are also originally derived from prior sensory experiences) to those sensory experiences.

What this means for our writing is that what we know is not restricted to the things which have happened to us in our lives; what we know extends to things like the stories we have heard from our families and friends, the research we do in various fields of work and study, the way certain pieces of music affect our moods, the things we assume about strangers we see in the street, the ways we interpret our relationships and the relationships of others, and the language with which we express ourselves and understand each other.

For example, when I was 19 years old, I met a famous guitarist at a concert and the band ended up back at my house after the show. The guitarist, as it turns out, had been a junkie for five years until he overdosed and wound up in hospital a few months earlier. He said something to me about his experience which stuck with me for the rest of my life: "A drug addict will

---

[1] Immanuel Kant, *Critique of Pure Reason*, unabridged edition, trans. Norman Kemp Smith (New York: St Martin's Press, 1965), p. 41.

steal your wallet and disappear for a few days; a junkie will steal your wallet and help you look for it." I took this explanation of his experience to be fundamentally about how the desperation of heroin addiction (in contrast with other drug addictions) makes it easy for a person to lie to himself, and how a person's whole identity becomes wrapped up in getting the next hit. It was a highly emotionally charged conversation to have with a stranger about his life experience and the conclusions he had drawn from them, and his revelations made us close friends very quickly. I have never taken heroin myself, nor have I ever stolen anybody's wallet, but this story told to me at 3 a.m. one morning c. 2001 forms part of what I would refer to as my knowledge. I unconsciously applied my prior judgments about dishonesty, desperation, reckless abandon, money, drugs, friendship, and the nature of reverie and regret to a 25-word story told to me by a new friend, conjured meaning out of it, and committed it to memory and later to words on a page.

The following exercises ask you to think critically about some of the things which constitute your knowledge. These are things which you might not think about every day, but which play some part in making you who you are and what you understand about the world and about people.

Keep the work you complete in this chapter somewhere close at hand; it will help you if you find yourself getting stuck in the chapters which follow.

The *Writers' Block* Myth

If you have ever sat in front of a blank page with a blank mind and the pressure of needing to produce a piece of writing, then you know what people refer to when they whinge and whine about *writers' block*. The author of this book rejects the principle of writers' block, and here is why.

First, as soon as the writer has everything she needs to proceed with the process of putting words down in coherent and connected sentences and paragraphs, nothing will stop him or her. If you have a project to write and the first thing you do is sit in front of a fresh new Word document, then you are doing things in the wrong order. You need to prepare yourself for any literary undertaking before you try to start writing. Different projects require different types of preparation. You may need to go to the library to research and read first. You may need to plan the broader structure by plotting chapters or subtitles or a storyline. You may need to sit down and collaborate with somebody who you know is the right person to bounce ideas off of. But beyond all these practical methods of preparing to write something, you also need to do that other thing that writers cringe about all the time: you need to procrastinate! Yes. Why? Because what you are actually doing when you are cleaning your whole apartment top to bottom, walking the dog for the ninth time in one day, making another cup of coffee, or taking your third shower for the day is that you are allowing your mind to synthesize all the components of the project, both consciously and subconsciously. You are thinking about how the final product should read, you are thinking about a piece of research that you know you want to work in but aren't sure how to, you are thinking about the criteria you need to meet, you are even processing your feelings on the content and the task itself, and what it means for you personally and professionally. So, if you have sat down in front of the empty page before you are ready, then naturally you aren't going to be ready to start writing straight away; that is not a block—that is simply a premature attempt at beginning to write. Some projects take years of gradual conceptualization (like a novel or a thesis); others take one minute of focused thinking (like the exercises in this book).

Secondly, there is nothing useful about the term *writers' block*. As soon as you start fretting that the reason no words are coming out is because you are irrationally blocked somehow, you are loading anxiety on top of your state of unpreparedness. This is not going to help you. In most cases, if you decide to either go for a walk, or do some reading, or cook a meal, as long as you make a deliberate effort to think about the best way into the piece that you want to write before sitting down again in front of that looming blank page, you will come back to it ready to start something. In some cases, especially when you want to write something which is especially personal and private, or something which requires you to do a bit more living or a bit more writing in other areas before you can do it justice, you can begin to collect your ideas slowly over a period of time while you work on other projects for which you are more ready. Regardless of the circumstance, there is no literal block, there is no immovable obstruction between you and your words, and so abandoning the notion of *writers' block* could be the difference between completing something and never starting it in the first place.

So, the essential element to overcoming the Anti-artist Formerly Known as Writers' Block is often just time and rumination. But what happens when you need to pump something out in a limited timeframe and you have too many distractions or no idea of quite where to start? Well, the natural antidote to not writing anything is writing *something*.

Exercise

This exercise is called Stream of Consciousness Writing (sometimes it is referred to as Free Writing). There are many different approaches to this exercise. Some authors have used stream of consciousness as a method for writing entire novels. Ideally, you might begin all your writing tasks with five minutes of stream of consciousness writing. You can do it on a regular basis to strengthen your ability to write without censoring your thoughts or trying to grammatically alter your natural voice.

This exercise is timed and it should take exactly five minutes to complete. The premise of Stream of Consciousness is simply to put pen to paper and write continuously anything which enters your mind without censoring yourself or trying to use perfect spelling and grammar. Your goal is to fill as much of the page as possible in a timed five-minute period. If you look at that terrifyingly white page and your imagination doesn't kick in straight away and you think, "what the hell am I going to write, what am I even doing here," then you should write the words, "what the hell am I going to write, what am I even doing here," and keep writing exactly what pops into your head continuously for five minutes. Soon your creative consciousness will emerge from the panic or tiredness or distractions of the day and you will begin to come up with some very interesting spontaneous writing.

You don't need to show anybody what you write in Stream of Consciousness exercises. The point of it is to practice deliberate awareness of your conscious thoughts and allow them onto the page without fear of judgment.

Focused procrastination

'Focused procrastination' may sound like an oxymoron, but it is an art form unto itself! The following series of tasks will help you practice dedicating the time you spend performing otherwise mundane activities to conceptualizing a piece of creative writing with a little help from one of the tidiest poetic forms: the haiku.

A haiku is a short poem which originated in Japan. It consists of only three lines, and usually deals with themes of nature and life. Because the haiku form is so short, it inevitably describes a single tangible image with a corresponding mood or tone. This requires the poet to consider the order of information presented in the haiku. For example, here is a haiku called "Blowing Stones" by the Japanese master poet, Matsuo Basho (note that it is a translation from the Japanese, and so the syllable scheme is not consistent with the English haiku standard):

> Blowing stones
> along the road on Mount Asama,
> the autumn wind.[2]

Here the image is of the windy road on the mountain in autumn. The mood might be described as sombre or solitary, the autumn wind blowing stones almost the same way a person might kick a can while walking along a path. The subject of the poem is not revealed explicitly until the last line, but it is alluded to through the object in the first line. Implementing innovative ways of exposing subject matter is a feature of the haiku form.

Traditional Japanese haiku (or hokku) consists of a total of 17 "on", which loosely translates to "syllables" in English. The first line has five "on", the second line has seven "on", and the third line has five 'on'. English language haiku is a little more lax about syllable counts, but it can help with composition and memorization in this particular exercise to restrict your haiku to the approximate breakdown of five syllables for the first and third lines, and seven for the second line.

Exercise

This task will get you to practice writing without writing. You could do it at home while you are doing laundry or some other mundane task. You could do it while you are in transit on public transport or in the car or walking through the city.

Your task is to compose a haiku poem in your head while you are away from your desk, and memorize it. You will need to keep it in your mind for one week before committing it to paper.

---

[2] Matsuo Basho, "Blowing Stones," in *Short Poems*, Jean Elizabeth Ward (ed.), trans. Robert Hass (Lulu.com, 2009) http://books.google.com.au/books/about/Short_Poems.html [accessed August 18, 2013], p. 18.

are doing some regular daily activity, compose a haiku. The haiku needs to be inspired by a scene from your everyday life. It needs to be three lines long and adhere to the conventions of English haiku form. Begin to compose your haiku and try to memorize it. Recite it aloud. Tell it to a friend. You can modify it as you think more about it over the course of the week by rearranging the lines, replacing adjectives with more relevant or accurate nouns, tightening the syllable count, and playing with the communication of the image you want to convey. Keep the haiku in your mind, but do not write it down.

After having mentally worked on your haiku over the course of about a week, write it down in its final polished version. If you happened to get really into the exercise and composed a few haikus, then write them all down now.

Workshop

Share your haiku with your study or workshop group and talk about your process. Was it difficult to compose something without being able to look at it and scrutinize how it appears on the page? Was it then difficult to remember it? Did you think of your haiku at strange times during the week—for example, before falling asleep at night, or in the shower, or at dinner with friends? When did you find you were thinking about it most clearly? Did you find yourself mentally writing lots of haikus during the week instead of just one? And how might this exercise of writing when you are not writing help you in other writing projects?

Knowing

Everything you *know* combines to form your life and your personality. In your writing you will inevitably draw from many of the things which occupy your mind and your attention at various stages in your life. The older we get, the more knowledge we acquire and the more diverse our experiences become. What you might have written about in the first grade at primary school was probably quite different from what you want to write about now—even if you are reflecting on a moment from your childhood: your perspectives have changed.

One of the things I knew before I was ten was that my family was a little bit different from most of my classmates' families. We spoke a different language at home, we ate different food, and most of our relatives were overseas and I never got to see them much. This made me feel a little bit left out of certain things at school sometimes and I wished my home life was more like my friends'.

I now know that my heritage is responsible for my affinity with poetry, my appreciation of other cultures, and my ability to learn other languages. Growing up bilingual has enriched my writing practice in ways I probably can't objectively imagine. I also now have a Persian tattoo on my arm from a book of poetry by Sohrab Sepehri which my mother gave me, which reads: "Live large, and independent, and modest, and unyielding." Finally, I have inherited something of a travellers' gene from my parents, which has meant that I've been able to meet the cousins and aunts and uncles whom I grew up missing.

Exercise

Write a list of five things you "knew" before you were ten years old. You might outline each thing in a few short sentences.

Once you have your list of five things, write a short one-paragraph response to each "knowing" from your perspective as an adult.

Workshop

Share with your workshop group one of the things you wrote about. The point of this workshop is simply to listen and to be heard. Take this opportunity to reflect, as a group, on how it felt to separate what you once knew with what you now know, and how you think your perspective on some of the topics you wrote about might continue to change and develop as you get older and, say, have your own children or grandchildren, or begin your career.

Exercise

Write a list of ten things you "know" which you have acquired through first-hand or second-hand experience, and the ways in which you have imposed your judgment on those things. They could be moments in your life when you had a revelation, stories told to you by family or friends or teachers, what it feels like to be in a physical fight or a car crash, books, music, or artworks which influence you, your preference in fashion and how you came to it, your first crush (mine was on the red Teenage Mutant Ninja Turtle when I was four years old). An example of this is given above in my description of meeting the famous guitarist when I was in my late teens and the thing he said about being a junkie, which stuck with me. You should be able to sum each of the ten things up in no more than three or four sentences.

Workshop

Share your list with your workshop group, and reflect on the process of verbalizing some of the things in your life which you might have previously taken for granted. Did you find any patterns in the ways in which you ascribe experience to your knowledge? Was it difficult to remember details in some instances? If so, how did you compensate for this? How do you think that affects what you have learned from that experience? Do you think if somebody else experienced some of the things you did they might take it in a totally different way?

Memory

As John Slattery said in an Interview Mag interview, "Memories are just stories we tell ourselves about the past ..."[3] In a sense, the way we string together our memories to formulate our sense of identity is the first and last story we ever write. We depend on a sequence of significant events

---

[3] Katie Fischer, "John Slattery is a Natural," Interview Mag www.interviewmagazine.com/film/john-slattery-in-our-nature [accessed June 13, 2014].

which happened to us at various ages to tell us who we are, what we know about the world, why we believe in the things we do, where our attitudes to different things came from. These events start with our earliest memories.

Until I was around seven years old I lived next door to a little girl who was my age and we used to play together almost every day. We pulled out two wooden posts from the backyard fence which separated our houses and we would call out to each other when we wanted company, then climb through the fence for the day's adventure. This is a memory which defines my life between the ages of about four and seven, which was when my family moved away. Why does it stick with me? Well, it was the first time in my life that I established a sense of community in my neighborhood for myself. As an adult, community is something which I value, and it might have started the day my little friend and I discovered a way to connect with each other independently whenever we wanted to.

Exercise

This one is about consolidating memories which consciously define your experience at various stages in your life. We all exercise our memories in different ways, and the things we remember in relation to certain times and places are often the things which we use to explain our vision of the present.

The following is a list of approximate age groups. For each one, write down one memory which defined that time in your life, and why those memories stuck with you: birth to age 4; age 5 to age 9; age 10 to age 13; age 14 to age 17; age 18 to age 21 ... And if you can keep going, write one memory from every five years thereafter. Each memory and its consequence should not be longer than one paragraph.

Exercise

The above kind of "letter to my sixteen-year-old self" has been done before by numerous professional and amateur writers in many different formats. Your task is to write an alphabetized list of key words pertaining to your life and an accompanying piece of advice to yourself about each word. Write one for every letter of the alphabet.

Example

Here is the first part of my alphabetized "letter to my sixteen-year-old self".

Dear Tara,

A is for art. Just because you're better at writing doesn't mean you shouldn't experiment and learn painting and sculpture.

B is for bastards. The world is mostly populated with these. Some of them are quite charming and attractive – beware.

Speaking of which, B is also for boys. Pretty much all the ones you secretly like like you back. So, don't be afraid to talk to them.

C is censoring yourself to please others. Don't do it. It's bad for your writing and you'll inevitably disappoint those people somehow anyway.

D is for depression. Be prepared to conquer this over and over again for the rest of your life. And make the most out of the times when you're alright.

E is for emancipation. You'll achieve it sooner than you think and after it happens the world will be your oyster. You'll also swallow it whole and get food poisoning from it.

F is father. Nothing changes in that department; your relationship will always be the same. The sooner you learn to give yourself what you think you need from him, the better.

G is for girlfriends. You need to get more of them. They're very good value.

H is for hair. Don't perm yours a second time, at least not until the first perm has completely grown out.

The idea here is using letters as prompts for memories about past anxieties, insecurities and missteps in life. Not all of these are serious or life changing, but all of them contribute to the details of my life story in some way. The details of our lives are the things that make our experiences unique and interesting.

Your writer self

The next exercise is called "Angel versus Devil." A few variations on this exercise exist in other books and on the web. The point of it is to consciously break out of your polite, social self, and activate your ruder, franker, writer self. Most good writing does not work because it makes the reader comfortable. Most good writing works because it says outright what we ponder in private and in doing so makes us feel validated and human. This means that as often and as proudly as possible we need to—as poet and publisher Lawrence Ferlinghetti put it—"subvert the dominant paradigm."[4]

Although, in its original poetical context, Ferlinghetti was talking about how a writer has a responsibility to draw attention to and challenge socially accepted principles and policies, to subvert paradigms requires us to regularly think outside of our daily politics to find the roots of the anxieties which force us behave in certain ways. For example, say you want to catch a bus from your home into another part of town, and after you get on and pay the fare you go to look for a seat and find that there is only one other passenger on the bus. What do you do? Chances are you don't go and sit next to that one other passenger. Chances are you will instinctively pick a seat on your own a comfortable distance away from that other passenger. Then what happens when the bus stops again a few blocks away and another passenger gets on? The third passenger will likely pick a seat which is an equally comfortable distance away from both you and the first passenger. This demonstrates the politics which exist in our mundane everyday activities. We behave politely, we behave in a way which will establish a basic degree of trust between ourselves and the people we share spaces with, we often only speak to strangers when we have an excuse to do so, and then we rarely open with, "Hey mate, your girlfriend is a hottie. Do you think you might be punching above your weight? You also look about twenty years older than her—you must make a lot of money! Say, are you in banking?"

This is all to avoid confrontation and to conform to our surroundings. It is learnt behavior. As children we behaved very differently in public. We were free from an awareness of dominant social paradigms which force us to act in certain ways. The older we get, for better or worse, we become encumbered by an awareness of social norms.

As writers we need to find ways of going deeper than the superficial politeness of daily activities, otherwise our writing lacks sincerity and becomes as mundane and disinterested as the act of catching a suburban bus—which might be alright, but only if you are forcing your reader to sit right on top of the only other passenger on board and see out what happens!

---

[4] Lawrence Ferlinghetti, *These Are My Rivers: New & Selected Poems 1955-1993* (New York: New Directions, 1994), p. 13.

Although the object of this exercise is to tap into your own inner "Angel" and "Devil" so that you can start thinking about how to embrace your darker side, in many novels and short stories there is a complex tension between a character's internal workings and the ways in which they modify their "Devil" self in their interactions with other characters. A literary example of this tension between the polite "Angel" self and the less socially acceptable "Devil" self is George Orwell's character Gordon Comstock in the book *Keep the Aspidistra Flying*.[5] Gordon scrimps and scrounges every penny, obsesses about his state of poverty, but his pride in being able to fit into the society who he begrudges so much for the irrational value it places on the idea of being able to "make a good living" won't allow him to ever take handouts or let a friend buy his beer. We see the tension between Gordon's public life and his private life, which causes a lot grief for Gordon and for everyone around him. However, Orwell dedicates the overwhelming bulk of the narrative to Gordon's compulsive obsessing over money and lifestyle—we spend far more time with his inner "Devil" than we do being exposed to his politer "Angel" self, because that is what is really interesting about the character of Gordon Comstock.

But it doesn't have to stop there. Sometimes tapping into our "Devil" or our impolite selves can lead us into the realm of the delightfully absurd. A former student of mine once wrote a short story assignment about a man who always wore a helmet everywhere he went. This makes him stick out, and so he feels quite isolated his whole life, until one day he walks into a cafe and meets a waitress who, incredibly, also walks around with a helmet on all day. In a sense, although the helmet functions as a symbol for the ways in which everyone is a little bit exceptional and vulnerable, its omnipresence means that we stay with the protagonist's private and socially unacceptable self the whole way through the story until the very end when he finds some validation and understanding from another character. My student tapped into the awkward truth of trying to find somebody who can love us for who we are by merging a bit of manifest madness with the mundane facade of daily life.

---

[5] George Orwell, *Keep the Aspidistra Flying* (Florida: Harcourt Inc, 1956).

Exercise

Draw a line down the centre of your page. Write "Angel" at the top of the first column, and "Devil" at the top of the second column.

Under the column you have labeled "Angel," write a list of ten things you do in an average week where you are making some kind of effort to *fit in*. This could be sitting on your own on the bus, being nice to customers at the cafe where you work, regularly calling that friend who always seems to be having some crisis or another, dressing up for a night out, etc.

Now, under the column "Devil," for each "Angel" thing you wrote, note down what you really think or feel about having to do those things and the equal opposite action or private thought you have in relation to each "Angel" thing on your list. This could be the urge to sit down at a table at work and take a fork and start picking at your customer's food, telling your friend that actually she is the common denominator in all her many life dramas, or wishing you could skip the preparations and go out completely naked one night.

Embracing the strange

Another part of "subverting the dominant paradigm" is looking outside of ourselves to embrace the stranger aspects of social life.

Once in the electronics district of Osaka in Japan, I walked right past an old man masturbating on the side of the street under his baggy old jeans. On another occasion on a tram in Melbourne, Australia, I witnessed a very large man begin to squeal, apparently out of the blue before standing up and slapping another passenger on the back of the head. In New York's East Village, I was at my favorite spot with friends when two girls who were clearly underage and very drunk began screaming into the window of our bar that the cops were going to arrest them.

Perhaps the masturbating man in Osaka had been on the streets so long he was genuinely convinced he was actually invisible. And maybe the squealing man realized that the man he slapped was, in fact, the devil incarnate out to cause the tram to short-circuit and crash. Perhaps the underage girls neglected to mention that they'd actually just taken out a pact to murder all of their boyfriends and that's why they were sure the cops were after them. I could explore any of these ideas in some detail.

Exercise

This exercise is about embracing the absurd.

Think about times when you have witnessed the shocking behavior of strangers. Make a list of five instances when you've seen something which genuinely shocked you, even if just for a moment.

Once you have your list, impose your imagination onto the characters you've written about and try to find a subjectively "logical" but absurd explanation for what that person was doing. The idea here is to use the real person as inspiration for a fictional character (not to make fun of, or cast wild aspersions on the real person's character).

For each of your five instances, write a paragraph which would explain your characters' motivations for behaving the way they did, within the realm of the absurd universe you create for them.

Workshop

Share with your workshop group your favorite observation of shocking behavior.

After each person reads, have a brief discussion on how the now-fictionalized subject of the real-life shocking behavior ended up wherever it was that you observed them. Imagine where they might have directly come from? What might have happened to them a week earlier? What might they be doing right now?

Once you have explored some of the possibilities, you can share the absurd situation you came up with to explain the shocking behavior, and see if it fits in with the fictional history your workshop group came up with for your subject.

Exercise

This one is about knowledge through language and communication.

Just like the guitarist junkie story mentioned earlier in this chapter, often the things we know are things which are told to us by others and which stay in our minds verbatim for a long time. Sometimes these come to us in one-off conversations with friends. Other times they are a line of song lyrics, or a quote from a book or an interview. Sometimes they are things which have been repeated to us over and over at various times in our lives by a parent or sibling.

Come up with a list of ten quotes which have informed your life in some way, and write them down verbatim. You might be surprised how many quotes you can reel off word for word without having to try too hard to remember them. Each quote should not be longer than one or two sentences.

Then, pick your favorite quote and write a short piece describing how you heard it, who said it or wrote it, what stage of your life you were in at that time, and what prior judgments you ascribed to your understanding of the quote. This shouldn't take longer than ten minutes.

Workshop

This workshop is an improvisation exercise.

One person begins by reading out one of their quotes. If you find that you have a quote written down which relates to the quote you have just heard from your group mate, then you should quickly respond by reading out your corresponding quote. Then another group member needs to respond to your quote with one of their quotes. You should move from quote to quote without pausing if possible. The idea is to create kind of an abstract conversation with your quotes to see how each one is interpretable in relation to the judgments of others and the ways in which your group mates associate your key words and ideas with their own. Keep shouting out quotes in response to the quotes of your group mates until you have used all of them once.

Emotion as material

Often the inspirations which drive our creative writing are those intense but intangible and pesky experiences we call *emotions*. From an early age, and especially into adolescence, we learn to use writing for catharsis; that is, we learn to translate our intangible emotions into language and record it either for ourselves or for somebody we trust with our innermost feelings. This kind of writing is best suited to journals or letters, but these days it quite regularly pops up on our Facebook and Twitter feeds. What is this compulsion we have to disseminate our most personal emotions through language? How does cathartic writing actually function to help the writer? And does catharsis have a place in writing literature outside of journals, letters, and status updates?

In some ways, cathartic writing is similar to talking about our emotions with another person. The intangibility of emotions renders the experience of them overwhelming and hard to understand, at times. It helps to pull the emotions out of yourself and place them in the context of real life in order to gain some perspective on how big or life-changing they really are. Quite often when we elect to talk about our feelings with somebody, all we really want is to be heard—that is to say, we don't need our friends to give us their analysis of our innermost experiences, we just need them to listen. In the case of blurting out our frustrations via social media, there is a sense that we have released some pent-up emotion out of our minds and into the ether. It is easy to forget who is actually reading our posts and even easier to forget that anyone can respond and disagree with us, misunderstand us, judge us, or invalidate what we are feeling. Essentially, while cathartic writing is helpful to the writer, unless it is carefully crafted or intended for a specific readership, it generally won't make for a very satisfying read.

However, this does not mean that emotion can't make for an inspiring starting point for a piece of creative writing. It just means that, in order for the emotion to translate effectively into a literary work, you need to consider the more tangible aspects of the emotional experience and apply your creative writing techniques as you would normally, rather than limiting yourself to diary-style writing which can be solipsistic and ultimately irrelevant to your readers.

The other important connection between emotions and creative writing is that all of the characters you conjure and write about are necessarily emotional beings, one way or another. If they weren't, they would have very little motivation to act and react within the plot unless they are bona fide psychopaths with almost purely intellectual motivations (but, even then, they are likely to experience things like frustration or anger). Like real people, characters are often driven almost entirely by their emotions. Sometimes it is useful to draw from the emotions you have experienced which caused you to spring into action and do something you might not have done had you cared less.

For example, in Charles Dickens's novel, *Great Expectations*,[6] Miss Havisham's jilted heartbreak motivates her action of manipulating Estella into breaking Pip's heart in a deluded effort to reap revenge on all men. Had she not felt this heartbreak so deeply, she would have had no motivation to act in such a way. Dickens demonstrates his knowledge of those emotions by writing such a convincing and evocative character. In order to adequately portray such complex emotions, Dickens surrounds the character of Miss Havisham with richly symbolic images. She never changed out of the wedding dress she wore the day she was left at the altar and she lived in a rich but almost haunted house. In these two descriptions alone, Miss Havisham's overwhelming jilted heartbreak is exposed in tangible ways which depend upon the reader's imagination and ability to interpret their symbols, while allowing for a necessary degree of mystery about her most internal workings which are essential to the telling of the story.

Exercise

Think about the ways in which emotions sometimes manifest in objects or scenery. For example, there is something inherently lonely about a child's stuffed bear which is poorly looked after and abandoned, and there is something hopeful about the first shaft of sunlight to emanate from between rainclouds after a storm. Think of the image of an object or a scene which you might associate with each of the following emotions, and write them down in one or two concise sentences:

Loneliness; hopefulness; regret; anticipation; alarm; desire; angst; fear; belonging.

---

[6] Charles Dickens, *Great Expectations* (London: Penguin Books, 2012).

Workshop

Choose one of the objects or scenes you have described, and, without revealing which emotion it is meant to elicit, read it aloud. It is up to your workshop group to guess which of the emotions you were writing about.

2

Writing the Self

Self-writing encompasses more than just autobiographical texts. Self-writing extends to genres such as the personal essay and reflective writing, as well as elements of journalistic feature writing, and creative nonfiction. The exercises in this chapter will show you some techniques and starting points for all of these genres, and the thing they all have in common is that you—the human behind the writer—are the protagonist and/or the narrator in each piece you will produce. The stories you write here will come from your life and your point of view, which means that, for now, you don't have a fictional protagonist or narrator to hide behind. Whereas with other literary forms we usually accept that the writer and the characters within text are separate and exclusive entities, self-writing puts the writer into the text alongside the other characters. The move away from strictly fictional genres (in which a little bit of imagination goes all the way down the rabbit hole and deep into your created Wonderland) means that the subject matter for the exercises in this chapter will draw exclusively from your life experience.

Students of creative writing since the beginning of time have been advised by professors to "write what you know." The interpretation of this advice is commonly, but perhaps inaccurately, that the student should limit her writing to first-hand experience. While first-hand experience is an important starting point for much of what you write, it isn't everything. The exercises and discussions in the chapter on Writing and Knowledge demonstrate that knowledge reaches far beyond the confines of the more obvious examples we can give of things that constitute first-hand experience.

We are now beginning to redefine the previously misinterpreted notion of "what you know" and acknowledge that, actually, the advice to "write what you know" is merely stating the obvious: we can only write what we know, even if it is knowledge derived from second- or third-hand experience, sensory stimulation, subjective memory, lies, or knowledge from imagination. In this chapter, you will be asked to dig deeper into some of the knowledges which you have begun to identify, and to frame those knowledges into short, self-contained pieces of prose in a variety of genres. Ultimately you will be asked to find within that process a long answer to the short question: Why do you write?

So, what is the value of trying to answer a question like that, especially so early in your writing career? Why does a person become a medical doctor? Why do people dance? Why are some students better at mathematics than English? Why does anybody do anything?

In the introduction to this book, we looked at the ways in which the writer's life is not necessarily a conventional one. We have started thinking about the greyscale spectrum of writers: from everyday written communications, to developing writers engaged in tertiary studies, to professionals who write as part of their jobs, to published authors, screenwriters, poets, and other practicing creative writers. You were also warned of the exigent journey from discovering that you want to write to achieving substantial success as a professional writer. A healthy degree of confidence and tenacity is paramount to the development of your writing in terms of essential skills and also in career terms. In his own essay titled "Why I Write," George Orwell cites "Sheer egoism" as the first of his general four great motives for writing.[1] By actively looking for meaning in your writing practice, you are effectively formulating a kind of personal manifesto substantiating your values and beliefs, which you can revisit and add to as time goes on and your writing practice develops. Directing your attention to the relationship between your writing practices, the beliefs you hold about writing in general, and who you are as an individual with distinctive experiences and perspective, will help you to solidify writing as a constant in your life. Once you start to build your confidence as a writer, the challenges of the career ahead of you will begin to feel more manageable.

Even if becoming a novelist or screenwriter is not your goal, and you are in the process of discovering what writing means to you, consciously making the effort to identify your history with writing and the ways in which it has shaped your knowledge, what you derive personally from writing, and what influences and inspires your writing will be useful in identifying your particular creative processes.

The following exercises require you to work from reminiscence, first in the composition of a piece of memoir. From there you will work on infusing

---

[1] George Orwell, "Why I Write," orwell.ru http://orwell.ru/library/essays/wiw/english/e_wiw [accessed September 7, 2013].

subjective memories with elementary research in the development of a short autobiographical work. It will take considerable courage for you to choose parts of your life to write about which will engage your readers and to write honestly about your experiences.

The important thing to remember is that memoir and autobiography are necessarily different from a personal journal where the goal is to achieve catharsis which sometimes requires us to write out our irrationalities and insecurities in a way which makes us completely vulnerable. Self-writing which is designed to be published and read is about telling our stories for the reader's sake instead of purely for ourselves. Remember that, as well as being the subject of the self-writing text, you are also its creator—you can control the presentation of the true story. This chapter will help you think about techniques for using real life as raw material for a well-crafted and compelling literary work.

The exercises on reflective writing will prepare you for an introduction to the more structured practice of a specific kind of feature writing which is increasingly coming into prominence in major newspapers internationally: feature articles in which the emphasis is on personal experience, usually of a private nature, such as relationships, illness, and family. Finally, you will complete a series of short exercises leading to the composition of your inaugural and distinguished personal essay, which will—like so many others before it—conveniently rip off the title of Joan Didion's essay, which conveniently rips off the title of George Orwell's essay, "Why I Write."

Memoir and autobiography

The distinction between memoir and autobiography is open to interpretation, and the popularity of both genres in commercial publishing is palpable. It's impossible to walk through an airport bookstore without feeling followed by a thousand pairs of celebrity eyes on the expansive biography shelves. Increasingly these books are being referred to by their authors or publishers as memoirs, even when they are more likely straight-up ghost-written autobiographies, perhaps because that makes the book sound more intriguing. In fact, there are better ways than looking at the blurb on the back jacket cover for working out whether a book is a memoir or an autobiography. In this section of self-writing you are going to begin to differentiate between the two, based on a few essential criteria. The basis for these criteria is the assumption that memoir can be thought of as being literary in its values, whereas autobiography is not. But what exactly does being literary entail? How do we know when we are and aren't being literary?

Remember this quote from the introduction, on literature as independent from everyday forms of utterance:

> The literary text does not enter into a referential relation with the "world", as the sentences of everyday speech often do; it is not "representative" of anything but itself ...[2]

Elucidated here is a foundational value of literature, and concurrently also a clue as to the type of writing not generally considered literary. Literary texts seek to work as something free from the crutches of true life, even when true life is the inspiration behind the text to a great extent. Whereas the news article is interesting to read because it represents something of the real world and has some practical application (even if that just means informing our understanding of current events), the literary text values autonomy from the real world as an art form. This idea is as vital to creative writing technique as it is to evaluating existing literature. It reminds us writers not to get trapped in the confines of reality when we're trying to tell a story. Just because something looks a certain way in real life doesn't mean we can't make it sound much more interesting in our writing by layering the memory of observation with our subjective reflections and creative responses.

As a literary form of self-writing, memoir is not written merely to record a series of real events in the author's life for the purpose of informing the reader of an objective history. Instead, memoirs might be written to explore the personal or existential significance of certain events, to illuminate the poetry of the everyday and turn something that is necessarily real into something that is engaging, regardless of whether or not it really happened. As Ian Jack wrote in an article for the *Guardian* in 2003:

> The memoir's ambition is to be interesting in itself, as a novel might be, about intimate, personal experience. It often aspires to be thought of as "literary", and for that reason borrows many of literature's tricks – the tricks of the novel, of fiction – because it wants to do more than record the past;

---

[2] Tzvetan Todorov, "Literary Genres," in *Twentieth-Century Literary Theory: An Introductory Anthology*, Vassilis Lambropoulos and David Neal Miller (eds) (Albany: State University of New York Press, 1987), p. 195.

it wants to re-create it. If a memoir is to succeed on those terms, on the grounds that all lives are interesting if well-enough realised, the writing has to be good.[3]

This idea of recreating history is terribly emancipating. As the writer, it gives you the opportunity to turn your past into an adventure story, and as the reader it means you don't have to get bogged down in the frustrating nuisance that is often the reality of somebody's life story. Think Grampa Simpson:

> One trick is to tell them stories that don't go anywhere. Like the time I caught the ferry over to Shelbyville. I needed a new heel for my shoe. So, I decided to go to Morganville, which was what they called Shelbyville in those days. So, I tied an onion to my belt, which was the style at the time …[4]

The challenges for writers of memoir and autobiography, then, are relative to this idea that memoir aims to be literary and autobiography does not. The memoir writer needs to take a story from her real life and find a way to apply literary conventions like metaphor, figurative language, and foreshadowing to the life story to make it compelling in its own right. Moreover, the memoir writer has something to say, a theme to examine, a world to build above and beyond the process of relaying a series of historical factoids.

The autobiography writer, on the other hand, needs to write in a style that represents the truth of what really happened in a way which sustains the reader's interest—even when all the facts aren't necessarily interesting. The emphasis is on setting the record straight.

The following exercises will give you some techniques for meeting the challenges of both memoir writing and autobiographical writing. They should also help to demonstrate the similarities between these two self-writing genres and give you a point of reference for the criteria which differentiate them. While you are working on these, bear in mind Todorov's definition of literary texts; see if you can identify how it is as relevant as a creative writing technique as it is a theory of literature.

---

[3] Ian Jack, "Memoirs are made of this – and that," in the *Guardian online edition* (AU: February 8, 2003) [accessed August 31, 2013].
[4] Jay Kogen and Wallace Wolodarsky, "Last Exit to Springfield," *The Simpsons* (Los Angeles: 20th Century Fox, 1993) Television.

Autobiographical writing

In Anthony Kiedis's (so-called) memoir, *Scar Tissue*, he describes how he arrived at a new school on the first day only to be told by the school counselor that the school had discovered he was lying about his address, and so he wasn't allowed to enrol. The next day he turned up to the local school, Fairfax High, where he didn't know anybody. He felt alone and began befriending some of the other unpopular kids, including Tony Shurr, "a ninety-pound weakling."[5] Kiedis describes how one lunchtime in the courtyard another kid jumps on Tony and puts him in a headlock. Kiedis assumes his friend is being picked on, and dives in to rescue him, only to discover the other kid was just joking around. Kiedis and that other kid become inseparable even though they almost came to blows right from the beginning. Turns out that kid is Michael Balzary, better known to some of us as Flea (the bassist of Red Hot Chili Peppers), and the rest is history.

Exercise

This exercise asks you to practice autobiographical writing. You are going to write about the day you first met someone very important to you—a close friend, for instance.

The first thing you need to remember is what was happening in your life right before you met this important person, and what happened specifically on the day you met him or her. Once you have a handle on how it all came about, start writing from the first significant thing that happened to you that day and work your way through the important details which led to the fateful meeting.

The meeting itself should be described towards the end of your piece as a kind of climax (the most dramatic moment in the prose), and an allusion to its significance should be your denouement (which is the moment the drama settles and a sense of renewal or change marks the end of your prose).

Your goal is to write as factually as possible, including all the essential information, in the first person (from your point of view).

---

[5] Anthony Kiedis and Larry Sloman, *Scar Tissue* (London: Time Warner Books, 2004), p. 57.

To write factually requires some attention to the pertinent details which comprise the story. To make factual writing interesting, you should try to keep your readers right there with you through the experience—make them see things the way you saw them. There is no need for elaborate detail at this point; the thing you want to draw your reader in with is the situation itself.

To make the situation compelling, you need to think about how each thing you remember from that day worked as cause and effect to lead you to that significant event, and express that with appropriate transitions between paragraphs. You want to show your reader how that event might never have happened had it not been for a certain series of events that came immediately before it.

This shouldn't be longer than about one page.

Workshop

Begin by having a discussion about the Kiedis example and what makes it work.

If Kiedis hadn't been turned away from his first choice of high school, or if he'd started out at Fairfax High as one of the popular kids, Red Hot Chili Peppers might never have gotten together. Note how it is essential for the reader of this text to care about the band in real life to really be engaged by the crux of this story.

That isn't to say that a factual account of how two people became friends is inherently uninteresting unless they happen to be rock stars, it just means that the emphasis would have to be on something more intrinsic to human nature, rather than on the beginnings of a famous band's formation.

How do you think it would have read if it was a story about any other two teenagers making friends? What parts of the story would you need to emphasize in that case to make it engaging? What are the most interesting parts of this meeting aside from the identities of the two teenagers in question? What else would you want to know about this meeting that isn't included in the existing text?

Once you've thought about these questions, workshop your "first meeting" exercise by reading your piece aloud without explaining it first, and then have your group mates answer the following questions about your story. Make sure you note down any constructive feedback you receive so you can revise this piece later on.

- What could you have included in the first paragraph that would have strengthened the impact of the meeting in the climax?
- What are the nuanced significances of this meeting, aside from the fact that the person you met was obviously important to you?
- What is the larger significance of your story? What makes your story special?
- How do your group mates find it relatable and relevant?
- Can you identify the cause and effect sequence of events that led to the meeting? Could these events be modified to make for a better read?

Memoir writing

In his *Chronicles: Volume One*, Bob Dylan describes having to sit down with the publicist at his new record label as a newcomer to New York having just signed his first deal. Dylan clearly doesn't think much of the publicist, as evidenced by the way he introduces the guy:

> Billy dressed Ivy League like he could have come out of Yale—medium height, crisp black hair. He looked like he'd never been stoned a day in his life, never been in any kind of trouble. I strolled into his office, sat down opposite his desk, and he tried to get me to cough up some facts, like I was supposed to give them to him straight and square.[6]

The conversation that ensues between the two men consists of Billy stiffly trying to interview Dylan, and Dylan underhandedly making fun of the situation by lying or giving stock answers. Eventually Dylan gets bored and distracted:

> I gazed past Billy, past his chair through his window across the street to an office building where I could see a blazing secretary soaked up in the spirit of something—she was scribbling busy, occupied at a desk in a meditative

---

[6] Bob Dylan, *Chronicles: Volume One* (New York: Simon & Schuster, 2004), p. 7.

manner. There was nothing funny about her. I wished I had a telescope. Billy asked me who I saw myself like in today's music scene. I told him, nobody.[7]

The meeting described here seems to have no real significance to the life and times of Bob Dylan. It is unnecessary for the reader to be invested somehow in the author's life's work to find this vignette engaging; it's engaging for its own sake, on its own literary merits. The way it provides exposition of the protagonist's experience of a major life event, and the relative awkwardness and boredom of these two men who would otherwise want nothing to do with each other colliding in an office as a result of that major life event, makes this compelling to read.

Exercise

This exercise is about memoir writing. You are going to write a short piece about another time in your life when you met somebody new. This time the person you met is not necessarily as important as the circumstances surrounding the meeting itself.

First, think back to a time in your life of significant change. Perhaps you were in a new physical location, or you were involved in some kind of big accident, or there was some major shift in your family dynamic, or maybe you'd just experienced a breakup with a boyfriend or girlfriend or best friend.

Then think about how that significant change led you to meeting somebody new—even if you never saw that person again in your life. Consider how your new life circumstance brought that meeting about, and how what you were going through influenced your attitude towards that meeting. Ask yourself what was preoccupying your mind at the time of the meeting and how that might have reflected in your behavior during the meeting.

Your challenge is to write about the scenario in which this meeting takes place. Write from the moment you meet the person through to the moment you leave them. Let your reader in on the broader context of the meeting, but let the meeting itself be the focus of this piece. Emphasize your reactions, your preoccupations, and the way you felt about being there at that time, and include the most

---

[7] Ibid. p. 8.

important part of the conversation you had as dialogue.

In this piece you can spend time describing sensory detail about the person you meet and about the setting. Point out any ironies or oddities you observed during the meeting. Feel free to use metaphors or analogies to describe what the meeting was like for you. This time, the emotional truth of the meeting trumps the basic facts.

This should be about a page long.

Workshop

Begin by discussing the Dylan example. What literary conventions can you identify in just the two quoted excerpts? How does the language employed to describe Billy differ from the language employed to describe the secretary? Is the language literal or figurative or a combination of both? How do we know how the protagonist feels about either of these other two characters? At what points does the narrative divert away from informing us of the facts?

Once you've had a chance to reflect on the example, you can start workshopping your own exercise. Swap your piece with a partner's, and, without talking about it first, read each other's work quietly. When it's your turn to workshop, your partner will ask you a series of questions about your intentions for this piece. Here are some possible questions you can ask each other.

- What was the overwhelming feeling you had when this meeting occurred? And how were you feeling immediately before and after it?
- What was your first impression of this person you met? And how would you evaluate that impression in hindsight? (For example, were you being overly critical of that person because of the situation? Was your judgment clouded because you were excited about something?)

Ask each other whatever questions you can think of pertaining to the details of the meeting and write down the answers your partner gives.

When the interview process is done, go back over your partner's piece. Make at least three editorial notes in the margin suggesting how your partner might more fully achieve her intentions for the piece now that you know more about the meeting.

Once you're done, swap back and go over the notes your partner has made for you. Keep your partner's notes in case you decide to rewrite this piece later.

Reflective writing

Reflective writing extends beyond the realm of the stories which make up our personal histories and enters into our unique responses to the knowledge we have acquired. Whereas the point of memoir and autobiography is to tell our life stories, whether literally or literarily, reflective writing hinges on our thoughts and thought processes, the way we learn, the way knowledge changes us, and our emotional and intellectual responses to the things we bear witness to.

It's interesting to note that reflective writing is used in a whole range of different professional and academic capacities. If you have taken university courses in the humanities or the sciences you might have been instructed at one time or another to keep a journal and write a little bit each week on what you discovered in class—what processes you took in your research for papers, or what you understood from your set readings. This is one kind of reflective writing which has a very practical application, because by recording your progress each week you are able to:

- Track your advancement through the course of study
- Find out which learning methods suit you the best
- Illuminate the specific topics which interest you the most
- Process all the content you are being given and begin committing it to memory
- Decide what your stance is in relation to any topical issues
- Identify the question on the subject that you wish to raise with your professor in class
- Know where your weaknesses lie and seek extra tuition if you need to

The common thread that connects all these points is that reflective writing is as much about the input of existing knowledge as it is about the output of newly synthesized knowledge. The reflective writer is simultaneously recording information and finding new depths of meaning within that information. However, reflective writing need not always pertain to brand new information, like keeping a weekly journal for class.

Consider what the word *reflection* really means. Here are some words that might come up if you looked up the word *reflection* in the thesaurus: thinking, contemplation, rumination, deliberation, musing, manifestation, indication, signal, expression, suggestion, likeness, mirror image. The idea is to take raw data and think about what it means both subjectively and objectively, what it signifies, what aspects of life it mirrors, what it is in opposition to, what all its elements do individually and how they function together, and, finally, what it represents to you. Given the inherent complexity of what reflection really entails, sometime the best reflections are the product of weeks or months or years of consideration about a particular subject. Other times, it is more useful to write a reflection on something we have just recently encountered as a way to avoid kneejerk reactions and to deeply engage with our new subject.

The content of reflective writing merges literal representations of real life with the author's imaginations inspired by the subject of the reflection and speculations about what might be entailed by the subject. The point of reflection is to explore possibilities and to be mindful of your personal responses.

The exercises in this section ask you to do a little bit of all of the above. The trick to getting the most out of the following tasks is to try your hardest not to censor yourself. Allow your writing to take tangents in the same way you would during a stream of consciousness exercise, without getting too distracted from the central point or theme of your subject. The challenge is not to restrict yourself to retelling what you already know about the subject at hand, but to use your writing process as a way into new knowledge, and new understandings.

Exercise

This exercise is about reflecting on something you recently read.

Think about all the reading you have done in the past week. Perhaps you read a chapter of a book either for your own enjoyment or for a class. Perhaps you read an interesting article in the newspaper or online. Choose the one thing you read that really stuck with you and focus on that. It might be helpful if you can access it readily now, as you're doing this exercise, but it's not essential—you can go off what you remember.

In the first five minutes, consider how you might answer the following questions. It might help to take some initial notes as you go through these.

- What was the text about? How would you sum it up in a few sentences?
- What were the features of this text which made it memorable or important to you?
- What were the overarching themes of the text? What questions was it seeking to answer, and why?
- What is your past experience with those themes? What new ideas occurred to you about those themes after reading the text?
- What do you think of the subject matter of the text? How do your evaluations of the subject differ from the author's? How are they alike?
- What other current events, stories, and memories does the subject of the text remind you of? How are they similar or different to the ideas presented in the text?
- What does the text mean to you in a broader sense? How would you sum up its overall significance to you?

After you have attempted to answer the above questions, start writing your reflection. You may not need to include all of the answers to the above questions in your reflection, and you may have found more relevant questions you want to explore the answers to as you write. There is no special structure you need to follow, but if you feel stumped for an opening you can start the piece by writing down your answer to the first question above and aim to conclude the piece with a few sentences on the last question.

The challenge is to discover something new about the text's meaning, significance, or how it affects what you already know, through the process of writing this reflection. That means you are not just regurgitating prior knowledge about the text—you are actually uncovering new knowledge through your reflections.

Your reflection should be approximately a page long, and it shouldn't take longer than 20 minutes to complete.

Workshop

Briefly describe three things to your workshop group: what the original text was, what your initial ideas about the text entailed, and, finally, what you discovered about the text and its impact on you through writing this reflection.

Discuss the possibilities of where reflection writing of this sort might be helpful or important, and why.

Reflections using visual stimulus

The following three exercises are all to be completed in any art gallery.

Initially you can spend 15 or 20 minute exploring a section of the gallery. As you move through the space, take a mental note of the location of the artworks which interest you the most.

When you are ready you can start on the first exercise.

Gallery exercise 1

Choose a large painting which you consider to be "powerful." It can be anything you like, anything that moves you.

Your task is to do ten minutes of stream of consciousness writing using the painting as stimulus. Sit in front of your chosen artwork, open up a fresh page in your notebook and begin writing straight away. You can write about the painting itself, or any thoughts or feelings it evokes. You can write about the colors and textures in front of you. You can write about the task of writing in a gallery. You can write about how you have to remember to feed your neighbor's cat later. You can write anything you like. Any time you run out of words, look up at your painting and let it inspire you. Don't censor yourself; just write continuously for 10 minutes.

When your ten minutes is up, spend two minute observing your painting. If there are people near you, also (subtly!) observe their reactions to your painting. Note down the artist's name, and the title and the year of the painting. Then move on to the next exercise.

Gallery exercise 2

Choose a painting or sculpture which reminds of you of something from your past.

Sit in front of your chosen artwork and, for five minutes, just observe it. Look for things you didn't necessarily notice at first glance. Consider the kind of mood it evokes through its shapes and colors. Identify its major and minor subjects and how they work in unison.

Begin to think about how all these elements happened to elicit a particular memory for you. How do you relate your memory to the contents of the artwork? What was the first part of the memory that came to mind when you witnessed the artwork? Which parts of the artwork are akin to your memory and which parts of it are unexpected?

After five minutes of observation and thinking time, start writing a reflection which somehow connects your memory of something from your past with the artwork. You might describe your memory using cues from within the artwork, and you might describe the artwork using cues from your memory. It's completely up to you how you merge these two stimuli (the memory and the artwork) in your reflective piece.

Once again, your challenge here is to find new meaning through the reflective writing process. Ask yourself questions about why the artwork in front of you is significant to your current self. Try to work out what your relationship with that past memory is now, and why it might have resurfaced today. What is its relevance? How does it make you feel? What new perspectives do you have on that memory, having spent time observing this artwork?

Write for 20 minutes. When you are finished, write down the artist's name, and the title and year of the painting, then bid your artwork farewell and move on to another part of the gallery.

Gallery exercise 3

Choose a painting, this time which depicts a curious setting.

Sit in front of the painting and, for five minutes, just observe it. Look for things you didn't necessarily notice at first glance. Consider the kind of mood it evokes through its shapes and colors. Identify its major and minor subjects and how they work in unison. This time, also begin to imagine what the artist was thinking and feeling while painting this setting. What social and personal issues might have preoccupied the artist's mind in order to paint this setting? What do you think the painting is really about? What might the artist reveal to you about the painting if you had a chance to ask him or her about it?

After your observation time, write your reflection based on the following scenario: You have mysteriously found yourself inside this painting. Suddenly you are an occupant of this curious setting. You are looking for some kind of a way out when a voice from above greets you and introduces himself as the painter of this work. You have an opportunity to reason with him to let you out of the painting, but, before he grants you leave, he wants to know why you wouldn't want to be an inhabitant of his painting (aside from the fact that you have a life back in the real world).

What is it about the setting that unsettles you, overwhelms you, disturbs you, or irritates you? What anxieties does the setting elicit? Make references to the details of the painting you observed and explain how they affect you, what emotions and thoughts they evoke for you, and why you couldn't tolerate being among them indefinitely. Write about what the issues communicated in the painting mean to you.

Write your explanation to the artist for approximately ten minutes. When you have finished writing your reflection you can leave the setting behind. Don't forget to make a note of the artist's name, and the title and year of the painting.

Workshop

First explain to your workshop group which of the three exercises you are going to share, and introduce the painting which inspired the reflection, then read your work aloud to the group.

Have a discussion about the experiences you had writing in the gallery.

- How easy or difficult was it to write in the gallery environment? What were the factors which either helped or posed challenges?
- How did you find working with a visual stimulus?
- What would you do differently to improve this experience next time?

Then discuss the specific exercises.

- What new idea, emotional response, or perspective did you discover in the second two exercises? How did the artworks help you to come to these discoveries? At what point in your writing process did these discoveries begin to emerge? And how did you include them in your prose?
- Were you able to include physical details about the artworks to emphasize your points throughout each of the three exercises? Or were the themes and ideas behind the paintings of more interest to you?
- In each of the three exercises, how much of your writing would you class as imaginative? How much of it would you class as speculative? How much of it was literal?

Exercise

This exercise requires you to write a reflection on an aspect of your own personal history.

Think about the different types of relationships you have had over the course of your life. These might include familial relationships with your parents, siblings, or extended family, friendships you've had since childhood, and romantic relationships from your first crush to your most recent partner. The one thing all of these relationships have in common is that they are inherently dynamic; relationships tend to grow and change and influence our understanding of the world.

First, choose one of these types of relationships from which you have learned an important life lesson recently. Think about this relationship both in general terms (for example, romantic relationships in general), and in specific terms (the particular relationship which taught you a life lesson).

Then, spend ten minutes writing two or three sentence responding to the following questions.

- How would you describe this relationship, generally?
- How did you first encounter this person / relationship? What were your early impressions of this person or this type of relationship?
- What is the biggest challenge this relationship has posed for you? What was the outcome of this challenge?
- What new attitudes towards life have you developed as a result of this relationship? How do they differ from how you used to feel?

Once you've answered these questions, write a one-page reflection which articulates as clearly as possible what this relationship means to you. You can include your answers to the above questions if you like. Conclude your reflection by elucidating what larger lessons this relationship has taught you about yourself and about the world.

The key is to verbalize your feelings and instincts about the person with whom you share this relationship and the type of relationship you enjoy as something which is tangible and relatable for a potential reader who doesn't know you personally.

Write neatly and on a clean page that you can rip out of your notebook. Don't put your own name anywhere in the reflection.

This shouldn't take longer than 15 minutes to complete.

Workshop

Each workshop group member should rip their one-page reflection out of their notebooks. Make sure your names don't appear on them. Put all the reflections in a pile and shuffle them. Each group member should randomly select a reflection which they will read out for the group.

When your reflection is being read out, don't let on that it belongs to you and don't interrupt the reader. Just listen to the way it sounds being read by someone else. Which sections do you notice sound laboured or clumsy? Which sections do your group mates give non-verbal responses to as they listen? Does the piece as a whole sound overly sentimental, or have you tried too hard to be objective and come off sounding detached or dispassionate?

After each piece is read out, you might reveal who authored which piece and have a general discussion on the strengths and weaknesses of each. Bear in mind everything you learned from listening to the readings.

Human interest features

Contemporary newspapers and magazines, especially those which are actively staying relevant and viable by providing more and more digital content, depend on human interest feature articles to appeal to the broadest possible range of readerships. As such, the range of topics which form the basis for feature articles is as diverse as the readers of the articles, and, although they are often concerned with matters of the zeitgeist, they are not limited to examinations of current affairs.

The more personal or confessional forms of human interest features are often the ones which amass the most reader comments on online publications; they can be motivational, comforting, inspiring, give hope, or encourage understanding and empathy. Although these articles aren't doing the important job of disseminating news, they are arguably a reflection of one of humanity's brighter sides: the compassionate urge to share experiences candidly and listen to the experiences of others in the hope that they can show us something of ourselves, or at least help us to feel a little less alone.

The style of confessional human interest feature articles borrows from the reflective writing you practiced in the last section's exercises and the memoir and autobiographical genres you encountered earlier in this chapter, but they tend to follow a format which is common to all feature writing, including news features and opinion editorials. The aim is to communicate a story from your life that has a theme of social significance which readers will be able to relate to. This requires a combination of narrative techniques, reflection, and some research to bear out your conclusions.

In case you are wondering why a section on media writing has mysteriously found its way into a creative writing coursebook, the explanation comes back to the issue raised in the introduction about the multiplicity of work a professional writer needs to be able to produce in order to survive. As you begin working on the first exercise in this section, take note of the authors of some of the feature articles you read in major newspapers. You will find that many of them are novelists, nonfiction writers, and screenwriters. Sometimes freelance feature writing is a lucrative and comprehensive way of publicizing or complementing your other work. Considering that millions of people read the world's major newspapers online and in print every day, it is likely that, of all the texts you have published during your career, the feature articles you produce will attain the largest readerships—by a long shot!

Exercise

You can do this task all in one sitting, or you may wish to do a little bit each day, perhaps over your morning coffee.

Visit the *New York Times* website and survey all of the sections which include human interest feature articles—that is, all the articles which are about human experiences and emotions. You will find that different sections have subsections which are dedicated to these types of article—for example, within the Opinion section there are a number of series dedicated to specific topics, regular columns, and letters to the editor, many of which have human interest angles.

Your task is to first make a detailed inventory of all of the sections you can find. Do not include sections dedicated to hard news—although these can be emotive at times, their purpose is to inform rather than to emote.

After you have scoured the *New York Times* for human interest articles, think about the sections which interest you personally. You might find them interesting because the issues they explore directly relate to you, or because the topics are important to you or the people close to you.

Your next task is to browse through the sections which interest you for articles which are written in the first person voice.

You can tell something is written in the first person voice when the narrative begins with "I," as in "I walked down the street," as opposed to the third person voice which has an omniscient voice, as in "she walked down the street."

Carefully read ten human interest feature articles which are written in the first person voice and which interest you. Take note of each article's title, author, and the section in which you discovered it. You may also want to bookmark the URLs of the articles you like the most so you can revisit them later.

Print out your favorite article and bring it into class along with your notes so you can work on the following series of feature planning and writing exercises.

Feature planning exercise 1

You are going to analyze your favorite article for its various parts and their relative functions. Identify the following sentences or paragraphs in your article and write a few sentences for each, explaining how the article employs the following techniques.

1 Lead (sometimes referred to as "lede"): This is the first sentence or paragraph of the article. It has multiple possible functions including setting the scene, raising the focal topic of the article, and establishing mood. Generally, the most important function of the lead is to provide an effective hook—the thing that makes the reader want to continue reading. Sometimes this is in the form of a question which the article promises to answer later, sometimes it is through an absurd assertion which inspires curiosity, and sometimes it's simply a compelling way to start telling a story.

2 Nut Graf (sometimes referred to as "nut graph"): This is the sentence or paragraph which states the facts which form the point of the article. In hard news articles, the nut graf and the lead are usually one and the same. In feature articles, the nut graf usually appears somewhere between the third and sixth paragraphs from the top and works to consolidate the opening narration of the article into a tangible point. It tends to include the "who, what, where, when, why" details which the remainder of the article is about.

3 Body: These are the paragraphs which tell the story and are bookended by the introduction (which might start with the lead paragraph and end with the nut graf) and the conclusion. The body paragraphs consist mostly of a central narrative in which the author describes her experience, or they might intersperse narrative with tangential details and facts derived from research.

4 Conclusion: This can sneak up on the reader. Sometime the conclusion is alluded to close to the middle of the article, and the author uses the subsequent body paragraphs to exemplify it before restating it more definitively at the end. Other times, the conclusion begins where the body ends. Wherever you find it, the conclusion is about what the author makes of the experience which she has described, its significance to her, and perhaps even its broader significance to society.

Feature planning exercise 2

Now that you are a human-interest-first-person-voice-feature-article aficionado, the time has come to prepare the beginnings of a pitch for an article of your own.

Come up with an idea for a feature article based on one of your personal experiences which fits into one of the *New York Times* sections you discovered during your homework task. Think of the experience which forms the foundation of the article you want to write, how it relates thematically to your chosen newspaper section, and how you might underscore its emotional significance. Also consider whether the topic of your article might call for some element of background research.

Once the idea is established, write a compelling lead, a clear nut graf, and a final concluding paragraph. Try not to exceed three sentences for each of these elements. Remember that you are writing in the first person voice—that is, from your own point of view.

Workshop

The idea of this workshop is to quickly pitch your idea. Read out the lead and nut graf for your proposed feature article and specify which section of the *New York Times* the article is intended for.

Once each group member has read, have a general discussion on which ideas you found especially compelling and why. Take note of any feedback you receive on your article.

Feature planning exercise 3

To conclude the workshop process, do five minutes of stream of consciousness writing with the topic for your article in mind.

It's alright if you take a tangent and start writing about something else as long as you keep coming back to your main topic.

The point of doing this exercise now is to freely explore the ideas and feelings you associate with your topic without censoring yourself or trying to write to a predetermined structure.

Exercise

This task picks up where the series of feature planning exercises left off.

You should now have not only an idea for a human interest feature article, but also drafts of the lead, nut graph, and concluding paragraph. This is a solid foundation for you to write up the whole article, which is exactly what you are about to do.

First, write up the body of your article according to the presentation of narrative and background research you came up with during the conceptualization of the piece. Continue writing this in the first person voice and make sure that the tense you are writing in (past, present, or future tense) remains consistent. Write the body paragraphs to fit around the three paragraphs you have already drafted. If you need to include research but you don't have the sources you need close at hand, leave space to inject your findings later and focus on the narrative.

This should take approximately 20 minutes. Don't worry if you haven't had time to include all the details you wanted to—you can come back to it later.

Secondly, write up the conclusion of your article, which will end in the final paragraph you have already drafted. Remember that the idea of the conclusion is to bring all the information you have relayed about the experience together and formulate some reflections which show the emotional and actual significance of the experience. Bear in mind what you particularly appreciated about the article you analyzed earlier; aim to emulate the best things about that conclusion in your own conclusion.

This should take around 10 minutes.

Once you are finished, assemble the parts of your article into a whole. The lead goes at the top. The nut graf should slot in neatly somewhere in the first six or seven paragraphs. The conclusion starts where the body ends, and the prewritten final paragraph (remarkably) goes at the end!

Workshop

Read your article aloud to the group, from the lead through to the final concluding paragraph.

Give each other feedback on the following points.

- Do the lead, nut graf, or final concluding paragraph need to be revised in order to better service the body and conclusion?
- Does the body follow a logical structure? Does it narrate a coherent and engaging story?
- Is there sufficient reflection on how the issues raised throughout the article have significance? Does the conclusion ring true with your partner? Does it offer a new perspective? Is it emotionally satisfying and relevant?

Personal essays, and "Why I Write"

The personal essay is one of the oldest forms of literary nonfiction, and in contemporary contexts it tends to reject the numerous accepted essay-writing rules and conventions even more regularly than it borrows from them. What this means is that the personal essayist has a whole lot of freedom with which to present the subject matter in question.

This is not (entirely) to say that now is a terrific time to forget everything you learned in your foundational composition classes—rather that here is an opportunity to take a creatively selective approach to your use of thesis statements, introductions, narrations, affirmations, negations, and conclusions.

Why leave all that regimented goodness behind? Well, because the personal essay is just that: personal. The form and style you administer should be specific to your method of reasoning and examination of the topic. You should use all the writing skills you are honing to give the reader an insight into your way of thinking, your tactics for engaging with your chosen subject.

The aim of the personal essay is to scrutinize your subject from every possible angle in order to present a considered thesis on that subject from your personal point of view. The personal essay author applies the breadth of her knowledge—every way of knowing that we have explored so far in this course book—in her deliberations on the subject at hand before starting to write. And, just as in reflective writing, quite often the crux and the climax of her investigation of the subject emerge through the writing process. It's alright to begin your personal essay before you are certain of how it's going to conclude as long as you have spent enough time thinking on it first.

There are infinite potential topics for personal essays, but, for the purposes of this chapter on self-writing, you will be zeroing in on the undoubtedly complicated answer to the question: why do you write?

In 1946 *Gangrel Magazine* published a personal essay by George Orwell titled "Why I Write."[8] The essay comprises bits of memoir, reflections on the influence of politics and literature on his writing practice, a poem, and a thesis in four points positing the most important reasons for anyone to

---

[8] George Orwell, Peter Hobley Davison and Ian Ang, *Smothered Under Journalism: 1946* (London: Secker & Warburg, 1998), p. 316.

5

write, from Orwell's point of view. The tone of the essay is a kind of assertive meditation on life and the place of writing in life.

Joan Didion wrote an essay of the same title which was first published in the *New York Times Book Review* on December 5, 1976.[9] Numerous other authors have written essays and manifestos describing their rules and reasons for writing. These essays, of course, are invaluable reading for aspiring writers—but there is also value in the writing of such essays in terms of finding out the place of writing in your world, knowing what you hope to achieve whenever you put pen to paper, and understanding yourself and what motivates you a little better.

The following few exercises are all lead-ups to the last exercise in this chapter, which asks you to write the first draft of a personal essay titled "Why I Write."

Exercise

This is a guided stream of consciousness writing task.

Think for a minute about everything that annoys you about writing and every negative experience you have had in and around the pursuit of writing. This could include trouble you have with particular types of writing such as research papers or job applications; or the times teachers or family members behaved in a less-than-encouraging way towards your writing; or the inherent dangers of trying to communicate using text messages, emails, and social media; or perhaps that lurking terror of writing dedicatedly for decades, never to be published (oh dear).

Once you have incensed yourself into a state of mild to moderate rage over all of these thoughts, it is time to start writing for five continuous minutes.

As usual with stream of consciousness writing, the goal is not to censor yourself and to fill as much of the page as possible in the five-minute time span. It's alright to go off on tangents as long as you return to the subject at hand when the tangents wear thin.

When your five minutes is up, read over your rant. Be sure to keep it somewhere safe.

---

[9] Joan Didion, "Why I Write" (Bridgewater: Bridgewater.edu). http://people.bridgewater. edu/~atrupe/ENG310/Didion.pdf [accessed June 7, 2013].

Details of a writer's life

Everyone has their own weird ways of doing things. Writers can tend to be a little more particular than the average bear about how they like things done, especially when it concerns work habits. Here is my list of writing rituals.

1 Always carry an A5-sized black spiral lined notebook and pen.
2 Write by hand using only black inky pens. No blue. No biro. No thanks.
3 Set goals in terms of word lengths. This month it's 2,000 words a day, five days a week.
4 A giant refillable cup of coffee and the newspaper (online usually) is the only way to begin every writing day.
5 When the coffee runs out, the writing begins.
6 A desk facing a window with a view of the street is the coveted ideal workspace. Sometimes this requires rearranging hotel room furniture. And that's alright as long as nothing is bolted to the floor.
7 Try not to forget to eat. But if the words are flowing, all those basic needs (eating, drinking, trips to the bathroom, stretching, exercise) nosedive into oblivion—sounds wrong, but it's for the best.
8 Never reread over things straight away. Give them a week to breathe.
9 Plan ahead, even though plans often change. Give subtitles to everything. Break big projects down into small parts. Revise the plan as needed.
10 Read constantly—but avoid reading in the genre I'm writing in at the time so as not to inadvertently start sounding like somebody else.
11 Red wine. Preferably as a reward at the end and not as an inducement at the start. Preferably.

Exercise

This one is about identifying your personal writing rituals. Make a list of all the rituals (however seemingly inconsequential) you have relating to how you write. These can include things you do before, during, and after writing.

Exercise

This one is about finding inspiration in the writings on the topic of writing by an author you admire.

Do some research online to see if your favorite authors have ever written about their own rules or reasons for writing. Make sure whatever you find is from a credible source and that it is possible to determine where the text was first published (you may want to avoid random memes prepared by goodness-knows-who on Facebook, for example).

Keep track of everything you find which inspires you. You might create a page of quotes and attributions and keep it wherever you do most of your writing.

Choose a few sentences from everything you have found which inspires you the most, copy them out verbatim and bring them into class.

Exercise

This one uses an inspiring quote you selected and copied out in the previous exercise.

Your task is to write a one-page reflection on one of the quotes you have chosen. Describe your first reaction to it, explain how it makes you reconsider your existing beliefs about writing, how it is relevant to your writing practice, and what it is you particularly admire about the author.

This should take no longer than 15 minutes.

"Why I Write"

All of the previous exercises have been building up to the last exercise in this chapter which will ask you to write a personal essay which interrogates the theme: Why I write. Now is time to synthesize your reflections on your history with creative writing, your writing habits, your peeves, and your inspirations.

Here is how Joan Didion begins her essay "Why I Write":

> Of course I stole the title for this talk, from George Orwell. One reason I stole it was that I like the sound of the words: Why I Write. There you have three short unambiguous words that share a sound, and the sound they share is this:
>
> I
>
> I
>
> I
>
> In many ways writing is the act of saying *I*, of imposing oneself upon other people, of saying *listen to me, see it my way, change your mind*. It's an aggressive, even hostile act.[10]

Didion acknowledges Orwell up front and then proceeds to connect the title they share with the beginnings of her answer to the central thematic question of the essay: why do I write? The style and tone are conversational but articulate and the remainder of the essay has an unfussy but discernible structure.

Here is the opening of George Orwell's essay "Why I Write":

> From a very early age, perhaps the age of five or six, I knew that when I grew up I should be a writer. Between the ages of about seventeen and twenty-four I tried to abandon this idea, but I did so with the consciousness that I was outraging my true nature and that sooner or later I should have to settle down and write books.
>
> I was the middle child of three, but there was a gap of five years on either side, and I barely saw my father before I was eight. For this and other reasons I was somewhat lonely, and I soon developed disagreeable mannerisms which made me unpopular throughout my schooldays. I had the lonely child's habit of making up stories and holding conversations with imaginary persons, and I think from the very start my literary ambitions were mixed up with the feeling of being isolated and undervalued.[11]

As you can see, Orwell has a more linear approach to his interrogation of the question at hand, and opts to begin with an autobiographical account of the earliest moments of his writing life.

---

[10] Ibid., p. 1.
[11] George Orwell, "Why I Write," orwell.ru, http://orwell.ru/library/essays/wiw/english/e_wiw [accessed September 7, 2013].

Both of these examples demonstrate how their respective authors chose to attack the central question in ways which would best introduce the reader to the crux of their theses. For Didion, writing is about ideas and exploration. For Orwell, writing is a negotiation between his private self and his social self.

Exercise

This is the last one for this chapter—it is the exercise you have been working up to.

Your task is to write the first draft of a personal essay. The title and topic of your personal essay is "Why I Write."

If you haven't already, now might be a good time to read George Orwell's essay in its entirety.

Revisit the pieces you wrote for the other exercises in this section on the Personal Essay. You can use as much of the material you composed as you like. Also look back over the exercises in the other sections of this chapter. It is completely up to you how much autobiography, memoir, reflective writing, or feature writing technique you include in your personal essay, as long as you come up with something honest and considered.

Workshop

Once you have completed the first draft of your personal essay, read it aloud to your group without prior explanations or disclaimers.

After you have read, your group can share their responses with you, point out the strengths and weaknesses in your writing, and suggest ways of developing the essay further. Ask your group if they have any questions based on what you read, and indicate the areas you particularly struggled with, in order to direct the feedback you receive. You can implement all the workshopping techniques and lines of questioning that you found useful in previous workshop sessions. After each group member's work has been discussed, spend five minutes noting down (either on your draft or on a separate page) the areas of your essays that you want to work on later.

Whatever else you do, hold on to this essay so you can revisit it in the future. It will be interesting to discover how much your relationship with writing evolves over the years.

3
Poetics and Poetry Composition

Poetry and its composition is likely the most polarizing topic in an introductory creative writing course: students either swoon over it or feel sick at the thought of it.

Note the way that last phrase used rhetoric parallelism to emphasize the point about how different students react to poetry:

Students either swoon over it

[Or]

Feel sick at the thought of it

Also note the alliterated repetition of the *s* sound at the beginning of each of the key words:

Students

Swoon

Sick

Did you also happen to notice the way, if you divided it into two logical phrases, both the lines would consist of exactly eight syllables each, and of those eight an even four syllables in each line are emphasized when spoken in a natural, conversational tone:

<u>Stu</u>dents <u>ei</u>ther <u>swoon</u> over <u>it</u>

Or <u>feel</u> <u>sick</u> at the <u>thought</u> of <u>it</u>

If you did not notice all of these things and more (the use of analogy, the juxtaposition of two equal and opposite sensations, the repetition of the *s* sound, the internal identical rhyming of the word *it*, and so on), it might be because the effortless way in which the techniques blend to form a phrase which is communicative and evocative is so effective that it fails to draw attention to itself.

Now that you are aware of them, I can boldly reveal the disturbing truth of all of their origins: all of these are poetic techniques. And, clearly, they all have applications extending far beyond the composition of poetry.

The thing that distinguishes poetry from prose is that while prose is purely discursive (which means that it is linear, logical, limited by syntax and grammatical principles, and in order to understand it you read from start to finish), poetry is partly discursive and partly presentational (it has physical form, shape, space on the page and is not limited by syntax and grammatical principles),[1] which is how we usually think of visual arts. To a degree, in order to understand a poem you have to read it through from start to finish. However, the way the words are arranged into deliberate line of lengths unencumbered by the margins of the page, and the lines are separated into stanzas of particular lengths, as well as the particular use of syntax and grammar which draws our attention to certain parts of the poem automatically—these are all presentational features which make poetry different from other genres of creative writing.

As we read along, the line and stanza breaks inform our interpretation of the poem more instantly and intuitively than the words and phrases themselves, whether we trust our immediate responses to the poem or not. A terrific example of this occurs between the first two stanzas of Stevie Smith's poem, "Black March," part of which is discussed later in this chapter.

Whether you have been writing poetry daily in a journal since puberty hit (oh dear), or whether the mere mention of the word poetry onsets symptoms of post-traumatic stress with flashbacks to Shakespeare classes in high school (also, oh dear), it's important to eventually acknowledge that poetic techniques are essential to all of your literary endeavours in one way or another. To comprehend the functions and applications of different poetic techniques is the first step in seizing more creative control over all of your writings. If you can use poetic techniques intentionally to give rhythm and pace to your prose, to emphasize certain ideas and images, and to simultaneously incite intellectual and intuitive responses in your readers, then you have the potential to produce really great work. Subsequently, it is

---

[1] Susanne Langer, *Philosophy in a New Key: A study in the symbolism of Reason, Rite, and Art*, 3rd edn (Cambridge: Harvard University Press, 1957), pp. 76–89.

likely that your readers' interpretations of your work will be closer to your intention for the work, which is always rewarding for any writer.

As well as favorably influencing your writing practice, a firm grasp of rudimentary poetic techniques will improve your ability to analyze virtually every different kind of text, from literary novels to political speeches. Poetic techniques are used both intentionally and subconsciously by writers across every genre as a scheme of verbal communication which is intrinsic to how we manipulate language. The more poetic techniques you pick up on in the work of others, the more aware you become of how useful they can be. It (almost) goes without saying that understanding why you like or dislike certain things about literature is concurrent with crafting your own work so that it more closely resembles the kinds of writing you admire (in technique only, of course; your voice should endeavour to remain your own).

Of course, if poetry is your passion then the topics covered in this chapter will provide you with a strong foundation for developing your craft. All the writing exercises in this chapter, including the ones on more traditional poetic forms like the sonnet, are built on modern and contemporary examples. The simple reason for this is that you are training to become a writer in a contemporary world with contemporary language and contemporary social constructs and inspirations. There is nothing stopping you from writing a sonnet, but there are some 400 years looming between you and a classical Shakespearean sonnet; why should you compromise your voice in order to conform with the modes and conventions of another time?

Additionally, the beginning of Modernism transformed the scope of English language poetry in ways which have been sustained over the past 140-odd years, and the new generation of poets (that means you!) are direct descendents of all the influences that have emerged since that time.

In the first section we take a whirlwind tour of poetic movements through history to give some background to the examples and exercises in the sections which follow. The second section is dedicated to the core of what poetry actually is; as former poet laureate of the United States Rita Dove famously said: "Poetry is language at its most distilled and most powerful … you carry it around and then it nourishes you when you need it."[2] The exercises in this section are dedicated to exploring the economy of language in poetry. The third section contains exercises which will introduce a range of sound techniques (including some of the ones mentioned at the

---

[2] Clara Villarosa (ed.), *The Words of African-American Heroes* (New York: Newmarket Press, 2011), p. 5.

beginning of this chapter) and their effects on the reader. The fourth section deals with one of the most popular presentations of poetry in many parts of the Western world—performance poetry. The fifth section guides you through experimentation with poetic form and discusses the ways form affects meaning and the communication of ideas in poetry. The final section is dedicated to finding poetry in the everyday and using sensory stimuli to inspire your poems.

The best advice for getting the most out of the examples in this chapter without becoming overwhelmed or frustrated (or homicidal) is to stop expecting the meanings of poems to leap off the page and slap you in the face.

Achieving instant comprehension is not the purpose of reading poetry. You are not expected to fully understand every line and every stanza on first or second or even third reading. And if you begin to panic because you think you're just not getting it you are almost certainly cultivating a delightful little self-fulfilling prophecy by doing so.

A much less painful alternative to repeatedly banging your head against a wall (or the desk) is this: read the poem at a natural pace from start to finish without stopping or rereading the lines that cause you consternation. As you read, let the sound of the words, and the images and feelings the lines evoke, wash over you—almost like a reverse stream of consciousness exercise in which the free thoughts are brought on by reading, instead of by writing. Once you have read over the poem for the first time, put it down, reflect on the parts of it that made you think. Then you can start to revisit the lines which didn't occur to you much on first reading.

Most importantly, bear in mind the principle of the hermeneutic circle which explains the dilemma of understanding a poem: in order to understand the poem as a whole, one must understand its parts—but in order to understand its parts, one must understand the poem as a whole. Finding your way into a reasonable interpretation of poems is necessarily a journey of methodological experimentation and contemplation, which is going to be a serious challenge if you're too busy freaking out.

Poetic movements: An abridged whirlwind history

A poetic movement—like other literary and arts movements—is a group of poets who practiced in a given period of time and whose work is distinguished by particular styles, feelings, or forms of poetry. Much of the poetry produced during each of the survey periods epitomizes certain values shared by poets at that moment in history. Often poetic movements are marked by the political and social contexts in which they emerged. The poetic techniques we will study in the remainder of this chapter were all derived from or gained prominence through different poetic movements in history, so a quick enumeration of a few of the key movements and eras will offer some necessary perspectives on the sections which follow.

Oral traditions of poetry

Before poetry was a written genre it was performed, spoken, recited, and sung. From the Ancient Greek oral poetries of masters like Homer and Sappho we can glean the beginnings of narrative poetry rich with characters and adventure and epic retellings of traditional stories about the gods. These stories are believed to have been memorized and performed before being transcribed later.

Very importantly, the Ancient Greeks' uses of poetic conventions like meter, rhyme, and alliteration to aid memorization and enhance the performative quality of the poetry are the foundation for all the techniques we use and apply to analysis today. Likewise, the philosophical literature about poetry from the Ancient Greeks, including Aristotle's *Poetics* and Plato's *Republic*, formed the beginnings of all the Western literary theory which followed.

Poets of the English Renaissance

The printing press became commonly used and the Elizabethan era culture established the importance of literature to England and to the English language. The English Renaissance was the setting for the earliest English sonnets. Sir Thomas Wyatt's sonnets were written between 1503 and 1542, Edmund Spenser's epic "The Faerie Queen" was written in 1596, and Shakespeare's sonnets were first published in 1609.

Classicism, which is literature inspired by classic mythology (for example, Shakespeare's poem "Venus and Adonis"), emerged during the English Renaissance.

Metaphysical Poets including John Donne, Andrew Marvell, and John Milton wrote in the lyric style consisting of conceits and speculations about love and God.

Shape Poetry such as George Herbert's "Easter Wings" (1633) emerged in the later part of the English Renaissance.

Romanticism

The Romanticist ethos of poets and artists was a revolt against the scientific and rationalized nature of the Enlightenment and the Industrial Revolution at the end of the eighteenth century. Romanticist poets including William Blake, Persey Bysshe Shelley, Mary Shelley, William Wordsworth, John Keats, and Samuel Taylor Coleridge embraced emotion over rationalism and, like the painters of that era, created an aesthetic both of the sublime and of gothic horror.

The Romantics used conventional form and regular rhythm and rhyme schemes, but it's worth noting that the first identifiably free verse poem was written by a Romantic poet. "The Argument" from William Blake's *The Marriage of Heaven and Hell* (1790–3) uses half-rhymes and unmetered rhythms and varied stanzas, all of which are techniques common to the free verse which came into prominence during the Victorian and Modernist eras.

Victorian era

This was the period of transition and transformation for English Language poetry from the Romantic to the Modern. Alfred Lord Tennyson's inherent musicality in poems such as "The Lady of Shalott" (1832) is an example of the influence drawn from Romantics such as Keats, and is also a clear precursor to the free verse of the Modernists.

Meanwhile, in New York, Walt Whitman's *Leaves of Grass* (1855) was revolutionary for modern and postmodern American poetry. Written in long-line stanzas inspired by the King James Version of the Bible, Whitman's meters relied on distinctively American accents and phrasings as opposed to English standards, essentially giving American poetry thereafter its own voice and identity.

Imagism

The Imagists formed the first modern poetic movement, in 1912, partly as something of a marketing ploy, and partly as a revolt against the traditions of the Romantics. Ezra Pound, Richard Aldington, "H. D." (Hilda Doolitle), and William Carlos Williams were the founders of Imagism:

In the spring or early summer of 1912, "H. D.," Richard Aldington and myself decided that we were agreed upon the three following principals:

1. Direct treatment of the "thing" whether subjective or objective.
2. To use absolutely no word that does not contribute to the presentation.
3. As regarding rhythm: to compose in the sequence of the musical phrase, not in sequence of a metronome.

–Ezra Pound[3]

The Imagist rejected poetry which was overly flowery, philosophical, or which described scenes and landscapes at great length (which Pound denounced as a vain attempt of the poet to do the job of a painter).[4] Note that all these features which were so undesirable to the Imagists are common to Romantic poetry. The Imagists wrote in free verse and defined an *Image* in their manifesto thus: "An Image is that which presents an intellectual and emotional complex in an instant of time."[5]

The Imagist poets, especially Ezra Pound, took inspiration from Eastern poetic traditions, especially the haiku form. One of the most famous Imagist poems, "Red Wheel Barrow," written by William Carlos Williams, almost takes the physical form of a poem written as a set of four connected haikus.

Harlem Renaissance

For more than a decade spanning before and after the 1920s after the post-World War I migration of great numbers of African Americans from the South to cities like New York, Chicago, and Washington DC, this movement was inspired by new economic and artistic opportunities, and celebrated African American culture, heritage, language, and religiosity. The poets of this movement contravened the pervading white literature and publishing culture of the time to write in styles and on topics which gave a voice to later African American writers. The scope of influences from which these poets drew ranged from the desire to create something completely new, to Anglo-American and English poets, to Southern folk music and sermons.

The Harlem Renaissance poet Langston Hughes experimented with a hybrid of lyricism, black everyday vernacular, and the blues in his works

---

[3] Ezra Pound, "A Retrospect," english.Illinois.edu, http://www.english.uiuc.edu/maps/poets/m_r/pound/retrospect.htm [accessed September 9, 2013].
[4] Ibid
[5] K. L. Goodwin, *The Influence Of Ezra Pound* (Oxford: Oxford University Press, 1966), p. 3.

on working-class life.[6] Jean Toomer also took inspiration from musical rhythms and structures in his explorations of racism and sexuality.[7]

The Beat Generation

The Beat Generation poets who wrote and published during the second half of the twentieth century are arguably responsible for delivering oral poetic traditions to a contemporary generation. Allen Ginsberg, Jack Kerouac, and William S. Burroughs were three prominent Beats whose writings share a spontaneous, rapid, rhythmical, stream-of-consciousness-like quality. The poets used innovative methods for composing poetry, aside from drug use, like recorded oral composition which was then transcribed, and writing continuously for extended periods on rolls of pulled-out butcher's paper. Their poetry was sometimes decidedly activist and often confrontational in subject matter and language; Ginsberg's poem, "Howl", famously landed its publisher, City Lights Books, in an obscenity lawsuit when it was first released.

As unique as the Beats were, they were a product of the times and of generations of poets who preceded them. Ginsberg was especially inspired by William Blake's visionary poetic exploits and the notion that one could "write poetry 'unfettered' by habitual tradition and contemporary critical standards."[8] Walt Whitman was something of a spiritual guide for several of the Beats, both in terms of his fearless treatment of sexuality in his poems and, for Ginsberg especially, for his long-line style which, as noted above, was in turn influenced by the King James Version of the Bible. It is worth noting also that Ginsberg was mentored by William Carlos Williams, who wrote the introduction to "Howl." Additionally, many of the Beats took inspiration from Eastern theology and poetics, especially things pertaining to Buddhism.

Confessionalism

The Confessional poets of the 1950s and 1960s were interested in dealing with deeply personal subject matter—often the darkest and, at the time,

---

[6] George Hutchinson, "Harlem Renaissance," brittanica.com, http://www.britannica.com/EBchecked/topic/255397/Harlem-Renaissance/272827/Poetry [accessed September 12, 2013].
[7] Ibid.
[8] Paul Portuges, "The Poetics of Vision," in *On the Poetry of Allen Ginsberg*, Lewis Hyde (ed.) (Ann Arbor: University of Michigan Press, 1984), p. 132.

taboo experiences such as sexuality, adultery, mental illness, the physical body, and drug abuse. Although most of the Confessional poets wrote in free verse, form wasn't essential to the movement. John Berryman, for instance, wrote a series of sonnets about an affair, titled *Berryman's Sonnets* (1967). What is common to all the Confessional poets and what necessarily distinguishes their work from other poetry is that the speaker of the poem is assumed to be the poet herself (or himself), whereas when we talk about most other poetry we separate the speaker in the poem from the identity of the poet.

Two compelling poets of the Confessionalism movement are Sylvia Plath and Anne Sexton, who enjoyed a friendship and wrote of their shared obsession with suicide, among other topics. After Plath died, Sexton wrote an ode to her friend, "Sylvia's Death."

The New York School

The New York School poets were something of a reaction against the Confessional poets. Their subject matter was decidedly observational rather than personal, worldly, sometimes light-hearted, other times violent. The New York School overlapped in terms of technique and the poets themselves with the Beats, writing in a stream of consciousness, spontaneous style.

The New York School poets were inspired by Surrealism and avant-garde visual arts and their poetry was rich with imagery. Frank O'Hara, Kenneth Koch, and John Ashbery are the key poets of the New York School.

There are numerous other prominent and grassroots poetic movements which emerged all over the world, especially in the past 100 years. They all have one thing in common: every movement is attached to some ideology, some way of thinking of the world and of the place poetry has in the scope of human existence. All poets, even the lone wolves who never associated with any movement, and even the less overtly political ones, are instrumental in shaping unique worldviews in one way or another.

Exercise

This is a research and reading task.

The descriptions above of different poetic movements and eras are necessarily tremendously abridged, since this is a creative writing coursebook and not a literature coursebook. Chances are you have already learned something about the history of poetry in your complementary studies.

Your task is to use the resources at your disposal to find one poem from each of the aforementioned poetic movements. You may start by researching one of the poets mentioned from each summary. Read the poems you find and write a two-page reflection about the poems, what you liked and didn't like, the techniques you observed in each, and how the readings might inform your own composition.

Workshop

Let your reading exercise stir a general discussion about the poems and poets you discovered, the techniques you observed, the eras and movements you are the most affected by, and how much (or how little) the task of finding poems you wanted to read altered your preconceptions about poetry. You might also begin talking about the kinds of poetry you hope to experiment with writing during the remainder of this chapter.

Poetry as "language distilled"

> Poetry is language at its most distilled and most powerful ... you carry it around and then it nourishes you when you need it.[9]

This famous quote by Rita Dove sounds almost like it is referring to the contents of a pendant vial full of some kind of deliciously refreshing drug. Dove's quote is quaint given the physicality of most poetry: the way the lines usually don't extend all the way to the margins of a page, the way poems tend to be self-contained literary works which start and finish in a single page or less, and the diminutive presentation of many books of poetry (think City Lights Books' Pocket Poet Series). And yet, Dove was not solely talking about the idea of distillation as something that is chiefly physical.

---

[9] Clara Villarosa (ed.), *The Words of African-American Heroes* (New York: Newmarket Press, 2011), p. 5.

The distillation of language is—to dine off the metaphor a little longer—the mental process of boiling down an idea to its essence. The challenge of poetry is to discard all the superfluities we often employ as crutches in our prose and strike directly at the truth in the heart of our subjects. Suddenly poetry is sounding more like an act of violence than a biochemistry experiment.

To digress from a largely analogous conversation and think about how this idea of "language distilled" tangibly works, it might help to look at what the Japanese haiku taught modern English language poets. You will recall from the haiku exercise you did in Chapter 1 that the haiku, at three short lines in total length, is one of the most "distilled" forms of poetry.

The following is a poem mentioned in the section on Imagism, William Carlos Williams's "Red Wheel Barrow":

so much depends
upon

a red wheel
barrow

glazed with rain
water

beside the white
chickens

This poem consists of four couplets, each of which consists of four words and either six or five syllables in total. Each couplet is focused on a single part of the whole image presented in the poem. The second line in each couplet contains the key image or idea, while the first line in each stanza contextualizes the image. The opening stanza is the one which shows us the significance of the poem's subject. The word 'red' in the second stanza is striking against the implied setting of a rainy day in the third stanza, and the wheelbarrow's steadfastness is contrasted by the whimsy and movement of the white chickens in the last stanza—thus demonstrating the point made about the wheelbarrow's inherent dependability at the beginning.

Can you see some similarities between this poem and a traditional haiku? They are short poetic forms, to be sure. Arguably, William Carlos Williams could not have communicated his intellectual and emotional image of a red wheelbarrow more effectively had he written a poem spanning 50 lines. Often students hate this poem on first reading because they feel certain they've missed something—but the beauty of the work lies in its commitment to the bare essentials. A reader does not necessarily have to give the poem a close reading in order to intuit its meaning, but that doesn't detract from its effectiveness.

There is a lesson in this poem about the potential for distilled language to pack a punch. This principle applies in the utterance of the everyday, too. Think about how much more powerful it can be when, in conversation, a person is able to make his point succinctly and eloquently rather than babbling and beating around the bush. Poetry is effective for the same reasons. Furthermore, the ability to use language in its most economical form is essential to writing and editing prose. Although in creative prose we have the freedom to elaborate on ideas, take tangential leaps back and forth, and spend time describing every sensual detail of a scene, the more we are capable of techniques which distil our language the more powerful our writing becomes.

The first important technique to master in the quest for language economy is simple: be specific in the first instance to avoid the tedious layering of detail over ambiguities.

Rather than writing "it was dark," why not say "a naked ten watt globe plugged into an outlet at one end of the corridor provided the only light source"?

At first glance, the second option is clearly longer than the first, so how is it more economical?

Well, not only does the second option show us that it's dark rather than merely telling us (yes, that old chestnut), it also conveys the challenge ahead, enhances the sense of tension, and establishes the scene at the same time as indicating how dark it is.

Of course, this is a judgment call and, for a particular style of prose, "it was dark" may be sufficiently compelling. The main thing is that it will help you make the best choice during your creative process if you understand the difference between the unembellished "it was dark" approach and the more descriptive "naked ten watt globe" approach. The philosophy of poetry as language distilled, once mastered, can be applied to your writing across the genres.

Exercise

The challenge of this exercise is to reject the use of superfluities and figure out what you really want to say, in a poem about a familiar object.

We all have objects in our daily lives which, for practical or sentimental reasons, give us comfort (perhaps for William Carlos Williams, for a moment, that object was a red wheelbarrow). It might be an old chair, or a piece of jewelry, or a well-used kitchen appliance, or a car, or something else.

Select an object that gives you comfort to be the subject of your poem.

Your task is to write a poem of four couplet stanzas (stanzas which consist of just two lines each) about this object.

The challenge is to communicate the essential significance of this object in the most economical way you can. Let Williams's way of juxtaposing the sturdy wheelbarrow with contrastingly lively fluttering chickens, and direct treatment of the fact of the wheelbarrow's dependability, inspire you.

Once you have written the first draft, go over it and see where you might cut back on excess descriptions or unneeded words, and how you might better communicate your meaning by using more specific language (for example, "beat-up blue sedan" instead of "the old car").

Workshop

Read your poem aloud, taking note of places which feel unnatural to annunciate or which come out sounding awkward.

Your group can give you general feedback on what they gleaned was the significance of your object, and where they noticed you used analogies, juxtaposing of contrasting images, and direct treatment of the central point.

Note down any changes you wish to make based on your group's feedback so you can edit this poem later.

The haiku, distilled

The art of the haiku form is contingent on the idea of language distilled, but not in a strictly quantifiable sense. The development of a strong image in a haiku emerges from a delicate balance of word choice, manipulation of line lengths, and the order in which the different elements of the image are presented. Even after you have composed three careful lines, you are left with the difficult choice of how to arrange the lines. The first incarnation of a haiku is not necessarily the best possibility. You might structure the lines so that there is a turn (similar to a volta in a sonnet) in the third line. Or you might open with an isolated movement in the first line and give the significance of the scene in the last line. Whatever structure you decide on, it's possible to mess around with the possibilities to see how the line order changes the communication of meaning.

Exercise

This exercise is about figuring out all the possibilities of a single haiku.

First, write a haiku in which one line describes an object, another line describes a movement, and a third line provides a setting or a context. The specific subject matter is your call.

Once you have your first draft, rewrite the haiku six different ways by simply rearranging the three lines into possible alternative orders. Put them all on one page, and write legibly.

When you are done, number each of the versions of your haiku.

Example

Here are six different versions of "Sad Haiku":[10]

1.
River of white headlights
Shine on raindrops, spattered pane
City-bound on the dusk M2

---

[10] Tara Mokhtari, *Anxiety Soup* (Melbourne: Finlay Lloyd Press, 2013), p. 31.

2.
Shine on raindrops, spattered pane
River of white headlights
City-bound on the dusk M2

3.
Shine on raindrops, spattered pane
City-bound on the dusk M2
River of white headlights

4.
River of white headlights
City-bound on the dusk M2
Shine on raindrops, spattered pane

5.
City-bound on the dusk M2
Shine on raindrops, spattered pane
River of white headlights

6.
City-bound on the dusk M2
River of white headlights
Shine on raindrops, spattered pane

The first version here is the one I settled on for publication, but it was not the first version I wrote.

Workshop

Form a circle. Each group member should pass their six haikus to the person on their left. When you receive a new page of haikus, read through each version and write on the back of the page which version you liked the best. Then pass the page along to the left again, and keep going until you have read and marked all your group mates' pages.

When you get your own page of haikus back, see if there was one version which your group mates agreed was the best. See how that one compares to your original haiku. What is it about the preferred version or versions that is more effective than the original?

Exercise

This task is meant to illuminate the difference between the language of prose and the distilled language of poetry.

Pick a scene from a chapter of your favorite book—just one coherent scene which describes a single action or even a single setting. It may be between one paragraph and two pages long.

Reread the scene, and then write a stream of consciousness piece inspired by what you feel the scene is really about, its significance to you, the tangents of thought it incites, and anything else that comes to mind.

Exercise

Based on the scene you chose and your stream of consciousness piece on that scene, your task is to compose a poem of between 8 and 16 lines.

Your challenge is to balance the physical details of the scene with their greater significance and your emotional response to it. You might take phrases directly out of your stream of consciousness piece, or you might temper certain sentences and rewrite them in your composition process. Whatever you do, try to compose a poem which would move a reader who had never read that book the same way the scene moved you.

Workshop

Read your poem aloud to your workshop group, taking note again of the parts which feel unnatural to annunciate or which come out sounding awkward, so you can edit these. Sometimes when you misread a first draft of something you have written, the misreading itself is a clue as to how the thing should read.

Have your group mates discuss the following questions about your poem.

- What does it seem to be about?

- What are the most striking images in the poem?
- What feelings do certain lines in the poem evoke?
- Which lines would your group mates like to hear again in order to better understand their meaning?
- Is there a discernible climax in the poem?
- Is the last line effective enough? Will a reader finish the poem and continue thinking about it?

Sound devices

Sound is an important component of what defines poetry and what differentiates poetry from the utterance of the everyday, even when everyday vernacular is the language used in a poem. The way a poem manipulates the sounds of words and phrases through various types of rhyming, rhythm, repeated consonant and vowel sounds in different parts of different words, repeated key words and refrains all contribute to the inherent sound of a poem.

It is not necessary for the poem to be written specifically for performance for sound devices to contribute to the structure and meaning of a poem—the feeling and understanding a poem conveys even when read from off the page depends somewhat on the emotional associations we have with certain sounds. For example, a long *s* sound might be interpreted as sensual, a crisp hard *k* sound might be jarring or violent, and a round *o* sound could evoke a flowing or rolling feeling. Of course, these are broad examples, and the real effect of the use of sound devices is activated when sounds are used to emphasize and complement certain words and phrases which communicate more literal meanings.

The following is the first part of a poem by Stevie Smith called "Black March." This poem was not written specifically for performance. You will notice that is does not contain regular end rhymes or a regular meter and the stanzas are all different lengths, so we can safely identify this as a poem written in free verse. That fact that this poem, like other free verse poems, implements sound devices solely for the purpose of helping to convey the intended meaning, rather than in forms like the sonnet which partly implements sound devices in order to adhere to the prescribed restrictions of the sonnet form, makes "Black March" a particularly good example of the function of different sound and poetic devices. Some, not all, of the sound devices have been annotated.

> I have a *friend*
> At the *end*
> Of the world.
> <u>His name is a breath</u>
>
> <u>Of fresh air.</u>
> He is dressed in
> **Grey chiffon. At least**
> I think it is chiffon.
> <u>It has a</u>
> **Peculiar look, like smoke.**
>
> It wraps him round
> It blows out of *place*
> It conceals him
> I have not seen his *face.*
>
> **But I have seen his eyes, they are**
> As pretty and bright
> As raindrops on black twigs
> **In March, and heard him say**
>
> I am a breath
> **Of fresh air for you, a change**
> By and by.[11]

The italicized words in the first and third stanzas are examples of end rhyme, which (incredibly!) is where there is rhyme at the end of a line. The underlined phrases are examples of enjambment, which is when a natural complete phrase is broken up from one line to the next (the opposite of end stop, where a phrase finishes and a new line begins). The bold lines all use caesura, or a punctuated pause occurring mid-line which affects the rhythm and pace of reading.

But there are many more subtle sound devices throughout these short stanzas. See if you can identify some of them.

---

[11] Stevie Smith, *Selected Poems*, James MacGibbon (ed.) (Middlesex: Penguin Books, 1978), p. 277.

Exercise

This is a quick test of your poetic observation skills.

Looking at the example of Stevie Smith's "Black March", see if you can identify where the following sound devices are used.

- Consonance: The repetition of a consonant sound at the beginning, middle, or end of any two or more words.
- Assonance: The repetition of similar or identical vowel sounds that do not necessarily perfectly rhyme.
- Refrain: A phrase which is repeated throughout the poem.
- Repetition: A word which is intentionally repeated through the poem.
- Alliteration: Two or more words in close proximity which start with the same letter or sound.

Workshop

Once you have found an example of each of the above, share your findings with your group.

In the introduction to this chapter, we discussed the thing that distinguishes poetry from prose: the combination of discursive and presentational symbols which inform our understanding of a poem. One of the points mentioned was that the space between stanzas can communicate meaning even more instantaneously than the words themselves.

Given this notion of the power of presentational symbols which are inherent to poetry, discuss the possible answers to the following questions: What is the effect of the enjambment between the first two stanzas (*His name is a breath // Of fresh air*)? What does the stanza break force the reader to do at that point in the poem? How does this convey the meaning of the words and phrases? What other art forms can you think of, if any, which can do this?

Exercise

Over the course of the week, whenever inspiration strikes you, write a free verse poem of 20 to 40 lines. The poem can be on any topic which happens to preoccupy your thoughts or emotions, any passing observation while you are out in the world, or any strange encounter you experience during the week. Be on the lookout for potential poetry in motion and write it down when it occurs to you.

Exercise

This is about editing your poetry with an eye (or an ear) for sound.

First, enlist the help of a partner. Have your partner read your poem quietly to herself first, ensure she understands it, and then listen while she reads your poem aloud to you.

Listen carefully for sound devices which you have already included, whether intentionally or incidentally, and think about how they could be exaggerated or tempered. Often repetitions of sound happen organically as we write and when we revisit the work we can find ways of making the most of them through editing.

Also listen for lines and stanzas which sound awkward when read aloud. Mark down where this happens and then rewrite those lines with a view to improving the way they sound. You may want to implement some of the devices mentioned earlier to emphasize certain words, force the reader to pause or slow down their reading, or repeat phrases, words, or sounds to convey certain meanings.

Do a complete rewrite of your poem based on everything you observed while listening.

Poetry and orality

The literature of Ancient Greece, especially Homer's *Iliad* and *Odyssey*, is the point of origin for Western poetry. The earlier section on poetic movements and eras alluded to the ways in which epic and pre-literate poems were performed through song and drama. Rhythm, rhyme, and other sound techniques helped performers to recall the poems. Oral story-telling is historically crucial to most cultures; the poetics therein assist with memory and preservation through retellings of traditional stories.

But the oral beginnings of poetry have manifested at many points in history since ancient times. Lyrics in music are a form of poetry (if you don't believe me, just ask Christopher Walken: http://www.youtube.com/watch?v=xy5JwYOlgvY, or Google "Christopher Walken reads Gaga's 'Poker Face.'" Then listen to a recording of Kurt Schwitters' sound poem, "Ursonate").

Rap and hip hop lyrics are arguably the closest thing we have to contemporary commercially viable poetry. And in the invention and reinvention of the coveted (in poetry circles, at least) Slam Poetry, where poets recite their work for audiences in a competitive arena, is prevalent in countries across the world, for better or for worse.

Besides these highly visible forms of oral poetry, at any given moment, in some bar or cafe somewhere in the world, an amateur poet is reading his soul for a half-empty room of his kinsfolk, and every time a small press publisher has a launch party for a new book of poems there is a reading or performance of some sort.

Poetry and orality have an enduring marriage, although it is lately sometimes fraught with identity crises when performers confuse the definition of their texts. Although spoken word and poetry share similarities, spoken word is written expressly to be spoken; that means that the words are expected to be colored by the performance, the personality, and the physicality of the performer. Poetry, on the other hand, should really be as effective on the stage as it is on the page. You know it's true because it rhymes.

The booming trend of Slam Poetry might be attributed to a number of modernist movements, perhaps most fervently the Beat Generation's influence on the new generation of poets. The Beats really emphasized the importance and effectiveness of the performance of poetry, through collaborations with musicians among other performative initiatives. As well as performing poetry, the middle part of the last century saw some poets experimenting with oral composition methods. During the 1950s, poets like Allen Ginsberg began recording spontaneous poetries on tape before noting them down later. These poets recognized the way in which oral improvisation augmented the creative process of composing poetry because of its inherent connection with sound. More importantly, this type of composition is quicker and more intuitive than sitting down in front of a blank page.

Exercise

You guessed right: your task is to experiment with composing something through recording improvised poetry.

This might feel unnatural or awkward at first. The following points might help.

- It could take a few attempts. If you try and give up, that's alright, just try it again later.
- Make sure you have time, space, privacy, and that you are feeling inspired when you start.
- If you have tried a few times and it just isn't working for you, change your environment. Do it in the dark. Do it on your phone while walking through the park. Put some instrumental music on and do it with the sound in the background. Do it in the shower or bath. This is beginning to sound more like love-life advice, but you get the idea.
- Treat it as a kind of verbal stream of consciousness exercise. Don't censor yourself in the improvisation stage. Whatever you hate you can delete later.
- You only need to spend up to ten minutes of actual recording time on this—although it might take some more time to prepare.

Once you manage to get all the way through a recording, go through and transcribe all the potentially usable bits.

It is up to you whether or not you feel you can turn the raw recorded material into a complete poem, but you are encouraged to at least try. You may find that, once you start writing things down, better ideas will surface and replace the exact words and phrases you came up with in your recording. That is alright, too!

If you do manage to come up with a poem, bring it, and your recording, into class.

Workshop

Share your poem and the recording with your workshop group, and have an open discussion about your experience. Try to answer the following questions.

- If you struggled with this task, what was standing between you and the illusive orally composed poem?
- What would you do differently if you were to attempt this exercise again?
- What are some possible variations on this exercise which still involve spontaneous oral composition, but which would be easier or more effective for you?
- What did you learn about your composition process by trying this method?
- Does the slight slowing down of ideas caused by the physical act of writing make composition easier? Or did you find that by recording yourself you were actually freer to keep up with your thoughts as they flowed?
- Will you use this method again?

Exercise

The following is a link to Jamaican poet Mutabaruka's performance on HBO's Def Poetry program; the poem is called "Dis Poem": http://www.youtube.com/watch?v=Pn-f8PgLVjU

After you watch "Dis Poem," think about the way Mutabaruka uses sound devices to emphasize the emotion behind some of the political messages of the poem. Also think about the use of melding of everyday and poetic language to create something that communicates on multiple levels. Consider the repetition of the title refrain "dis poem" and the way it punctuates scenes throughout the poem. And, finally, pay attention to the moment the poem becomes self-referencing and begins addressing the audience directly.

Your task is to write a poem for performance—that is to say, a poem which is both readable and aurally engaging. Make a concerted effort to implement sound devices which will keep the pace and contribute to the performance potential of the poem.

Start with a title. The title you choose will be repeated as a refrain to punctuate the scenes in your poem. Then begin writing. Every time you find you are moving into a new phase of the poem, repeat your title refrain. At some point, before the closing stanza, let your poem's speaker address its audience directly. Find a powerful ending which consolidates your central theme and somehow acknowledges the refrain and the audience.

When you are finished, go over your poem and edit it as you see fit.

Workshop

Each group member gets a chance to perform (or just read aloud). There is no need to give feedback on this one unless the poet specifically asks for it. The important part of this workshop is to experience reading your poem aloud to a large group, and feeling how effectively the devices you used through composition and editing translate in performance.

Form and meaning

So far in this chapter we have viewed poetic techniques and devices as they are used at the complete discretion of the free verse poet. However, from the brief descriptions of a few key survey periods and movements, we know that these techniques and devices are largely derived from particular forms—or prescribed styles—of poetry which came into prominence long before the advent of modern free verse. Some of the forms already mentioned in this chapter include the haiku and the English sonnet. Other forms you can research and experiment with include: the villanelle, the ballad, the canto, the ghazal (a Persian form), the epic, the sestina, and many more. All of these poetic forms have a unique set of tenets and physical restrictions calibrated by the linguistic, cultural, and artistic setting in which they emerged.

For example, we already know a haiku is three lines long, with a linear syllabic breakdown of 5, 7, 5. A sonnet can be identified by its three quatrains (a set of four lines connected by a rhyme scheme and a common subject) that lead into a closing couplet (two lines) from which we usually are able to gather the essential thrust of the whole poem. Of course, there are different types of sonnets: the Petrarchan sonnet, the Shakespearean sonnet, the Spenserian sonnet, as well as modern sonnets and sonnets written in languages other than English. While all of these sonnets commonly use the three quatrains and concluding couplet, they vary according to rhyme scheme (the pattern of end rhyming used throughout the poem) and sometimes according to meter.

The question is how are these classical forms relevant today? Why bother with them when we have free verse at our disposal which allows us not to follow any seemingly arbitrary rules of expression? Is not the point of poetry to use poetic devices to most effectively communicate our message rather than be hindered by them in a restricted form? After all, this is a creative writing course, not a literature course.

Some contemporary poets are naturally drawn to formality. In your workshops for this chapter, you may have heard students say that, as far as they're concerned, if it doesn't rhyme and have a meter, it isn't poetry. This is an objectively incorrect assertion, of course, but that does not undermine the creative preference for stricter form. For those poets who generally disregard classical forms in their compositions, occasionally forcing themselves to adhere to a particular stanzaic structure or rhyme scheme can actually be an interesting exercise in restraint. More importantly, if you understand how to make the most out of the boundaries form provides, you have yet another opportunity to improve the control you exert over your free verse. The challenge here is to communicate as expressively as possible within a framework, and once you can do that, you can begin to make the framework bend to convey your intended meaning.

Additionally, not all forms are wholly prescriptive. As well as experimenting with a traditional sonnet in this section, you will be introduced to concrete (or shape) poetry—a form which is as presentational as it is discursive.

Sonnets

The rhyme scheme for a Shakespearean sonnet is: a, b, a, b, c, d, c, d, e, f, e, f, g, g. If you look at the last word of every line of a Shakespearean sonnet you will notice this rhyming pattern, which separates each quatrain by a new set of two end rhymes, and a rhyming couplet at the end.

The meter of a Shakespearean sonnet is called an iambic pentameter, which means that there are five stressed syllables on each line (on average in the English Language we naturally stress every second syllable we utter).

Here is Shakespeare's Sonnet 130:

My Mistres eyes are nothing like the Sunne,
Currall is farre more red than her lips red,
If snow be whit, why then her brests are dun,
If haires be wiers, black wiers grown on her head;
I have seene Roses damaskt, red and white,
But no such Roses I see in her cheekes,
And in some perfumes there is more delight,
Than in the breath that from my Mistres reekes.
I love to heare her speake, yet well I know,
That Musicke hath a farre more pleasing sound
I graunt I never saw a goddesse goe,
My Mistres when shee walks treads on the ground.
    And yet by heaven I thinke my love as rare,
    As any she beli'd with false compare.[12]

Note the rhyme scheme: sunne, red, dun, head; white, cheeks, delight, reekes; know, sound, goe, ground; rare, compare. Also see if you count either nine or ten syllables in every line. In this particular example, the quatrains are also punctuated with either a semicolon or a period.

Of course, poetic forms evolve with time. Here is a contemporary sonnet about Melbourne, Australia. Check how closely it resembles a Shakespearean sonnet:

Stupid Sonnet II

Her granite-black streets soaked
mist abound at every gutter
floating above sidewalks, boots and cloaks,
coffee brews and voices mutter.
Gothic shadows wake from dreams
of European romances and Rioja wine,
oak-tree hems and tram-track seams,
regular rhythms and sporadic rhyme.
Lime and lemongrass emanate from little Bourke lanes,

---

12 William Shakespeare, "130," in *Seven Centuries of Poetry in English*, 5th edn, John Leonard (ed.) (Oxford: Oxford University Press, 2003), p. 501.

beats and riffs pulse underground
through dark hours the warmth remains
she holds my hand and walks me 'round.
She holds my heart, recites poetry,
and inspires mine – Melbourne, my obsidian city.[13]

Exercise

Your task is to write a Shakespearean sonnet about your city or town.

Try to restrict yourself to the rhyme, rhythm, and stanzaic structures set out in the classic and contemporary examples above.

The challenge here is going to be to capture the essence of your city and evoke its unique sensory pastiche, its mood, its significance to you, and convey all of that in a limiting framework. It's alright to break the rules a little bit, but try to produce something as closely resembling a Shakespearean sonnet written in contemporary English as possible.

Exercise

Now that you have attempted a conventional sonnet, your next task is to write a kind of hybrid free verse poem which implements two of the conventions common to the Shakespearean sonnet.

You might choose to write a poem with four quatrains and a closing couplet that neither rhymes nor follows a meter. Or, you might choose to write a longer poem which has a closing rhyming couplet and consists of approximately ten syllables per line. There are many possible variations.

The only other requirement is that this poem should explore the theme of death.

---

[13] Tara Mokhtari, *Anxiety Soup* (Melbourne: Finlay Lloyd Press, 2013), p. 6.

Exercise

Revisit the absurd happening exercise from Chapter 1.

Your task is to write a poem about that absurd event you witnessed and later wrote about. You can use the prose you produced in the earlier exercise as a starting point, or you might want to give the topic some fresh perspective.

The first thing you will need to do is to figure out what you want your poem to say about this absurd happening, and make sure that you write to that thematic goal. Whatever you decide about the central point of your poem might inform the composition of your closing lines.

Your only other challenge is to incorporate one device common to the sonnet form, and one other sound device mentioned earlier in this chapter.

Concrete poetry

In the 1950s in Europe, poets like Eugen Gomringer and Augusto and Haroldo de Campos began writing a kind of poetry which might be described as being even more presentational than discursive in form. Concrete poetry has its roots in the shape poetry of the seventeenth-century poet George Herbert, who wrote poems like "Easter Wings" in the shape of a pair of wings which were originally published on their side. Concrete poetry takes poetry which is arranged in a strikingly visual form to the next level by experimenting with the possibilities of what meaning can be derived purely from presentation. Here is Eugen Gomringer's famous concrete poem, "silencio":[14]

```
silencio    silencio    silencio
silencio    silencio    silencio
silencio                silencio
silencio    silencio    silencio
silencio    silencio    silencio
```

---

[14] Eugen Gomringer, "silencio" (first published 1953).

It is possible to have an immediate intellectual understanding of what this poem is about simply by looking at it on the page; however, taking the time to read it aloud and pausing for the length of time it takes to say "silencio" in the space in the middle of the poem is equally effective in communicating the point of the poem.

In a way, concrete poetry is simultaneously the freest and most instantly recognizable poetic form. There are no restrictions in terms of how you must use poetic devices or presentational symbols to communicate meaning in a concrete poem. You can repeat a single word or phrase or you can use many words and phrases in your composition. And the arrangement of the words is at the creative discretion of the poet, as long as it somehow contributes to the meaning of the poem.

Exercise

This is about collaborating with a co-poet in the composition of, yes indeed, one or a short series of connected concrete poems.

Working with a partner, first decide on a subject that interests you both. Then start by having a general discussion on the associations you make between that subject and the physical world. When you feel ready, figure out how your concrete poem will look on the page, the kinds of words you will use to help convey your intended meaning, and what the first thing is that you want your reader to notice about the poem.

Once you have sorted out those details, each of you can compose your own version of the concrete poem. Then compare your individual attempts and see if you can use the most effective parts of each to create one new draft of the concrete poem.

Workshop

Make a pile of all the concrete poems your workshop group have composed, and have each partnership select one at random. You should not worry about identifying the creators of the concrete poem you are working on.

Your job is to look at, read, and interpret the poem you found and then show your findings to the class.

Once everyone's concrete poem has been presented, the creators of each can talk about the intention behind the poem, and the class can have a general discussion on the efficacy of the presentations.

Finding your poem

So now you understand the application of some poetic techniques, and, chances are, having practiced composition through the exercises in the earlier sections of this chapter, you are beginning to find a place for poetry in your repertoire (if it did not already exist). This last section is about ways of recognizing the potential for poetry in the everyday, and using sensory stimuli to inspire your poetry.

The following homework tasks are best completed in moments when you are living your normal life and opportunity strikes. Sometimes that means pulling your pen and notepad out to write while you are out in the world. Other times it means forcing yourself to write when you are alone and perhaps not feeling particularly like writing.

Exercise

This one requires you to pay attention to your physicality in a moment of heightened emotion and write a stream of consciousness style poem in the moment.

At some point when you are feeling an overwhelming emotion, pause, grab a pen and notebook, and sit somewhere comfortable. Whatever you do, don't try to shake yourself out of the emotional state, just spend some time observing how it feels.

Think about your posture, your breathing, the tension in your face and shoulders, and your body temperature. Also pay attention to the speed at which thoughts are churning through your mind.

When you are ready, start writing. Let the rhythm of the sensations flowing through your body dictate the poem to you. While we usually talk about stream of consciousness as an observation of every thought running through your mind, this stream of consciousness poem should focus on the many simultaneous physical experiences of the emotion.

Keep writing until the poem feels complete. Then set it aside, do whatever you need to do, and revisit what you wrote another day when you are feeling calm.

Exercise

This one is about finding poetry in strange encounters.

The next time you have a strange encounter of the silent variety with a stranger, take some mental notes about the finer details we don't always look for when we are in the thrust of everyday weirdness. Look at what the stranger is wearing, his or her hairstyle, posture, idiosyncrasies, and what you think the stranger is thinking about, what certain looks or expressions seem to communicate. They might be very obvious in their body language or they might be trying to conceal something.

As soon as possible after the strange encounter is over, write a poem about what happened—how the encounter started and how it ended—including something of a character sketch and something of the dynamics between you and the stranger.

Keep writing until you feel you have a poem which encompasses the essence of this strange encounter. Set it aside for a day or two and then reread what you have written. Does revisiting this poem evoke the sensations of the strange encounter? Are there things you remember about it upon rereading that you forgot to include in the actual poem? Are there parts of it which detract from the main feeling you had about the strange encounter that you can cut?

Rewrite the poem based on your explorations of the above questions.

Exercise

The next time you have plans to meet somebody in a restaurant, bar or cafe, show up 20 minutes early with your notebook and pen.

Your task is to write a poem about your observations of the sights, smells, sounds, and sensations surrounding you as you sit quietly by yourself in a room full of activity. Try to identify your core emotion at that moment—whether you are feeling lonely, apprehensive, tired, anticipatory, self-conscious, or frustrated— and make that emotion the epicentre of all the sensory action happening around you.

The challenge is to write something that a reader will be able to relate to in some way. We all have moments of being alone in a crowd, even if we have different experiences of it at different times. Your poem should stir up the emotion you are feeling in the moment you wrote it for your reader.

You may want to edit this poem when you have some free time, and then take it in to class for workshopping.

Workshop

Without first providing the background or context of one of your poems from the above exercises, read it aloud to your group. What overriding emotion did your group mates sense throughout the poem, and what kind of setting did they envisage as you were reading? See if your group grasped your intention for the poem and ask them for feedback on what you could do in terms of enhancing or rearranging the order of information, the line lengths, the sounds, and the sensory details in the poem.

4

Fiction Conventions

This chapter might have been presented as two separate chapters: one dedicated to short stories and another to novel writing. While there are obvious distinctions between the two most common forms of prose fiction, they share enough essential fiction writing conventions and creative processes that it's possible to learn something significant about one by practicing the other, and vice versa.

The curious beginning followed by a quick building of dramatic tension which might characterize the structure of an entire short story is useful in constructing a powerful climax in a novel. The brushstroke style of character development in a novel, where a character is exposed through layers of plot, dialogue, and internal monologue rather than exclusively through narration, is important for maintaining the pace of a short story (as opposed to stopping short to describe the character in her entirety before moving on to developing the plot). The treatment of a central theme, the presence of hooks to entice the reader to read on in the beginning, the allusion to back story in exposition, settings, characters—all of these things are the body parts of most prose fiction forms; it can be handy to dissect them to understand their functions in the life-force of a good novel or short story and to understand how they work differently in each.

The thing is, though, all the aforementioned techniques are about as useful as the body parts in a cadaver if they are learned independently from the art of finding stories. Sure, you can identify each one and articulate its definition, but really—since this isn't brain surgery, it's creative writing, nobody is going to be harmed in the reading of this chapter—you want to mess around with the possibilities of these techniques in real potential starting points for new pieces of fiction writing.

So, providing real starting points for new pieces of fiction is precisely what the exercises throughout this chapter are designed to do. You can approach the exercises purely for technical practice if you want to, but you can also use what you write for each exercise as markers for a novel you might be working on (or want to start), one or a series of short stories, or even a novella.

If you have a creative project in mind, the exercises will help you to explore the potential of the application of each of these techniques—to try a new way of describing a setting or developing a character. The idea is to break out of your usual approach to fiction writing, and, in doing so, discover a whole new set of possibilities for your plot, character, and your treatment of the theme.

If you are starting fresh, use the exercises to inspire ideas for complete short stories, or even the beginnings of a novel. Try to imagine the "what ifs" of the bits and pieces you work on so you can expand on them later if you want to—imagine more than just the one or two pages the exercises ask you to produce as you formulate your ideas.

Whatever you do, bear in mind that the *idea* is the skin of your story; it is the largest, all-encompassing organ, without which all the other parts would be exposed, ugly, and in grave peril. Of course, the idea for a story can come before you put fingertips to keyboard, or it can come as a result of experimentation with a technique. The important thing (as in life and love) is that it does, indeed, come.

If you find yourself uninspired with the outcome of an exercise, think about the reasons why it wouldn't work as an idea for a story: Where is the blockage? What could you have done differently? What kind of character would you rather have worked on? What do you really feel like thinking deeply about at this moment? How can this preoccupation become a new idea you can actually get on board with?

Fiction and creativity: The anecdote, the muse, and the visionary

In the chapter on self-writing we began to elaborate on the key differences between literature and utterance of the everyday. We drew from the theory that literature works only to signify itself, whereas everyday speech works to signify something else in our real lives. The next mystery we have to debunk about the connection between literature and the everyday is this:

Where does fiction come from? If literature is literature and life is life, how is literature created inside of life?

Whereas in previous chapters you have worked more directly from life experience, this chapter asks you to begin to find the parts of your thought processes where imagination comes from.

Although there might be a bit of you in every character you create, and a bit of your life and the places you've been in every story you dream up, you are no longer depending solely upon memory for your writing.

The anecdote

Anecdotes have a complex relationship with writing and fiction; they are taken from everyday life, and retold in everyday life, as well as within the context of literary fiction, essays, memoirs, blogs, and feature articles. Sometimes fiction itself is derived from anecdote.

However, the object of an anecdote necessarily contrasts from the object of fiction. We read (or listen to) an anecdote for its punch line—which is the single most important reason the otherwise cursory characters, plot, and setting come together. On the other hand, we read fiction to enter the world of the characters, plot, and setting, and quite often the punch line is something we construe through our understanding of the narrative rather than something which is delivered to us on a silver platter.

When used as a literary device in a work of fiction, anecdotes can offer insights into the characters that tell them, and act as foreshadowing, symbolism, metaphor, etc. For example, in the first chapter of my novel, *Lion!*, I use an anecdote to help establish mood in the opening scene, to introduce the protagonist's way of thinking and his sense of humor. Importantly, I also use the anecdote to frame the whole chapter with an animal motif:

> So here they are, a little drunk and damp haired, ascending the cracked and scratched marble stairs to Len's second floor hotel room. She's telling him a story about a famous billionaire entrepreneur who built apartments a few blocks away along the Hudson River. When the apartments were finished, the unnamed billionaire let loose great orchestras of crickets in the park across the street. His big idea was that when people visited they'd think this area was something special; the night air all a chirp – an aural piece of upstate magic in the middle of Uptown Manhattan. Len is tired listening to this story and all he can think about is what the string section of a cricket orchestra would look like: a thousand little tuxedoed Jiminy clones each with

a tiny violin tucked beneath his chin playing Vivaldi's Four Seasons. They reach the second floor.[1]

The anecdote is the story about the billionaire and the crickets and it appears almost at the very beginning of the chapter. The crickets are revisited at the end of the chapter after the central hook of the story is exposed—the protagonist has found a lion in his New York City hotel room and he is in a state of panic:

> He runs down the hallway in his socks, reaches the elevator and punches the down button thrice before quitting and skidding down the stairs.
>
> In the lobby a high school sports team swarms around the front desk. Len runs past them hissing: "Lion!"
>
> The receptionist doesn't look up from the stack of room keys he's counting out and allocating. A small group of kids turn to see the weirdo tall long-haired guy barefoot running out into the street mumbling about animals. One kid soberly comments in a knowing Southern accent that, "all New Yorkers are like that."
>
> Cars and trucks fill the streets as rush hour starts on the Upper West Side. Len keeps running down West Seventy-Ninth in the direction of the Hudson not stopping to look for traffic as he sprints across the road, over the roundabout at Riverside Drive and into the park. He keeps running until his heart nearly explodes and then he lands in a heap on a park bench. A rat holding a cricket in his teeth scurries past and disappears into the shadows of the unkempt leaves of grass.
>
> Suddenly Len can feel his body again. Every muscle aches unbearably. To keep from losing it completely and weeping into the river, Len lets rip a roaring:
>
> "RAAAH!"[2]

The important thing to note is that while anecdotes are useful in fiction, they aren't fiction in and of themselves. Some anecdotes from our lives might translate well into fiction if you have a way of creatively approaching the treatment of the characters, plot, and setting involved; some anecdotes can be worked into our fiction as literary devices which expose information about our characters and further the exploration of our themes, whereas other anecdotes are better saved for happy hour.

---

[1] Tara Mokhtari, *Lion!* (manuscript, 2013), p. 1.
[2] Ibid., pp. 12–13.

The muse

The idea of the muse is one which transcends cultures and eras. By some definitions, the muse is necessarily a living person, often a beautiful woman, who inspires the writer and triggers the creative process. By other definitions the muse is something much less tangible or human—it's an autonomous spirit which inhabits the writer in moments (or hours) of spontaneously inspired creative productivity.

In practical terms, the muse is the philosophy behind the stream of consciousness exercise introduced in Chapter 1. The idea with stream of consciousness is that we can tap into new and unexpected possibilities for fiction by opening our minds and disallowing self-judgment or self-censorship so that the inspiration flows in (or out). So far in this book, for the most part, we have considered knowledge as it manifests through cognition and consciousness, our memories, our observations, our values. But, of course, creativity doesn't always work in so much black and white.

Quite often, when we are at our most creative and most productive, it's as though we unplug from reality and plug into an alternate state of mental functioning. It doesn't follow, however, that this alternate state should be relied upon to happen of its own accord and dictate when the writer does and doesn't work. Exercises like the stream of consciousness one are ways into the "muse zone," as is the act of mindful procrastination! The writers who ever actually finish a work of literature are generally the ones who are in touch enough with their muse to be able to conjure it regularly every day by being disciplined in their practice.

Some folks embrace the spiritual idea of the muse as something which inhabits the writer because they prefer to feel that they are not really responsible for the things they write—that some external universal force created the work and they were just the divine vessel for it. Some folks take a lot of exotic drugs to try to capture the experience of the muse synthetically, while others practice meditation, and work on their spirituality to attain increased contact with the muse.

Whether any of the above is for you is nobody's business. But the trend suggests that, for a writer, the feeling of being highly creative and productive is the best feeling of all—it is at these moments we feel like the greatest version of ourselves. So, it's no wonder the feeling can be addictive.

Suffice to say, fiction is derived from much more than everyday life and reality.

The visionary

The idea of the writer as visionary—someone who sees divine visions of God or the universe or who has psychic abilities—has been around at least since the Romantic period, when writers and artists became placeholders for God in society. Perhaps most notably, the notion of the visionary writer can be attributed to the poet William Blake, who claimed that he saw visions of ghosts and angels his whole life and these became the subject matter of his poetry and paintings.

William Butler Yeats, the Irish poet, experimented with automatic writing, which, in its most mystical state, assumes that the writer is inhabited by a spirit who is using her to send a message (the writer as human Ouija board?), and in its most practical state is linked with something like stream of consciousness writing, because the idea is that the writer is not in command of the words, the words just emerge. Yeats wrote *A Vision* (1925) based on his experimentations with creativity.

In 1948, in Harlem, the poet Allen Ginsberg reported that he heard the voice of Blake reciting poetry to him, and saw the hand of God outside the window, and he wrote the poem "The Lion For Real" inspired by the experience. This was the first of a few visions which he initially felt were God and later believed to be realizations of his mature self. Whatever the reality, Ginsberg's cult status sustains in the minds of many people today.

Whatever the truths behind these mysterious stories, it might be argued that all creative writers have something of a visionary inside their imaginations. Perhaps physical, external visions don't come to you, but unprompted ideas certainly do (you know what I'm talking about). A writer doesn't necessarily need to sit down and work at conjuring an idea for her next novel or screenplay or poem—quite often the ideas begin to play out without any effort in our minds through day or night dreams.

The point of having an awareness of the more infamous notions of visionary experience is to recognize that part of your creative existence when it's happening to you and learn to use it, rather than ignoring it. When you have a dream that moves you, even if it was disturbing and the first instinct is to try to forget about it as quickly as possible, write it down. When you hear music in your mind, write about it. If you happen to see things, describe them on paper (then perhaps, to your doctor).

Ideas and themes

Theme is really the reason for the characters, plot, and setting of a work of fiction to collide in the way that the author sets out to tell a story. It's the thing that makes the reader think after they stop reading. Themes tend to be broad and relatable topics about the human experience, but the way in which an author chooses to tell a story is a manifestation of his or her particular perspective on a broad theme. If you think about every novel that has ever been written on the "coming of age" theme, each one necessarily emphasizes its own original take on what it means to "come of age." So, the aim of the following exercises on theme is to get you to identify the original ways in which you might treat different common themes, and manipulate character, plot, and setting according to your unique perspectives on human experience.

The following exercises explore themes through micro-short stories. A micro-short story is less than 300 words in length, and it may either be entirely self-contained or it may be part of a potentially larger narrative. The important thing about a micro-short story is that it has to be engaging and dynamic from beginning to end.

Exercise

The following is a series of "beginnings." Each phrase could kick off a micro-story. Don't look at them all now, instead hide the list under a piece of paper, or your teacher can give you the phrases one by one at five-minute intervals.

Your task is to look at the first phrase, write it down and then continue it on, building the micro-story using the skills you learned in your stream of consciousness exercises. Spend five minutes writing on each phrase, and as soon the five minutes are up, move straight on to the next one. The key is to let each phrase trigger your creative response.

Phrase 1: Despite her adoration for him, she knew …

Phrase 2: Beneath the kitchen sink he kept a …

Phrase 3: She was perfect mess of a human being, her face …

Phrase 4: The fence was far too high to jump, there was nowhere left to …

Phrase 5: The monotonous beep of a heart monitor flat-lining was a sound she …

Workshop

Try to identify the theme and inspiration you took from each phrase and how they differed between group members. What were the clues in each phrase which were suggestive of theme? How did each group member interpret the clues differently? Also discuss the ways in which you felt compelled to explore each phrase according to your instincts.

Exercise

The following is a scenario with the theme of "secret relationships", with the details hollowed out. Your task is to write a short story (two or three pages long) which explores the way you imagine the scenario would play out.

Don't limit yourself to just filling in the blanks, expand the scenario out into a coherent story by adding extra details. Also, feel free to alter parts of the existing information if it would suit your telling of the story better.

> They were only (?) and (?) respectively the year that they met.
>
> (?) was from a (?) family and had lived in the same (?) since she/he was born. She/he had never seen a (?) before in her/his life. She/he felt confined by her/his (?) until (?)
>
> (?) had moved into the neighborhood after (?), and missed the (?) terribly. She/he felt like an outsider in her/his new town until one day (?)
>
> Because of the nature of their relationship, they had to keep it a secret. (?)'s family would never understand (?), and (?) could lose her/his (?) if the truth ever came out.
>
> One morning they met by coincidence at the local (?). In public they acted (?). Both of them were dreading their day ahead, but for very different reasons…
>
> (?) quietly joked that they should get on a bus to (?) and change their names and never look back.
>
> (?) said it actually wasn't such a bad idea…
>
> They looked at each other. They both knew it was the

answer to all their problems—they'd be giving up everything they know, but they would always have each other.

The agreed to meet back at the bus depot in thirty minutes…

At the bus depot, (?) waited under the big clock by the ticket counter holding two fares.

(What happens next?!)

That was a very long time ago. Now they are (?).

Everyone in that town who is old enough to remember what happened still talks about the day those two (?).

Exercise

The following is a list of general themes. Each theme comes with a short series of keywords attached to it. Your task over the course of the following week is to write a micro-short story (between 100 and 300 words in length) triggered by each theme and keyword combination. Write one of these each day.

Ideally, you should look at one of the theme/keyword combinations first thing in the morning, write it down in a notepad and carry it with you during the day. Any time you have a new thought or idea, note it down. Then at the end of the day, set aside 10 or 15 minutes and write up your micro-short story.

Theme 1: Death—absence, estrangement, goodbyes, accident, empty, relief, dreaming

Theme 2: Kindness—strangers, surprise, cruel world, faith, spirit, hands, empathy, loneliness

Theme 3: Spaces—home, public, shared, solitary, confinement, productivity, history

Workshop

The micro-short story is a genre which is gaining traction through social media platforms. It can be a welcome imaginative alternative to the usual kind of personal or current affairs-related posts users are used to reading on Facebook and Twitter.

Your workshop group might initiate a closed social media group where you can post your micro-short stories for comment by your peers for the purposes of workshopping these exercises.

Narrative structure

Narrative structure is a term that encompasses all the elements of story-telling, including the theme and the way it manifests through plot, character, setting, and point of view. Underlying all these narrative elements is the Aristotelian theory which has been in existence since the earliest analyses of Greek tragedy: that every story has a beginning, middle, and end. This might seem like fairly pedestrian advice to writers, but it can be worth thinking about your stories in the three-act structure early on in the composition process to ensure you are maintaining optimum control over how each act interacts and answers to the others.

In the chapter on Screenwriting, you will be introduced to some more detailed narrative structural maps which are overall more film and television specific. In this section, we'll focus on the essentials of the beginning, middle, and end.

Beginnings

The beginning is the set-up. Two key parts of the story happen here.

- Exposition: We are introduced to the main characters and the world they inhabit. This part of the story is a set-up of what is and isn't justified in terms of the protagonist's potential reactions, actions, and motivations, and also in terms of what we can expect from the world in which the story is set. In order to achieve suspension of disbelief for your reader, you need to honor whatever it is you've told or shown us at the beginning about who your characters are and the time and place they live in.

- Inciting incident: The inciting incident is the thing that throws our protagonist into the situation that will (however subtly) either make or break her/him. It is the beginning of the story's inevitable trajectory. In very short stories, the exposition and inciting incident can overlap. We learn about our protagonist as they enter into the centre of the action of the story.

Even in stories which open by showing us a flash-forward of the ending, we have a set-up that demands to be examined further in the middle and revealed as a resolution at the end.

Middles

The middle is the exploration of what was set up in the beginning. Two main things happen in the middle of a narrative.

- The rising action: The protagonist begins to respond to the inciting incident, and encounters a central conflict in doing so. That is to say, we realize that it's not going to be a straightforward task for our protagonist to overcome the situation introduced at the beginning. The central conflict might be brought on by another character or by circumstance, and is known as "the antagonist."
- The falling action: The protagonist changes her/his approach and begins to tackle the central conflict, albeit not without some subsidiary conflicts along the way.

Essentially, in the middle, you should let your protagonist suffer as much as possible as a result of the inciting incident, as she/he grapples with the unfolding conflict. As Kurt Vonnegut puts it: "Be a sadist. No matter how sweet and innocent your leading characters, make awful things happen to them—in order that the reader may see what they are made of."[3]

Endings

The ending is the resolution of what was set up in the beginning. In the end two things usually happen.

- Climax: This is the highest point of action in your story. It is at this moment that the protagonist is either triumphant or dead. All the

---

[3] Vernon Trollinger, *Haunted Iowa City* (Charleston: Haunted America, 2011), p. 80.

possibilities of the rising and falling action have been exhausted and there's only one thing left to do. The tension is stretched so tight at this point that it has no choice but to snap.

- Denouement: This is our closing, after all is said and done—where we leave our protagonist. Sometimes this is a lengthy examination of how the events of the beginning, middle, and climax have changed our protagonist for better or worse. In shorter fiction we end with the briefest sigh at the cessation of the climax and leave the details up to the reader to think about.

You can think of the relationship between the main elements of the beginning, middle, and ending as a kind of imperfect symmetry. The Exposition is resolved through the Denouement. The Inciting Incident is resolved by the Climax. The Rising Action is countered by the Falling Action. You could figuratively fold a story down the middle to discover the cause-and-effect relativity of each of these main narrative structural parts.

Of course, this is all very plastic narrative theory once you start applying it to the imagining of your fictional story. The three acts are totally open for manipulation and experimentation and some of the most compelling fiction bends the three-act rule to fit the story's intended aesthetic and thematic underpinnings. And obviously, we never sit down to write a story with all these parts in mind ... That is, until right now.

Exercise

Plot and write a six-paragraph micro-short story. Each short paragraph must correspond with each of the above points under the subheads, beginning, middle and ending: Exposition, Inciting Incident, Rising Action, Falling Action, Climax, and Denouement.

Bear in mind that you need to make each of the paragraphs relate to each other in the way described above: the Exposition is answered by the Denouement, the Inciting Incident resolved in the Climax, and the Rising and Falling actions directly opposing each other.

You should limit yourself to just one or two characters for the purposes of this exercise. You will need to decide who your protagonist is and who/what her/his antagonist is. You also may try starting with a single sentence description for each paragraph so you are clear on how each part of your story works in the context of the whole.

This shouldn't take longer than 25 minutes. Don't forget to look at the lists you made in the exercises for Chapter 1 if you feel stuck for ideas.

Workshop

Discuss the following questions.

1 How difficult or easy is it to force yourself to think of a story in terms of a three-act structure?
2 What kind of story did you come up with? Does it remind you of any other types of stories you have read? Does it mimic a fairytale or fable type of narrative, for instance?
3 What are the advantages and disadvantages of putting structure ahead of inspiration in the composition of a work of fiction?
4 Do you feel more or less inclined to pay heed to the functions of the three acts in stories you write in the future having now thought of them in literal terms? Why? Why not?

Narrative structure toolbox

Hooks

Similar to the hook in a pop song, the literary hook is the tantalizing piece of information given at the start of a work of fiction that attracts the reader's interest. Sometimes this is in the form of a question that needs to be answered later in the story. Other times it's an incomplete description of a character, event, or place which requires further explanation in order to satisfy the reader's piqued curiosity. We keep reading because we need to know more once we are hooked on the story.

Occasionally we are induced to keep reading when the author stimulates our voyeuristic inclinations, as in Anton Chekhov's short story, "The

Slander."[4] Chekhov concludes the opening paragraph, which describes the bustle and activity of a wedding party of elite guests, with the sentence: "Persons whose social position precluded them from entering were looking in at the windows from the yard," which indicates to the reader that some juicy piece of gossip must surely be simmering away inside the house. We want to know what the gossip is, and so we keep reading to find out.

Symbols

Symbols are used in fiction as denotations of deeper meaning. Symbols are established in our understandings of the world, so when we find them in a work of fiction we automatically take meaning from them within the context of the writing—often without even realizing it. In a way, symbols are a way for the story to speak to the reader's subconscious. For example, where there is a mention of water in a text we immediately understand it to denote cleansing or clarity. When we think of the color yellow we generally associate it with happiness.

In "The Slander," Chekhov particularly chooses midnight for the temporal setting of the part of the story where the protagonist unwittingly vilifies himself in a state of abject paranoia. The symbol of a clock striking midnight usually denotes the sense that something sinister is about to happen. When the protagonist suffers the consequences of his paranoia during the next day, we take the symbol of daytime to denote exposure or revelation.

Dialogue

Dialogue is the speech that takes place between two or more characters in fiction. Often, dialogue is most useful for indirect exposition of character, but sometimes dialogue is also used as a plot device. In "The Slander," the protagonist's dialogue is used to both advantages:

> "I've just been in the kitchen to see after the supper," he said to the Frenchman. "I know you are fond of fish, and I've a sturgeon, my dear fellow, beyond everything! A yard and a half long! Ha, ha, ha! And, by the way ... I was just forgetting ... In the kitchen just now, with that sturgeon ... quite a little story! I went into the kitchen just now and wanted to look at the supper dishes. I looked at the sturgeon and I smacked my lips with relish ... at the

---

[4] Anton Chekhov, "The Slander," in *The Horse Stealer and Other Stories* (New York: The MacMillan Company, 1921), pp. 221–8.

piquancy of it. And at the very moment that fool Vankin came in and said: … 'Ha, ha, ha! … So you're kissing here!' Kissing Marfa, the cook! What a thing to imagine, silly fool! The woman is a perfect fright, like all the beasts put together, and he talks about kissing! Queer fish!"

"Who's a queer fish?" asked the mathematics teacher, coming up.[5]

Clearly our protagonist is not the calmest or coolest fellow. We know from his dialogue that he lacks a degree of self-awareness. We know that he's happier to be cruel to his staff than to look foolish to his peers, and that despite this he is quite likely, in fact, somewhat of a pompous fool. Concurrently, we are shown a plot device here. Instead of Chekhov merely telling the reader that the protagonist went around the party telling everyone how stupid Vankin is, he shows us the protagonist in action.

Exposition

Generally exposition refers to information the author reveals about back story or character. When we first encounter a character in a story, we assume the character came from somewhere, had earlier experiences, lived in their world actively before the point at which the story began. Likewise, we assume the world in which the story is set was there before the beginning of the story. Exposition is either done directly, where the author explains the back story of a character or setting in literal terms, or it is done indirectly through the description of events and the dialogue.

In "The Slander," while we are given a few direct details at the beginning, most of the exposition happens through indirect descriptions of the wedding party, and the dialogue between the protagonist and his servants, wife, and colleagues.

Narrative point of view

The narrative point of view is the point of view from which the story is told. Although early in your writing career it's a good idea to practice keeping your narrative point of view consistent throughout any one piece of creative writing, as you develop more confidence you might start to experiment with split narratives that combine two or more incarnations of narrative voice. For now, here is an abridged list of some possible narrative points of view:

---

[5] Ibid., p. 23.

First person: Told from the perspective of the protagonist—for example: "I leapt up out of bed that morning with a fright, drenched in sweat."

Second person: Told from the perspective of the reader (this one is rarely used)—for example: "You leapt up out of bed that morning with a fright, drenched in sweat."

Omniscient third person: Told from the perspective of an all-seeing, all-knowing external narrator—for example: "Jesse leapt up out of bed that morning with a fright, drenched in sweat. Haunted by his nightmare of little blue and white aliens cruising the highways with machine guns, he contemplated the anxiety of his forthcoming journey over the border with no paperwork. It terrified him. What would his mother think if she knew? Meanwhile Margarite was in a deep sleep of her own, not dreaming after the drugs that were slipped to her a few hours ago, just sleeping in calm blackness."

Objective third person: Told from the perspective of a fly-on-the-wall type external narrator who can see everything that happens but doesn't enter the minds of the characters: "Jesse leapt up out of bed that morning with a fright, drenched in sweat. He wiped his brow as he checked the time. 4.04 a.m."

Subjective (or Over-the-shoulder) third person: Told from the perspective of a narrator who only knows the internal workings of the protagonist—not of the other characters in the story: "Jesse wiped the sweat from his brow still haunted by the aliens and looked over to find Margarite still sleeping soundly. He wondered if the drugs he'd slipped her the previous night were giving her strange dreams of her own, as he got out of bed, careful not to move her."

Tone

The tone, or mood, in fiction manifests through style, and combines creative choices pertaining to pace, vernacular, choice of symbols, imagery, and even punctuation. Where you have a lot of short sentences which move through details in quick succession, the pace of the story lifts and you give the impression of urgency or excitement to the reader. Conversely, if you have longer, meandering sentences which take the reader on a tangent, you give the impression of contemplation, sadness, the feeling of being encumbered by a problem. Add to this the use of words with "dark" connotations, evocation of sad images which juxtaposition contrastingly happy images, measured sentences which use a lot of caesura, and you are developing a distinctly melancholic tone. Here is an example from Virginia Woolf's novel, *To The Lighthouse*:

> Nothing stirred in the drawing-room or in the dining-room or on the staircase. Only through the rusty hinges and swollen sea-moistened woodwork certain airs, detached from the body of the wind (the house was ramshackle after all) crept round corners and ventured indoors. Almost one might imagine them, as they entered the drawing-room questioning and wondering, toying with the flap of hanging wall-paper, asking, would it hang much longer, when would it fall? Then smoothly brushing the walls, they passed on musingly as if asking the red and yellow roses on the wall-paper whether they would fade, and questioning (gently, for there was time at their disposal) the torn letters in the wastepaper basket, the flowers, the books, all of which were now open to them and asking, Were they allies? Where they enemies? How long would they endure?
>
> So some random light directing them with its pale footfall upon stair and mat, from some uncovered star, or wandering ship, or the Lighthouse even, with its pale footfall upon stair and mat, the little airs mounted the staircase and nosed round bedroom doors. But here surely, they must cease. Whatever else may perish and disappear, what lies here is steadfast ...[6]

Here is a manifestly gloomily nostalgic tone used to describe the Ramsay house in Woolf's famous novel. The long ambling sentences divided by multiple commas which slow the pace of reading, inclusion of words like pale, wandering ship, cease, perish, disappear, steadfast, detached, ramshackle, fade, and the images of torn letters, falling wallpaper, darkness, and contrasting red and yellow flowers ... All these elements contribute to the tone which helps to tell the story of this family and their friends and the tragedies of their lives in and around this house. The darkness setting in itself is both literal and figurative, serving as a symbol of the sadness of deaths in the family.

There is no one right way to implement tone to describe any one scene. The Woolf example above, had it used different pace, vernacular, and imagery, might have described the serenity of nighttime at the house, and this would have had a completely different effect on the rest of the story. Think of in how many different tones you might describe a character as he is waking up in the morning. Sometimes waking up in the morning is a peaceful event, other times it is disturbed or filled with dread. It can be sad

---

[6] Virginia Woolf, *To The Lighthouse* (London: Urban Romantics, 2012), p. 98.

and numb, mechanical, or confused. There is no one way to wake up in the morning. It is the author's responsibility to manipulate the description of a character as he wakes up so that the reader understands intuitively as well as intellectually what kind of awakening it is.

Exercise

Write just the first page (the beginning) of a short story, and include at least one of each of the following: a hook, a symbol, a line of dialogue, and some exposition. Also, remain aware of the tone you are setting with your choice of language, phrasing, and the length of your sentences and paragraphs, and stay true to one single narrative point of view throughout the whole piece.

You can write on any topic that you choose. You shouldn't need more than 20 minutes to complete this exercise. Make sure you hang onto this when you are finished in case you want to build on the story you begin.

Workshop

Swap your page with a workshop partner and read each other's work. As you go through your partner's work, identify and note down the exact places in the piece she has used hooks, symbols, dialogue, exposition, and narrative point of view. When you get your page back from your partner, go through it and check to see if your techniques were detectable and effective.

Plot and conflict

If theme is the element of fiction that makes the reader think, then plot is the element of narrative structure that makes the reader keep reading. In every work of fiction something *happens*, usually to the protagonist, in the context of the time and the place in which the story is set: this is called plot. The element that instigates the plot is conflict. Our protagonist is presented with a challenge from one or more antagonists. (An antagonist can be another character or an event or even "the world.")

What makes us care about what happens to a protagonist is often to do with how he or she responds to the central point of conflict they are faced with over the course of the story. We find it hard to care what happens to a character that is mostly passive and fails to respond in some genuinely surprising way to conflict—this character is the victim who is at the mercy of fate and we almost begin to want them to fail. We also find it hard to care about a character that is mostly in control of the conflict unfolding in the plot—this character is unchallenged and impossible to relate to.

However dramatic or subtle the central conflict of a plot is, the point of it is always to test our characters, to find out what they're really made of. For example, in William Carlos Williams's short story, "The Use of Force,"[7] the central conflict is relatively very simple in contrast with the dramatic tension that is sustained throughout the story. We have the plot: a doctor makes a house call to a family he is unfamiliar with, whose young daughter, at risk of diphtheria, bluntly (and eventually, violently) refuses to open her mouth to show the doctor her sore throat. The protagonist is the doctor, and the central conflict he must face is how to open the child's mouth to make a diagnosis—a scenario you might imagine must happen every day somewhere around the world. Williams treats the protagonist's response to the conflict with great care. He can neither allow the child to give in to the doctor, nor can he let the doctor leave the child to potentially die of diphtheria. What ensues is a totally exciting battle of wills resulting ultimately in *the use of force*.

A contrasting example is the character, Celeste, in Guy de Maupassant's short story, "Confessing."[8] Celeste faces two conflicts, one in the present— confessing to her mother that she is pregnant, and one which emerges during the confession, told in the past tense—that in order to save money getting into town to sell their farm produce, and after much resistance, she consented to having sex with the coach driver, Polyte.

Here we have a relatively shocking and dramatic plot, delivered in a contrastingly glib tone. The two conflicts are resolved simultaneously by the mother who curbs her fury long enough to devise a way to profit from their misfortune: she reasons that they'd best not tell Polyte, and, instead,

---

[7] William Carlos Williams, "The Use of Force," in *The Doctor Series* (New York: New Directions, 1984), pp. 56–60.
[8] Guy de Maupassant, "Confessing," in *The Hairpin and Other Stories* (Whitefish: Kessinger Publishing, 2004), pp. 51–7.

continue enjoying free rides into town with him for as long as possible. This reaction simultaneously quells Celeste's anxiety about telling her mother she is pregnant, and leaves her back where she started in terms of her troubles with Polyte.

Here we have a dramatic tension which builds as the details of how Celeste allowed herself to become pregnant become worse and worse apparently, and a surprise ending in which the two central conflicts resolve each other in a confounded and comical slap-in-the-face kind of way.

We care about Celeste because she did a stupid thing, she's afraid of the consequences, and she's forced to face up to her mistake which will inevitably change her life forever. We feel for her as much as we are amused by her, because of the absurdity of the whole situation and the way she manages to muddle her way through it.

The following exercises require you to think about the possibilities for conflicts which drive plot and how they shape your reader's relationship with your characters.

Exercise

Consider the complexities of the deadlock style plot in the above example of William Carlos Williams's "The Use of Force." Sometimes the most satisfying reads are the ones where we begin to think there's no possible end to the central conflict and then finally the protagonist surprises us by succeeding. These are often the most difficult stories to write because we can feel overcome by the conflict we are building. It becomes very hard to see past the struggle to a satisfying conclusion.

Your task is to brainstorm a scenario in which two characters are forced together by circumstance. They are in direct opposition in terms of what each of them *wants*, and so they find themselves in a deadlock which must be resolved one way or another.

You are only restricted by these three requirements:

1 Your characters must not know each other personally before they are forced together by your scenario. This means that they cannot use past experiences of each other to coerce one another to relent.
2 Your characters are in direct opposition with each other on an important matter and neither of them is willing to budge.

3 The deadlock must be resolved in the end—somebody must win. However, it may not be as result of either character's first or second efforts to overpower the other.

You might begin by drawing up a map of the different possible outcomes of the deadlock to help you brainstorm your way into and back out of the scenario you come up with.

When you feel you have figured your way out of the deadlock, write up the scenario either in dot points or prose form.

Workshop

Work with your workshop group to analyze the efficacy of the scenarios each of you has dreamt up. Without revealing the resolution, first introduce your characters, how they are forced together, and explain the deadlock they encounter. Then, let your group mates discuss the possible ways out of the deadlock you have designed. See what they come up with for your characters before you reveal the ending you've written.

Exercise

Consider the example above of the humorous treatment of a contrastingly serious and dramatic conflict. Often we are drawn to these stories because they remind us to make light of our darker experiences—a skill which is sometimes essential to our ability to overcome traumatic events in life.

Your task is to brainstorm a scenario for a plot in which your main character is challenged by something usually considered pretty serious or dramatic, and then to devise a humorous way for your character to respond to the conflict at hand. The idea here is not so much for the conflict to be fully resolved, rather, for the protagonist to discover a less threatening way in which to view the conflict so that he or she can have a hope at overcoming it.

The important thing to bear in mind is that, where a climax forms the tempering of some rising anxiety, the anxiety necessarily needs to be introduced as the hook at the beginning of the story.

Characterization

Characterization, even where you have an antihero (who tends typically to do bad things) for a protagonist, is the part of the story that the reader relates to. Quite often the stories we dislike are the ones with protagonists we can't identify with—we can't understand what motivates them to behave a certain way; we can't get on board with their overarching worldview. Good characters are the ones we root for—no matter how flawed they are, we ultimately want them to win.

In Sylvia Plath's *The Bell Jar*, even if you have strong feelings one way or another about the issue of suicide, you cannot help but empathize with Esther's feelings of detachment and disorientation at least in parts of the novel. We have all felt those things at some time or another. The characterization in this book helps someone who has never felt suicidal in their life to understand how somebody might come to the conclusion that killing herself is the only thing left to do.

In Harper Lee's *To Kill a Mockingbird*, we are able to root for young Scout's idealism and bravery in coming to terms with the realities of her highly flawed society. She becomes all the more relatable to us when we discover she is also prone to judging others and experiencing fear of the unknown in her dealings with Boo Radley. We're relieved to discover that she's only human.

What both of these characters (and many other well-written ones) have in common is that they are imperfect, and they are active, rather than passive, in their approach to their respective central conflicts. They don't always do the right things. They make mistakes. They unwittingly make life harder for themselves at times. There are things about the world they fail to understand or take into account and they suffer the consequences thereof. Importantly, they are keeping within the realistic limitations of who they are, and doing the best they can with what they have in the context of the plot that is unfolding around them.

The best characters are not limitless. Scout would never have walked into the courthouse with an air rifle and shot the prosecuting attorney no matter how frustrated she felt about the complex situation. Likewise, Esther would never have busted out of her shell to embrace the glamor of her internship in New York City and turned into a glittering socialite. Characters, like real people, don't get a vacation away from themselves. And, if they do, it's because the central conflict in the plot has overwhelmed them and they are in danger of becoming a lost cause—and it's very difficult for a reader to root for a lost cause.

Exercise

Come up with a character profile for the protagonist of a novel or novella you might like to write in the future. If you happen to be working on a project like this currently, you can write about the protagonist you have already begun to develop.

Begin by noting down the basics about your protagonist:

- Name
- Gender
- Age
- Occupation
- Relationship status
- Sexual orientation
- Domestic situation
- Family life
- Friendships
- General disposition

Once you have all of these, move on to your protagonist's inner workings. Write a few sentences on the following points.

- What does your character know about the world?
- What does your character mistakenly think she/he knows? How do these things manifest in her/his daily life?
- What is your character clueless about? What important lessons is she/he yet to learn? How does this inexperience manifest in daily life?
- What defence mechanisms has your character developed to deal with life's challenges? How do these defence mechanisms help and hinder her/him?
- What makes your character the most vulnerable?
- What gives your character the greatest feeling of strength?
- What is the worst thing that could ever happen to your character? What would her/his reaction be? How might she/he surprise her/himself?
- Ultimately, above all else, what does your character desire? Why can't she/he attain this thing?

Exercise

Based on the character profile you have just developed, write a short scene out of your prospective novel or novella which features your protagonist using the scenario below. Note that this does not have to be a scene from the beginning, nor does it need to be a particularly pivotal scene in the story.

Your challenge is to expose at least three of the points from the inner-workings part of your character profile. You can use a combination of direct (telling) exposition and indirect (showing through action and dialogue) exposition.

The scenario is as follows:

Your protagonist is out in the world (perhaps at work, or school) performing a mundane task he/she doesn't particularly enjoy, until something happens which interrupts his/her momentum and causes him/her to fail miserably at the mundane task, and lose something very important in the process.

Decide where this part of the story will be set, what the mundane task is and its significance to your protagonist. Then figure out who or what interrupts him/her, what is lost, how it is lost, and how it is even more significant than failing the task itself. Once you are ready, begin writing. This shouldn't take more than 20 minutes or so.

Workshop

Without introducing your character first, read your scene out to your group. After you have read, ask your group to answer some of the questions from the profile task about your protagonist based solely on the scene they have just heard. Pay particular attention to finding out whether or not they picked up on the three inner-working criteria you intended to expose within the scene.

Exercise

Characters (like real people) are often interesting because they are plagued by contradicting dualities. In *To Kill a Mockingbird*, Scout is both a tomboy who fights and also smart, sensitive, and a keen reader. In *The Bell Jar*, Esther wants to lose her virginity and live life on the edge, but she is always compelled to retreat and hide away from the world.

Write another scene using the same protagonist you have just been working on. This time, expose a contradicting duality your protagonist struggles with, using the following scenario.

Your protagonist has done something wrong and is now in trouble. He/She has been called in to see an authority figure and explain him/herself or be punished. The problem is, your protagonist wants to stand by whatever it is that he/she did and fails to see why he/she should apologise.

Bear in mind that this is a scenario that would cause some degree of anxiety, and so the tone you adopt should reflect this.

The scene can be about a page long, and should not take more than 20 minutes to complete.

Workshop

Have a workshop partner read your work over once before reading it aloud back to you. Listen to your descriptions of the characters' inter-action. Is your character's contradictory nature emphasized enough? Does it contribute to the complexity of the scene? Is your character likeable based on the information revealed in the scene? Why? Why not? Can your partner relate to your character's conundrum?

Setting: Time, place, and context

Often we think of setting merely in terms of the way a place is described through sensory detail. Actually, it is much more than that. Certainly, setting partly functions as a means to add to the imagery surrounding the characters and plot, but setting also gives context to the way your characters behave, their motivations, and the expectations imposed upon them by others.

If you think about a novel like Jane Austen's *Pride and Prejudice*, the different types of setting can actually be viewed as Elizabeth Bennet's main antagonists. Not only is the politics of the period in which the story takes place the reason why the Bennet girls are under pressure to find husbands, but the rules of social life in a small English town and the internal workings of the familial home are all fraught with challenges that Elizabeth and Darcy must overcome in order to find love together. This narrative reliance on setting is probably the reason why several authors have written alternate versions of *Pride and Prejudice*: to explore the contemporary cultural possibilities of a love story like Elizabeth and Darcy's.

Time

The period in which a story is set gives the reader cues about the limitations of the plot and characters. It is unlikely that we will encounter a UFO landing in a story set in the Middle Ages, for example. It is also unlikely that a character in a story set in current-day Los Angeles will be dressed by ladies-in-waiting for a ball that she will attend by way of horse and carriage (although, in Los Angeles, who knows?). If a character in a story set in the 1970s greeted a close friend with, "Mr Robertson, how do you do, sir?" we would likely assume it was said ironically. If Mr Darcy whipped out his iPad to Facetime with Mr Bingley we would be at a total loss. We rely on symbols, descriptions, and language tropes to indicate the period in which a story is set.

The span of time in which the plot events take place in a story is also a factor worth careful consideration. Where does your story really begin and end? Do you need to tell a whole life story, or will five days in your characters' lives suffice? How much can realistically happen to a person in the space of one year? In some ways, time is bendable in literature. Think of C. S. Lewis's *The Chronicles of Narnia*, which shows the four children's elevation to kings and queens in a secret world with a totally different sense of time to the one they normally live in. They can leave their normal world for just five minutes and have years of experiences in Narnia; and, as readers, we buy it completely because the concept of bendable time is consistent from the moment it is introduced to us, the very first time Edmund stumbles through the back of the wardrobe and into the magical land.

Exercise

Write a short scene of prose set in the present day in which your protagonist has to ask another character for something, perhaps a favor, or advice, or to borrow something.

The details of who your two characters are and whether or not your protagonist's request is honored are completely up to you. The only requirement is that you need to include five indications (a combination of symbols, descriptions, and language) that your story is set in the present day.

This can be between half a page and one page in length and you may include dialogue.

Exercise

Using the same scenario you came up with in the previous exercise, now write a short scene of prose where your protagonist has to ask another character for something again—this time, though, your scene will be set in another period of your choosing.

You might want to stick with a period you already know a little bit about. You are also free to set your scene in a futuristic setting, as long as you keep the details of that world consistent.

Include five indications (symbols, descriptions, and language) which will give your reader cues about the period in which the scene is set.

Workshop

Without first explaining your intention for the piece, read your scene aloud to your group. See if they can identify the period in which it is set, and ask them articulate the specific cues in the text which alerted them to the temporal setting.

Place

The place where a story is set is just as important to the reader's suspension of disbelief. If a scene is set at a party, the reader needs to know what kind of party it is: whether it is in a restaurant or a gallery or an inner-city studio apartment; whether there are 6 guests or 600 guests; whether it is a formal affair or an orgy; whether there is dinner or disco lights. All these details will give the reader cues about how the characters might interact.

Place is also important when a story is set outside of the realm of what we know of daily life. One common feature of fantasy novels is the inclusion of a map of the land in which the story takes place. This is a genre-specific method of demonstrating a consistent narrative progression through time and space which is important to creating a believable world.

Finally, in novels set in countries that are exotic to our experience, we want to learn about the sights and smells and sounds which are significant to that place throughout the story.

Exercise

Write half a page which describes a party setting. This can be any type of party you choose.

Make sure you include as much sensory detail about the setting as possible, including details about the guests, how they are dressed and how they are interacting, the room or space where the party is taking place, the smells and sounds, and the mood.

Be specific in your descriptions as much as possible, rather than relying on general information. Your task is to make the reader feel like a fly on the wall at this party.

Exercise

Think back to a time when you dreamt of a place that was partially familiar to you. Perhaps the dream was set in a place you have been to in real life, but some significant details of it were altered in your dream state. Or perhaps you have dreamt of this place many times in the past, but it is not somewhere from your memory of real life.

Write a page describing the dream with an emphasis on your experience of the place where it is set. Don't worry about trying to make this make sense. The idea is to capture the surreal quality of the setting and the events that took place there.

Context

The contextual premise of a story is the third factor of setting which symbolizes certain presuppositions for character and plot. Although a courtroom is technically a place which contains particular pieces of furniture and objects, the more important thing a courtroom signifies is a set of social and professional protocols integral to the purpose of that physical place. Our prejudgments about what happens in a courtroom, how the jury sit together, the judge on a kind of pedestal, prosecution and defence, the banging of the gavel, the swearing on a bible—all these things are cues about how characters in the story are supposed to behave, how they feel, what might happen to them, and what they value in that moment.

Exercise

There are many examples of contextual settings which have a determining impact on your characters' values, behaviors and motivations. Here are a few of them:

- The emergency ward of a hospital
- A classroom
- A prison cell
- Church
- Inside an airplane cabin
- A courtroom
- Inside a cinema or theater
- The checkout line in a supermarket
- An upscale restaurant

Your task is to pick three of these contextual settings, and plonk your protagonist from the exercises in the Characterization section of this chapter into each one. Think of one good reason why your protagonist would find themselves in each of the three contextual settings you have chosen.

When you are ready, write half a page on each contextual setting. Describe your protagonist's observations, emotional state, and interactions in the three different settings.

The object is to experiment with the ways in which different contextual settings affect your characters in unexpected ways. A character that is ordinarily very confident and self-assured might be reduced to a state of panic in a hospital emergency ward. A character that is normally rebellious might have trouble falling in line with the rules associated with being inside a courtroom.

Finding your voice

Whereas the previous discussions on fiction writing in this chapter are topics you can objectively learn, memorize, and apply to your creative practice, the subject of finding your voice as a fiction writer is quite another matter altogether. In practical terms, the only way to "find your voice," per se, is a steady regime of writing a lot for many years alongside a generous dose of reading widely.

George Orwell's voice is distinct in its precision and clarity of meaning. Walt Whitman's poetic voice is characterized by a long-line style and rhythm inspired by the King James Bible. James Joyce was known for his parodies of classic Greek literature and more generally for his stream of consciousness style—but then, so was Virginia Woolf, who added to this a strongly lyrical aesthetic. Authors become recognizable not just from the length and metric aesthetic of their sentences but also from their manipulation of words and word meanings, the way their sense of humor or irony or tragedy manifests in unexpected ways in their prose, the particular lenses they use to show the reader their characters' internal workings, their overarching worldviews, and the things that constitute their very identity.

One way to think of it is that anybody could tell the story you came up with, given all the important details—but only you can tell it the way it should be told. In other words, everything that makes a work of fiction charismatic and lively is what encompasses this idea of the writer's voice.

Finding your voice as a writer is no less challenging than, or complex as, finding yourself as a human being. We experiment in life just we experiment with our writing. We try new things, figure out what we do and don't like, what makes us think, what makes us feel things, and we forge a sense of self, as people and, simultaneously, as writers.

Next to exposing you to genres and concepts you might never have considered on your own, the only thing a textbook section on this topic can help with is to illuminate some of the moments you can look out for in your personal journey of cultivating a unique voice.

Reading widely

Anyone who tells you reading will stunt your growth as a writer is either himself a terrible excuse for a writer, or a psychopath, or possibly an idiot.

Reading is essential. Knowing what kind of writing turns you on is essential. Finding authors at different times in your life who make you want to be a better writer: also essential. Just as nobody writes in a bubble outside of the limits of their knowledge, nobody writes in a bubble outside the lineage of the thousands of great writers who came before them. To believe you are above everything Blake and Shakespeare and Auden and Arthur Conan Doyle and David Eddings (and even all the authors of romance novels and pop fiction) have to teach you about the power of words is nothing short of delusional.

Storytelling predates literacy. Your very existence is the product and the instigator of a whole series of stories, most of which you might never know about. Think of the value of storytelling in terms of how it helps us to find stories and meaning in our own lives. We read something new and take pleasure in the ways it opens us up to new perspectives on the topics that interest us. By reading widely, you are teaching your brain new ways of viewing and framing the life experiences which will later form inspiration for your own works of fiction.

Old rubbish and the adult brain

According to neuroscientists, our brains are not fully developed until about the age of 25. Dr Sandra Aamodt said in an interview on NPR.com, that, "one of the side effects of these changes in the reward system is that adolescents and young adults become much more sensitive to peer pressure than they were earlier or will be as adults."[9] So, it might be worth considering that this idea of no longer seeking approval from our peers, the sense of individualism and knowing oneself is not likely to be fully developed until well into our 20s. How, then, do we start to cultivate our voice as writers before that age? Is it possible to have comfortably established your unique style before the age of 25? Who knows?

Chances are your writer's voice will continue developing for the rest of your career to some extent. Malcolm Gladwell famously argued that it takes anybody 10,000 hours of practice to become proficient at a complex task,[10] but he surely didn't mean to stop at the end of 10,000 hours lest you surpass a place of mastery and end up back where you started. We keep learning and growing as writers. Even if you more or less plateau at some point, when your style becomes inimitably your own, you will continue to improve through experimentation.

The importance of looking back at the things you were writing one year ago and ten years ago (or more) and feeling encouraged that your voice has developed and improved, rather than feeling embarrassed that you ever wrote that story about a girl and her beloved pony in the sixth grade, is immeasurable. You may still be on a journey of finding your voice as a writer, but you have come a long way since the first time you ever put pen to paper. The worrying thing would be if you read back on your old work and felt that you might as well have written it yesterday—that would be an indication that you weren't growing as an artist. Have some pride in all the old rubbish you wrote in high school!

The following exercises combine the ideas about reading, revisiting old work, and experimentation in the development of the writer's voice.

---

[9] Tony Cox and Sandra Aamodt, *Brain Maturity Extends Well Beyond Teen Years* (transcript: NPR), http://www.npr.org/templates/story/story.php?storyId=141164708 [accessed December 21, 2013].
[10] Malcolm Gladwell, "Complexity and the Ten-Thousand-Hour Rule," in *The New Yorker* Online Edition (New York: 21 August 2013), http://www.newyorker.com/online/blogs/sportingscene/2013/08/psychology-ten-thousand-hour-rule-complexity.html   [accessed December 21, 2013]

Exercise

Who is your favorite author at the moment? How much do you know about this author from research and from reading his or her work? What do you want know more about? If you could tell him/her anything, what would it be? If you ask him/her anything, what would you ask?

Your task is to deliberately draw inspiration from the style of your favorite author and write a letter to him/her in experimental or creative prose.

Try to let your intimate relationship with the author manifest through your prose. Ask questions, explain things about your life that are relevant to the subjects of the author's work, and try to implement some of the stylistic elements that distinguish the author's work in your letter: that is to say, try to speak the author's language.

You can write whatever you like, and set the letter out any way that you wish.

Example

Here is part of a poetic letter I wrote to Allen Ginsberg:

Dear One, The plaque on our building says you died in 1997 the same year I wanted to die

For almost the first time; before I knew your name and before I knew my name

You wrote your last poem the same year I wrote my first poem something about the 'child inside is dying'

I was not knowing what I was really saying just as you were finally sure and ready.

Did you take your last walk down 2nd Avenue for the Ukrainian mushroom soup?

Did you stroll up the punk piercing and tattoo shops on St Marks and buy an oversized umbrella in an improvised downpour so you wouldn't have to

Rush home before making it all the way up to Washington Square Park where you'd marched against Moloch more than once

Sit down on a bench as the rain let up and hold Orlovski's hand or someone else's hand or look at your own hands or hold a paper cup of hot coffee?

Did you keep your beard long long after Memorial day when the clammy heat set into the city and began saturating all the apertures of all the city's denizen organisms?

Did your beard curl and frizz and stick to your neck and interrupt your meditations?

Did you still eat hot soup in the summer or did Cafe Orlin make cold green gazpacho back then too?

If they did could you stand the NYU bunnies waxing bumptious at the outdoor tables, oil and vinegar on the side, arugula, kale, and a camomile tea?

GS told me the first time we met that he saw you around the neighbourhood in Little Ukraine,

Tonight we went back to the same hole-in-the-wall Shochu place where we went after that night last June, sixteen years after your last night,

I wore a dress and sneakers and my hair curled and frizzed in the clammy heat that set into the city, saturating my calm then inflaming it

GS's heart lining was inflamed, they didn't catch it at Beth Israel, I told him an inflamed heart lining is romantic

He wrote his name in Sharpie red Katakana on the unfinished bottle of Kappa and I came home to

Ask you the afore-posed queries–please reply at your leisure. I'm not going anywhere.[11]

Here I use a mixture of things I know about Ginsberg, things I want to know about him, and parallels taken from my own life experience which link us together. I'm also allowing Ginsberg's long-line style (which, incidentally, he took from Walt Whitman) to inform my experimentation with long lines and meter.

---

[11] Tara Mokhtari, *Dear Allen Ginsberg* (manuscript, 2013).

Exercise

Revisit a couple of old stream of consciousness exercises you have done in the past few weeks or months. Read through them and underline passages that you particularly like the sound of. It doesn't matter if your favorite parts don't necessarily make a whole lot of common sense, the important thing is that they use certain kinds of phrasing, word play or rhythms that you would like to emulate in future writings.

Once you have captured four or five favorite passages from previous exercises, it is time to use them. Rewrite the first passage on a clean page, and use it as stimulus to continue writing using the stream of consciousness method for three minutes. When your three minutes are up, move on to the next passage.

The object is to grasp hold of the moments you are most vividly tapping into your developing writer's voice, and to try to sustain the style for longer periods of time.

Exercise

Many writers are known for having specific routines, methods, habits which drive their individual creative processes. Jack Kerouac famously wrote his novels on one long roll of teletype paper. In interviews he explained that it helped him to see the whole work and to write non-stop.

Your homework task is to experiment with some new ways to write, that move away from the upright desk and laptop or notepad or whatever you usually do when you go to write.

Each day for the next week, set aside five minutes of stream of consciousness writing time. Each day, your challenge is to find a position, medium or setting in which to complete your five minutes of writing. You might try writing on a long roll of paper. You might try writing on a whiteboard (or on your fridge!) in whiteboard marker. You might record yourself instead of writing manually. You might write in bed or on the floor or on the roof or at the kitchen table. You might write on post-it notes and fix them to the wall. Whatever you do, the point is to break habit.

Exercise

Writing what makes you uncomfortable in the most honest way you can is often as rewarding as it is difficult.

Often we write for escapism and we can become wrapped up in the glamor of the characters and settings we create almost for wishing we lived in that world ourselves. This can lead to a strange creative kind of mimesis of what is idealized rather than a unique reflection of what is your true voice as a writer.

By focusing away from ideal characters and storylines, and onto the opposite of what we consider ideal, it becomes harder, as a writer, to hide behind some glossy, unrealistic, unreadable voice.

Your task is to write a short, one- to two-page experimental story based on one of the scenarios below of your choosing:

- A family come together for the funeral of the protagonist's father or mother.
- The protagonist's dissatisfaction with being oppressed in some important way.
- The end of the world and its causes and effects.
- The protagonist falls in love and is rejected by the object of her/his affections.

Your story need not follow a conventional narrative structure. You might start in the middle of the action, or there may be very little action and a focus on your protagonist's internal life. You could write about just a few moments in time which explore the images, surrealism, associated metaphors, and rhythms at the centre of what has happened. Most importantly, embrace the horror at the centre of whichever scenario you choose. Don't try to make it better for your reader. Show us how it really feels.

Genre fiction

Genre fiction, or pop fiction, is generally identifiable according to the ways in which it adheres to specific plot-driven storytelling conventions. Whereas literary fiction explores complex characters and themes which are written to make the reader think, genre fiction focuses on plot and is designed to help the reader escape into a fictional world. You might think of the difference between the two in terms of how much mental work the reader has to do in order to fully appreciate the work.

Each genre has a set of plot points which usually drive the narrative. A romance novel normally consists of two people falling in love, overcoming a challenge that could break them up, and has a happy ending. Science fiction and fantasy novels are usually about a hero taking a journey of adventure in order to rescue somebody and alter their normal world for the better somehow. Crime, mystery and detective stories have a strong heroic protagonist and one central human antagonist.

The following are examples of popular genres.

Science Fiction: Set in the future, science fiction stories explore the possibilities of science and technology on human life.

Fantasy: Set in magical places and times, fantasies rely on the consistencies of invented worlds in order to achieve suspension of disbelief for the reader. This is why they often include a drawn map in the prologue and also why they have epic (literally) potential.

Detective: Detective stories, whodunits, and mysteries rely on a strong detective protagonist and the unraveling of an intricate plot to uncover the truth about a crime.

Horror: Scary stories! The efficacy of a horror story is measured according to how well the author uses a combination of suspense and relief to elicit fear in the reader.

Romance: Two people meet, fall in love, and overcome a struggle to live happily ever after. (Just like in real life. Ahem.)

Exercise

Pick one of the genres above which interests you.

Start by doing some guided stream of consciousness writing. Imagine a main character, a setting, and a point of conflict that would fit with the genre of your choice and write whatever comes to mind about those three elements for five continuous minutes.

Once you are in the zone of your chosen genre and you have explored your initial ideas about character, setting and plot, come up with an opening for your developing story. Where do we meet the protagonist? Under what circumstances? What is the first thing we find out about her/him and how is the conflict set up right from the beginning?

Write two pages which could act as the beginning of a genre fiction novel.

Workshop

Swap your work with a workshop partner. Without first discussing the genre you chose, read each other's novel beginnings. Is it clear to your partner what genre you were experimenting with? Is there a clear sense of a plot beginning to unfold from these first two pages?

5

Screenwriting Techniques

One of the few opportunities a writer gets to emerge from the solitary den of darkness and actually work interactively is in the technicolor world of screenwriting.

Television writers usually work as a round table of several writers all working together to plot out episodes and seasons. The reason for this might be inherent to the craft of screenwriting, above and beyond the obvious logistical issues of trying to get one writer to produce 12 complete 44-minute episodes each of which maintains the dramatic tension and dynamics of the series, while simultaneously manipulating the program's plot formula into something new and surprising over and over again indefinitely. Actually, there is something a bit special which happens when writers have to negotiate their visions (and they literally are visions) for the exploration of themes and the development of characters which do not live only in the imaginations of their readers—but whose journey is witnessed in elaborate physical (and sometimes three-dimensional) detail.

Since the sequence of events in film and television is fundamentally concerned with cause and effect—so, because Edward's girlfriend dumps him over the phone at the beginning of *Pretty Woman*,[1] he takes Stuckey's Lotus, and because he can't find his hotel or drive a stick-shift, he winds up meeting Vivien, and because Vivien discovers Kit has spent their rent money on drugs, she is motivated to score a big trick that particular night, etc—a round table situation forces the writers to justify the relevance of everything that happens in every scene. If, as a television writer, you can't bear to "kill your own darlings," your colleagues will do it for you.

Whereas in novels there is considerable leeway for artistic indulgence given the readers' prejudices and interpretations of the text, films are

---

[1] J. F. Lawton, *Pretty Woman*, film, directed by Garry Marshall (1990; Los Angeles: Touchstone Pictures/Silver Screen Partners IV, 1990), video.

comparatively rather naked. Films lay it all out in front of the audience in about 100 minutes of moving images, words, music, scenery, and lighting. So it helps to apply the kind of objective reasoning that collaborations usually command.

The other major difference between screenwriting and most other genres is the inherent *point* of a script. The point of a script is not to exist as an autonomous work of art like a novel or a poem. The point of a script is to act as a blueprint for a separate final product: a film (or a television show, or a play). The relationship is not merely between author, text, and reader; the relationship is between author, director, producers, actors, crew, set and lighting designers, composers, and audience.

It is for this reason that there are so many rules for scriptwriting, and not the kind of highly plastic rules we talk about in prose and poetry composition. A strong screenplay communicates very clearly the story and the key themes according to the writer's point of view. A lighting designer and a director of photography and a set designer must all be able to read the script and have a relatively unanimous understanding of what each scene will look like in order for the story to work the way the writer has envisaged it. To a basic extent, formatting rules about slug lines, action, and dialogue, as well as any necessary camera shots help writers to communicate their intentions to the cast and crew.

This idea that the screenplay is not an autonomous work of art is the cause of some heartbreak for any new writer. Imagine working for years on a feature film, crafting it to perfection, and finally landing a deal with a production company—only to hand over the script and let tens of other artists impose their visions for your story onto the production. The final cut may exclude your favorite scenes. The director may manipulate your denotations to suit the aesthetic for the film which was decided upon by the producer. Any number of changes to your original vision might occur during the making of the film. Ho hum.

The question is: how do you make sure the story as you wrote it is not lost during production? The answer is relatively simple: write consciously! Set concrete objectives for each scene and make sure that all the action and dialogue is working to achieve those objectives. Have no superfluous scene, and include only the details which are essential to the story you want to tell. By crafting a screenplay whose every part is crucial to the film as a whole, you are minimizing the opportunity for misinterpretation.

After you have done all you can to write a tight screenplay, there comes a time to accept that film is a collaborative medium: without the work of all the other artists involved, your screenplay will join the millions of screenplays all over the world which sit in millions of desk drawers gathering a whole lot of dust. Embrace the input of all the experts who work hard to bring your story to life on the screen.

The exercises in this chapter will introduce you to the fundamental techniques and standards for scriptwriting. By the end of this chapter you will have developed skills for transforming your ideas from the conceptualization of themes to the telling of a visual story.

The slug line

The slug line is the heading for every scene in a screenplay. Every single time you change locations in a screenplay—even if you are just going back and forth between two locations—you need to separate your scenes with a slug line.

Here are examples of two different, very basic slug lines:

```
1. EXT          SUBURBAN STREET          NIGHT
```

This slug line indicates, in order of appearance: that this is scene one, the scene is an external (outside) shot, it is set on a suburban street, and it happens at night.

```
2. INT          JAMAL'S HOME OFFICE          DAY
```

This slug line indicates: scene two, shot internally (inside), set in Jamal's home office during the day.

Action

Many scenes in films contain no dialogue, but all scenes in films contain action of some kind. The trickiest technical part of writing action is that you are restricted in terms of telling the reader what the characters are feeling and thinking.

In a short story or novel, it is common practice to write something like:

Angelina had been waiting for twenty minutes for Brad to arrive. She was always waiting for him; ever the supportive wife. All she wanted was for him to consider her needs from time to time. It was degrading to always be waiting around for a man who thought of himself as some kind of god.

She was finally losing patience. She wondered whether it was even worth hanging around. Perhaps his lateness that day was a sign. Perhaps she'd be better off alone.

In a script, however, you generally can't write anything internal without having a way of showing it visually. You also need to write the action in a way which will allow the scene to play out in an immediate way, which means using physical present tense and third person narration. So, you might write:

```
ANGELINA paces back and forth in front of the beaten up old
Mustang before leaning up against the hood. She has been
crying and she's trying to hide it.

She glances down at her watch, frustrated. She's almost
ready to give up.

She opens the driver's side door and gets in, puts the key
in the ignition.
```

The key is to think visually, and to know what you need to achieve in each scene. So, in the above example, my primary goal is to show that Angelina is at the end of her tether with Brad and she's ready to leave him unless he acts fast.

The particulars of the scene—that Angelina is supposed to meet Brad at the car and he is late—are merely the means to achieving the primary goal. Yes, Brad's late again. Yes, Angelina's left waiting again. But the point is to show the dynamic in their relationship and to indicate that their current situation is not sustainable; something is about to give. Depending on the emotional significance riding on this scene, I can intensify the drama in the action to reflect the heightened level of tension. Maybe this happens every day in Brad and Angelina's relationship, and they are miserable. Or, maybe something is going on in Brad's work or private life which has caused him to start treating Angelina poorly. Maybe one of them is having an affair. The way I write this scene will depend on whatever I am plotting to do with Brad and Angelina's story.

The action must be written in physical present tense, third person narration. This style is essential to the script as a blueprint to the film. If a director, a set designer, and a sound crew each read the prose example of Angelina and Brad, they would all have totally different images in their minds of what the scene looks like. It is the writer's job to eliminate as much uncertainty as possible about how the scene will work—without stepping on any of the other artists' toes, of course.

Sure, the general point of the scene might be to show that Angelina is ready to leave Brad. But, if I know that in the last scene of the film Brad runs over Angelina in his car, then having a moment in this scene where Angelina starts driving away just as Brad appears in her rear view mirror might strengthen the impact of that last scene. So, in this case, it becomes important for me to be specific about how we find out that at one point Angelina almost leaves Brad.

Note also that in the above example each individual action is given its own new paragraph. The point of this is to keep the action to a logical sequence of events and to make the script easy to scan.

Exercise

Imagine a scene that happens in one single location, in which you are the main character. You are trying to achieve a simple task but things keep going wrong.

Describe in physical present tense, third person, how the scene would play out from the opening shot, through to the climax wherein you either succeed or fail at your task, last shot.

Write this up to include a slug line and adhere to the screenwriting format guidelines as described above.

Example

```
EXT            GERTRUDE STREET            NIGHT

TARA (30) emerges out of the pub, handbag on her
shoulder, holding a half-empty pint glass.

The door opens behind her; somebody reaches around
and snatches the glass from her hand, and then the
door swings shut again as the lights inside switch
off.

TARA stumbles down the step and onto the stoop,
peering up the road for signs of a tram.

The street is empty as far as she can see.

From the opposite direction, a cab speeds right past
her, honking a warning as it knocks her off her feet
and backwards onto her arse. We see her mobile phone
slip out of her handbag and down a drain.
```

TARA picks herself up and makes her way across the street to the bus stop. She pauses to read the timetable, and then looks down at her watch—she's missed the last bus.

At that moment, a phone ring sounds.

TARA is startled, and begins rummaging through her bag.

Realizing the ring isn't coming from on her person, TARA listens intently…

She follows the sound back over the road and kneels down by the drain. The ring echoes louder and louder, until it abruptly stops.

TARA sighs, and sits on the stoop with her head in her hands.

Exercise

Your task is to revisit one of your favorite films and pick a scene that features the main character, but which contains no dialogue.

Watch the scene with pen and paper in hand, and note down in sequential order every physical thing that happens. Make a note of every pertinent action performed by the character, and every other relevant thing that happens around her/him. Pick a scene which does not depend too heavily on choreography (like dance or fight scenes).

Using your notes, write the scene of action you observed in your own words. Include a slug line and make sure all the action is written in present tense, third person narrative. Give each significant action a new paragraph and organize the scene sequentially.

Workshop

Without revealing the title of the film, read out your scene to your group mates and see if they can identify which film and scene you worked on.

Once everyone has read, you might want to search online for the original screenplay for your film and find out how the writer approached the same scene you rewrote. How does the language you used compare with the original script? What kinds of screenwriting devices did the writer include to denote camera angles and shots? What did the original writer consider to be the important actions to specify? What actions did the writer leave up to the director to figure out?

Exercise

Imagine a scene in which someone you know well is the main character. She or he is in the middle of a private and embarrassing act (like preparing to pig out on a feast of junk food, or dancing around the house naked), when she/he is interrupted by somebody.

Describe the scene in physical present tense, third person: the opening visual of your character mid-private act, the moment they are busted in on, and the immediate result of the embarrassing interruption.

Workshop

Have your workshop group close their eyes and imagine the scene while you read it to them aloud. How did each of your group members envisage the scene? Did everyone have a unanimous understanding of the most important details about the two characters? Is any of your action to readily open to interpretation?

Dialogue

In every exchange of dialogue onscreen, each character wants something—even if it's just a cup of coffee, or to be validated, or to get out of something they don't want to do. The interesting thing about this is that often the desires of two characters are in direct opposition to one another, there is a conflict, and so the dialogue becomes something of a power play.

A terrific example of power dynamics and conflicting desires in dialogue is found in the sitcom *Seinfeld*. If you read through several episode transcripts you might notice that in every scene of dialogue, the power shifts between every one of the characters at some point. Take the first scene of the pilot episode—Jerry and George are in the diner:[2]

JERRY

```
Seems to me, that button is in the worst possible
spot. The second button literally makes or breaks
the shirt, look at it: it's too high! It's in no-
man's-land. You look like you live with your mother.
```

GEORGE

```
Are you through? [Irritated]
```

JERRY

```
You do of course try on, when you buy?
```

GEORGE

```
Yes, it was purple, I liked it, I don't actually
recall considering the buttons.
```

JERRY

```
Oh, you don't recall?
```

GEORGE

```
[Pretends he's talking into a microphone] Uh, no,
not at this time.
```

JERRY

```
Well, senator, I just like to know, what you knew
and when you knew it. [A waitress approaches the
table]
```

WAITRESS

```
Mister Seinfeld. [She pours coffee in his cup]
Mister Costanza. [She goes to pour coffee, but
George stops her]
```

GEORGE

```
Are, are you sure this is decaf? Where's the orange
indicator?
```

---

[2] Larry David and Jerry Seinfeld, *The Seinfeld Chronicles – Pilot*, directed by Art Wolff (1989; Los Angeles: Giggling Goose Productions, Shapiro/West Productions, Castle Rock Entertainment, 1989), television.

```
                    WAITRESS

    It's missing, I have to do it in my head: decaf
    left, regular right, decaf left, regular right…
    It's very challenging work.
```

There are three distinguishable beats in this section of the scene. A beat is a chunk of scene in which the tone, topic and power balance stays the same before moving on to a new phase. Jerry has the power right at the beginning because he's actively making fun of George's shirt. At this point, Jerry wants to be entertained at George's expense, and George wants to be left alone. Then, in a new beat, George neutralizes Jerry's power play somewhat by instigating the interrogation bit with the pretend microphone. The next beat begins when the Waitress interrupts with the coffee, and briefly seizes the power when she makes George insecure about the decaf. Now George wants assurance about the decaf, and the Waitress wants George to give her a break (and, perhaps, to make George squirm a bit).

The throw-away line here which gives us insight into Jerry and George's relationship might be, "Oh, you don't recall?" We get no new information in this line, it's reiterating the obvious, but it also shows an underlying playfulness in Jerry and George's friendship—we understand here that it's not really about the purple shirt, it's about the shit-talk that characterizes every single conversation they ever have together.

Exercise

Remember back to a conversation you had with one other person which didn't go the way you wanted it to. Maybe the other person didn't listen to your point of view, or didn't understand it, or perhaps she or he lied or manipulated the conversation to get what they wanted.

Your task is to write a short reflection on what happened during this conversation, answering the following questions.

- What did you want from that conversation?
- What did your co-converser want?
- Who started off holding the balance of power?
- At what point in the conversation did the balance of power switch from one person to the other person?

- What were the throw-away lines uttered which, in some small way, worked to re-establish the relationship between you?
- Where did the conversation really begin and end, discounting the usual pleasantries, greetings, etc?

Once you've reflected on the conversation, write it as a scene of dialogue, including a slug line and some basic action at the beginning. Don't start at the very beginning with "hellos" and "how are yous" and don't try to write the conversation out verbatim. Instead start with the line of dialogue in which the exchange started to get interesting.

As you write it out, bear in mind who holds the power and when it shifts between characters, and include an occasional throw-away line which demonstrates the relationship between the characters.

Exercise

Over the course of the next week, take a few minutes while you are out in the world to eavesdrop on an awkward conversation between two strangers. Note down the reasons why it seemed awkward and what the conversation seemed to be about. Then answer the following questions.

- What was the conversation really about? Was it totally literal, or was there some underlying issue bubbling away beneath the surface?
- What kind of relationship did the two people seem to share?
- Do they trust/like each other? How could you tell?
- How did the more passive of the two people compensate for their lack of power in the conversation?
- Did they both always necessarily mean what they were saying? Could they have been withholding information or feelings, or even outright lying to each other?
- What could you glean about each of their characters?

Example

I recently witnessed a conversation at the university cafe at lunchti

Initially, the man, dressed in a suit and tie, was alone with some fi making phone calls. Eventually, a woman, well dressed, arrived, apolo ⎽ed for being late by saying it was silly she'd forgotten their meeting since they only arranged it yesterday.

The man was very forgiving, but then when she sat down and opened her laptop and they started looking at their work and she criticized an idea he'd had, the man said that she needn't worry about it today if she was too distracted. He even reached across the table to pat her arm, condescendingly.

It seemed like he was using her lateness to diminish her criticism of his idea. She impressed me by totally ignoring his attempt at power play and getting on with business without indulging his fragile ego.

Exercise

Using your eavesdropping notes, recreate the conversation you witnessed as a succinct scene in which your "eavesdroppees" are the main characters of either a sitcom or a drama. Once again, avoid greetings and pleasantries at the start unless they are essential to the story.

Workshop

Workshop your scenes of dialogue in groups of five or six. Make legible copies of your scene and hand them over to two group members of your choosing. Have them stand up and read the scene through as though they were actors auditioning for roles in your film.

How does the conversation play out? Are the voices of each character natural and believable? Do the two characters sound too much alike? As they read, mark down on your copy of the scene where the beats and power shifts occur.

Exercise

Think about the kinds of arguments couples often have. Most of the time, while the specific topic of the argument might change, the couple is actually having the same argument over and over again because of some underlying undealt-with issue.

Imagine a married couple who embody the following profile.

Partner One is always late. To everything. Compulsively. "One" always feels guilty about it but can't seem to get it together and actually be on time for once. Sometimes "One" conceals the guilt with humor or light-heartedness. "One" also tends to try to surprise Partner Two with unusual gifts or acts of kindness but fails to ever really impress Partner Two with them.

Partner Two is always on time. "Two" now expects "One" to always be late, but that doesn't necessary help the situation; in fact, it's a little damaging to "One"'s self-esteem. "Two" tries to show appreciation for "One"'s surprise gifts but sometimes they almost seem thoughtless (like, giving a massage voucher to someone who has an allergy to massage oil), and "Two" can't always conceal the feeling disappointment.

Join up into a group of four, and starting from the character descriptions above, develop more detailed profiles for the two characters and their relationship. Think about how they met, under what circumstances they decided to marry, what their individual upbringings were like, what made them fall in love, and who else exists around their relationship (children, family, ex-lovers, etc).

Once you have worked out who your couple is, come up with four separate argument scenarios for your couple. Each argument scenario should be about a different topic, but the underlying cause of the arguments should be essentially the same.

Once you have the four scenarios, allocate one scenario to each group member. Then, work independently and write up the scene you have to work with, with a focus on the dialogue between your two characters.

Give the scene a slug line, set the scene, and dive straight into the centre of the action—the moment the argument really begins. Write until the argument ends (or somebody walks out), but don't try to force your couple to resolve their underlying issues.

Workshop

Bring each of your group's scenes to the table. Cast two members of your group as the couple, and have them read out the dialogue in each scene, one after the other with just a brief silence between.

Once you have listened to the ways these underlying issues manifest in your couple's everyday lives, and how they have been represented by each group member, go through and co-edit the dialogue in each piece with a close eye for the following.

- Are there lines which could feasibly be cut or shortened?
- What are the throw-away lines which divulge elements of the underlying issue?
- Do both characters sound too much alike? Or do they sound too different for a married couple? Can you manipulate their voices through changing some words or phrases?
- Are there discernible power shifts between the characters? Can these be edited so that they are more dramatic or humorous?

Once you have edited all four pieces, do another read through so you can see the progress you've made from the first drafts.

Exercise

The following is a group exercise which will get you thinking about subtext. Subtext encompasses all the things which aren't literally spoken in a scene of dialogue, but which are implied, and exist on some deeper level that the audience senses intuitively.

A great example of subtext illuminated is the scene after the tennis match in the Woody Allen film, *Annie Hall*. The two main characters are on the roof of the apartment building talking together, but a curious attraction and a mutual self-consciousness is building between them. We are provided with subtitles which show what the two characters are thinking as they carry on this seemingly mundane conversation.

For this exercise in six phases you will need a recording device of some kind.

1 As a group, develop character profiles for two characters that are in some kind of new relationship. Decide on their individual biographical information, and then start working out their respective back stories, their values, their desires, their kinks.

2 After you have two character profiles, develop an idea for a scene in which your two characters must make an everyday, mundane decision, and realize that they may have very different views on life and how things work. However, neither character is willing to admit outright how they really feel. Figure out where the scene takes place, what decision they need to make together, and what their mismatched views of things are.

3 As a group, come up with three lines of dialogue for each character which they will utter at some point during the scene to mark a shift in power from one character to the next. These lines needn't necessarily be hostile; a character can seize power simply by actively reassuring another character, or cracking a joke, or changing the topic of conversation.

4 Then elect two people in the group to improvise the dialogue between your two characters, and record the improvisation. The idea is for the two characters to fail to say what they really mean, although their true feelings on the matter might begin to surface very subtly. For instance, they might be being overly kind to each other to avoid conflict, or perhaps they are using the decision at hand to glean information about a more important unrelated issue. During the improvisation, members of the class can interrupt the actors by feeding one of them one of the prewritten lines of dialogue. When this happens, the actors continue their improvisation from the line that's been fed to them. Once both characters have used all three of their prewritten lines, the conversation is over. Hit stop on your recording device, and have a group discussion on how the improvisation played out.

5 Now play back the improvisation, and, as you listen to it, individually write a scene of dialogue in which each of the characters is literally and bluntly saying what they are really thinking. If this were a Woody Allen style of film, the recorded version of the dialogue would form the visual/audible scene, and the scene you write in response to that would form the subtitles to go with it.

6 When you are ready, you can share your literal interpretation of the scene with the group to see how differently each of you reads between the lines of this semi-improvised conversation.

Characterization

Characterization for film and television shares the same essential goals as characterization for fiction writing, except there are certain conventions which limit the ways in which character exposition occurs on screen. In a novel or a short story, we have the luxury of opening with a lengthy description of the main character in the first chapter, which delves into their psyche and biography. Conversely, in film, everything we know about a character needs to be revealed either through physical action or dialogue. This naturally prevents us from starting a script with a lot of direct narrative about our protagonist's family life and their feelings about the world.

Of course, there are ways around this. We could, for instance, use voice over narration to reveal things about our characters which aren't necessarily evident from the scene we can see playing on screen. Think of a television series like *Sex in the City*, which uses the running narrative thread of the protagonist Carrie's voice over in relation to her weekly newspaper column. All of the episodes open with Carrie's voice over telling us what the theme for the week is, and what is preoccupying each character before we meet them at the centre of the action.

But beware of the all-knowing, all-telling voice over—it can get tedious for your viewers. There is a certain satisfaction we derive from putting together the clues in a film for ourselves. Don't deprive your audience of that by spoon-feeding them.

Exercise

Character exposition begins in scene one of your film or your television pilot, as demonstrated in the earlier *Seinfeld* example. This exercise requires you to write the opening scene of a pilot.

Your task is to take an existing show and re-imagine the first scene of the first episode.

Your challenge is to use everything you know about the main character from watching the series to guide your gradual exposition of him or her and adhere to the conventions of your show's format as much as possible.

The real writers did not have had the opportunity to write the pilot with the benefit of seeing how the plots and characters unfold over the course of several episodes and seasons—but you do! So, use everything you know about the show to your advantage.

Example

Take the character of Carrie in *Sex and the City*.[3] The first scene in the existing pilot episode involves two characters completely unrelated to the series, but it incorporates the repeated voice over convention—which is how we first meet Carrie.

I might re-imagine the pilot episode so that it is less about the general theme of love and sex in New York City, and more about the love and sex lives of Carrie and her four friends—which is the direction the show quickly takes from a few episodes into the first season. Instead of the opening scene being about Carrie's retelling of some other couples' love lives, I would make the opening scene about Carrie and her relationship with her friends.

```
1. EXT.          UPPER EAST SIDE — STREET          DAY

A wide shot of a street in New York's Upper East Side
closes in to the front steps of a typical brownstone
apartment building.

Through the first floor window we see a woman get up from
her desk and close her laptop before pulling off her
shirt and disappearing from view for a few moments.

Then the front door swings open and CARRIE emerges
wearing a day dress and high heels, pulling her hair up
as she skips down the front steps.

                    Carrie (V.O.)

          For some writers, meeting your friends
          for lunch at 2pm on a Wednesday is
          what you might call taking a break…

We follow CARRIE as she walks quickly down the street,
narrowly avoiding a postman and skipping around a lady
walking two poodles as she goes.

She turns a corner and pauses at a cafe window, looking
in.

We see from outside the window a group of three women
sitting at a table inside and waving her in.

She waves back and from our viewpoint on the street we
see her enter and join her friends.
```

---

[3] Darren Starr, *Sex and the City*, dir. Susan Seidelman (1998; New York City; Darren Starr Productions, HBO, Rysher Entertainment, 1998), television.

```
                     Carrie (V.O.)

          Not for me. For me, it's research.
```

Hopefully from this new first scene, first episode, the audience could glean something more essential about Carrie as the protagonist of this series. In my re-imagined opening I have shown: where the protagonist lives and works, what her lifestyle is like, what her job is, hopefully something about her sarcastic sense of humor, and the nature of her relationship with her friends.

I have also been faithful to the conventions of the show by: using voice over, and sticking to the same vernacular and phrasing that Carrie is known for, and replicating the familiar scene where Carrie goes off to meet her friends in a restaurant or bar.

Workshop

Join up with one workshop partner, preferably one whose television show you are familiar with (and vice versa). Swap scenes and take time reading your partner's work.

Write a list of all the things your partner exposed about his/her protagonist through action or dialogue: Are all the essentials there? Has your partner allowed enough mystery for the audience to be interested in getting to know the character better? Has your partner managed to stick with the conventions of the show as you know it? Swap notes and discuss your thoughts on each of the scenes.

Exercise

Work up a profile for a fictional character whom you might like to explore in your screenplay. Imagine everything about the character, from basic biographical information, to their private life, desires, and inner workings. Make it as detailed as possible.

Workshop

Join up with one workshop partner. First share your character profiles with each other.

Then, on your own, create a series of ten interview questions you'd like ask your partner's character. Don't show the questions to your partner yet.

When you're both ready, your task is to improvise a mock-interview. Assume the voice (and brain) of your character, and have your partner ask you the interview questions they have prepared. Do not prepare by first showing each other the questions you composed. The challenge is to improvise answers to your partner's questions as your character.

Bear in mind that characters sometimes lie and withhold information and feelings. Characters can be manipulative, they can feel threatened, and they don't always say exactly what they mean.

After you have both been interviewed, go back to your character profile and fill it in with everything you learned about her or him during the improvised mock-interview workshop.

Workshop 2

When you are ready you can workshop this character with the rest of your workshop group. Put a chair at the front of the room. Let's call that chair *The Hot Seat*.

Once again, you need to improvise the role of your character. But this time, you don't give the group any information about your character.

When it is your turn to workshop, you will go to the front of the room, as your character, and sit in *The Hot Seat*. Your group mates will ask you as many questions as possible to determine your character's personality and back story in the space of three minutes or less. They might begin by asking your character's name and age. Then they might start asking you more personal questions about your character's family, background, beliefs and values, and life experiences. You need to improvise the answer to each of these questions as quickly and convincingly as possible.

Have your original workshop partner take notes for you during this process, paying particular attention to the kind of language you use to answer *The Hot Seat* questions. You can use these notes later if your character makes their way into your next screenplay!

Theme and narrative

There are many interpretations of what is commonly known as the *narrative arc*. Narrative arcs help writers not only to plot a film, they also help us to identify what our film is really about, what the central themes are, what each of our characters symbolizes for the protagonist, and how we want to answer the questions we have set up in the beginning of our script.

The following is a breakdown of the main parts of a typical narrative arc structure, using the contemporary children's adaptation of "Little Red Riding Hood".

- *Starting Point:* The Starting Point is the moment we first meet the protagonist. We know instinctively that this character has a back story; that is, she or he came from somewhere, has some kind of established life, and that there exists a pretty good chance that that established life is about to be disrupted somehow. Simultaneously, at the Starting Point, we are introduced to the protagonist's fatal flaw— the character trait which she or he must either eventually overcome to succeed at the end of the story, or succumb to and fail at the end of the story. In the story of "Little Red Riding Hood," the starting point is when we meet Little Red Riding Hood, who lives with her mother and is always a good girl and does what she is told; so, arguably, her fatal flaw is her trusting nature.

- *Inciting Incident:* The Inciting Incident is the moment when we find out for certain that change is about affect our protagonist's life. It's the action which disrupts the character's normal life, however slightly. For Little Red Riding Hood, the Inciting Incident comes when we discover Grandma is ill.

- *Call To Action:* The Call To Action occurs soon after the Inciting Incident. Someone or something compels the protagonist to react to the Inciting Incident. Little Red Riding Hood is instructed by her mother to take cake and wine to Grandma, which entails a walk through the wood. Little Red Riding Hood is warned to stay on the path.

- *First Turning Point:* The First Turning Point is often the first deviation from the protagonist's intended journey after accepting the Call To Action. It is at this moment that we realize the journey won't be quite as simple as the character believed it would be. Little Red Riding Hood meets the Wolf in the wood, and, for the first time, her trusting nature betrays her. The Wolf convinces Little Red Riding Hood to stray from the path and pick flowers for her Grandma.

- *Mid Point:* The Mid Point is the moment the protagonist has an opportunity to alter her or his approach and redeem her or his self. If the protagonist fails to change, and continues trying to deal with the problem at hand in the same old way, chances are she or he will fail. Interestingly, Little Red Riding Hood is an example of a protagonist failing to change in time. The Wolf goes into Grandma's house, eats Grandma and puts on her clothes and climbs into her bed. When Little Red Riding Hood arrives and sees her Wolfish-looking Grandma, she is still somewhat trusting that this person in bed is actually Grandma, although her suspicions are aroused and she begins commenting on Grandma's strange appearance.

- *Lowest Moment (or, The Death Experience):* The Lowest Moment is when everything goes as wrong as it can possibly go for the protagonist. Whereas the First Turning Point was a challenge to show the protagonist that something needs to change, the Lowest Moment is the ultimate "do or die" moment. Little Red Riding Hood is convinced to come close enough to the Wolf in Grandma's clothing to be eaten herself! At this moment, all seems to be lost.

- *Climax:* The Climax is the highest point of action and drama in the story. All is either saved or lost in the Climax. For Little Red Riding Hood, the Climax occurs with the arrival of the Woodsman who sees the bloated Wolf in Grandma's house, puts two and two together, and hacks Wolfy open to free poor eaten Grandma and Little Red Riding Hood. Annoyingly, our protagonist in this story is completely passive during the climax. In a more satisfying climax, the protagonist, with the help of her friends, and having learned from everything that has happened to her so far, would pull herself out of her lowest moment.

- *Denouement:* The Denouement is the final moments of the story where we find out how this journey has altered the protagonist for better or for worse. Some stories end with the Climax, and the Denouement is merely implied. In the Brothers Grimm story, since it is established that when a wolf eats a person it doesn't necessarily follow that that person is dead, it is also within the believable realm of Grimm reality that, after a wolf is disembowelled, he will survive and immediately regain his appetite (of course). So, in the often glazed-over Denouement of popular adaptations of "Little Red Riding Hood," the Wolf tries to come back to eat Grandma and Little Red Riding Hood again, but this time Little Red Riding Hood and Grandma have their wits about them. They make a pot of boiling water and trick Wolfy into landing in it, and they make wolf soup. Little Red Riding Hood has learned her lesson about indiscriminately trusting everyone.

Arguably, in the Brothers Grimm version where the emphasis is on the revenge soup, the plot points would shift so that the Mid Point happens when Little Red Riding Hood and Grandma are freed by the Woodsman, and the Climax is the moment Little Red Riding Hood and Grandma capture the wolf. This version renders the protagonist an active participant in her own fate, which is favorable to the sugar coated Woodsman-saves-the-day adaptations.

The *Monomyth*, or the *Hero's Journey*, according to Joseph Campbell, describes the path the protagonist takes from the first moment we see them through to the plot's climax and the inevitable ending:

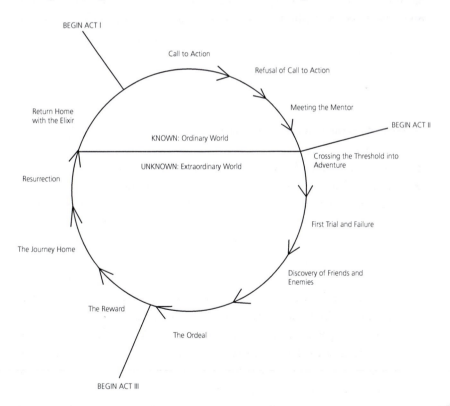

To break it down:

- The hero is called to action but she is reluctant until meeting her mentor who convinces her to leave her safe normal world for an adventure.
- She experiences her first challenge and fails.
- Then things intensify as she learns who her friends and enemies are, is tested, and learns new skills.
- Then the worst possible thing happens and with all the knowledge and experience she has gained,
- She comes good and reaps the reward, before journeying home again, reborn.
- She arrives home having realized her hero self.

Try applying the "Hero's Journey" to a film your class is familiar with. The original *Star Wars* film is always a good one. A more complicated example might be *Inception*,[4] where there are layers of interrelated action, and the protagonist's goal is ultimately to unpack the layers (reality versus dream, the job versus the estranged family).

Another very useful plot structure is Dara Marks's *Transformational Arc*, which describes the way the protagonist's external journey (plot) is mirrored by her or his internal journey (character), according to the writer's exploration of the main idea (theme).

The theme of any piece of writing is the answer to the question: What's it about? Being able to succinctly answer this question is not only useful in the pursuit of getting your work produced (or published) and promoted but also helps to keep the work on track as you labour through multiple edits.

Marks's "Transformational Arc" is simpler than the "Hero's Journey," and arguably also more widely applicable to any genre of film, whereas the "Hero's Journey" is better suited to more traditional styles of storytelling which consist of a cast of adapted archetypes. (Often genres like Science and Speculative Fiction, Fantasy, and other epic styles follow the format of the "Hero's Journey" quite closely.) Marks's "Transformational Arc" is founded on what she describes as "the single most consistent pattern that defines the nature of a great story."[5] The pattern that Marks describes is presented thus:

---

[4] Christopher Nolan, *Inception*, dir. Christopher Nolan (2010; Los Angeles; Warner Bros, Legendary Pictures, Syncopy, 2010), film.

[5] Dara Marks, *Inside Story: The Power of the Transformational Arc* (London: A & C Black Publishers, 2009), p. 29.

A person (character) succeeds or fails ...
To grow and change (arc) ...
Within the context of the conflict that is unfolding (plot) ...
From the writer's point of view (theme).[6]

At first glance, this seems like an oversimplification—after all, aren't all great stories original above all else? The answer is both yes and no.

The old argument that no story is original is sound in the sense that all stories contain at least one character, some semblance of plot, and a discernible theme or two. Arguably also, these three elements virtually always interact in a way that consists of a beginning, middle, and an end—which is the foundation for a narrative arc—even if those parts aren't presented in a linear way. On the other hand, the best stories are original in their treatment of all these essential elements, and they ask a specific thematic question and seek to answer it in a new way.

The next couple of exercises move away from the technical considerations of screenwriting and begin to explore the practice of theme, the macro-structure of scripts, and visual storytelling.

Theme is the first most important consideration for any screenwriter. Before we have characters or a plot or the first scene, we have a preoccupation with particular questions pertaining to life's general themes: love, friendship, the future of the Earth, illness, war, growing up, and infinite other themes that are the overarching ideas which form our specific experiences.

But it isn't enough to decide you want to write a story about friendship, this is just a starting point. The next question you need to ask yourself is: Why? What is it about friendship that interests you? What are the nuances of friendship that inspire or confuse or distract you? What types of friendships do you have or wish to have? And, finally, what are the questions about friendship that you want to explore?

Of those questions, which is the most important to you? Once you figure that out, you have the theme for your screenplay.

The story you come up with, once you've worked out all of the above, each of your characters, and every single scene will all work to answer that central question. And that central question is called the Thematic Point of View.

---

[6] Ibid.

Exercise

Six general themes are mentioned above, they are: love, friendship, the future of the Earth, illness, war, and growing up.

Choose the one of those six themes that interests you the most. If you have another general theme in mind which is not listed, you can work on that instead.

Your first task is to list five specific questions pertaining to the general theme you have chosen to work on. Think of the questions about that theme which preoccupy you the most. What are your beliefs about the theme and how might you challenge the beliefs you hold? What are your experiences of it and how do they compare with the experiences of others? What are the perplexing aspects of your theme? This should take no more than ten minutes.

Your second task is to pick write a short synopsis for an original screenplay which seeks to answer that question. You need to come up with a basic plot, a protagonist, and any other important characters, and you need to decide how you want the story to resolve. Most importantly, you need to make sure that each of these elements is working towards answering your specific thematic question.

You may wish to partially base your synopsis on personal experience. Alternatively, you might want to write an adaptation of an existing canonical work which deals with a variation on your specific theme, like a classic novel or a fairytale (think the connection between the Hollywood film, *Clueless*, starring Alicia Silverstone, and Jane Austen's novel, *Emma*).

This shouldn't be longer than one page, and it should take around 20 minutes to complete.

Example

Friendship is one of the main general themes in *When Harry Met Sally*.[7] The specific theme under the umbrella of "friendship" is elucidated within the first several minutes of the film through the kind of philosophical banter style of dialogue the two protagonists come to share on a regular basis. When Harry and Sally first meet and drive together from the University of Chicago to New York City, Harry posits that a man and a woman can never really be friends because sex always gets in the way. Sally disagrees with him at first, but eventually she concurs, although we get the sense she isn't entirely convinced. The specific thematic point of view on the general theme of friendship can be summarized in one simple question: "Can a man and a woman be friends without sex getting in the way?"

This becomes the rationale for why the two protagonists go their separate ways as soon as they arrive in New York. The theory is tested when Harry and Sally meet each other again several years down the track, and once again ten years later when they finally embark on a real friendship. The ultimate test comes after they have become close friends and they wind up in bed together.

It has been alleged that the original ending was that Harry and Sally mend their friendship—thus proving the theory about friendships between men and women wrong. In the ending we know (the more Hollywood-friendly version), Harry and Sally end up getting married—which proves their theory right: sex does get in the way of a friendship between a man and a woman, but not always for the worse.

So, at every plot turn, there is an attempt at answering the question posed by the thematic point of view.

Exercise

Your task is to articulate what your favorite film is really about.

Begin by writing a one-page synopsis explaining who the characters are and how the story unfolds chronologically. For the

---

[7] Nora Ephron, *When Harry Met Sally*, dir. Rob Reiner (1989; Los Angeles; Castle Rock Entertainment, Nelson Entertainment, 1989), film.

purposes of this exercise, you may want to avoid films with overly complex plots, like *Inception*. Write out the synopsis from the point of attack (the first moment we meet the characters) through to the climax and ending. This shouldn't take longer than ten minutes.

Now that you have your synopsis, answer the following questions using complete sentences.

1 Who is your protagonist?
2 What is it your protagonist is forced to ultimately learn, and
3 What is at stake that forces the protagonist to learn and change?
4 How would you pose the writer's thematic point of view as a question?

Example

If I were to answer the above questions for the film *Clueless*,[8] it would look something like this:

1 The protagonist is Cher, a spoilt Beverly Hills high school student
2 who is forced to learn a lesson about genuine altruism
3 in order to earn the respect of Josh, her former step-brother and the subconscious object of her affections
4 in a story that asks the questions: Can altruism illuminate our awareness of our fundamental needs and desires?

Exercise

This exercise is to be done as a workshop group.

First, allocate the task of head writer to one member of the group.

---

[8] Amy Heckerling, *Clueless*, dir. Amy Heckerling (1995; Los Angeles; Paramount Pictures, 1995), film.

Have the head writer draw up a table on the white board that looks like this:

Bartender	Rock Star	Murderer

As democratically as possible, fill in the table with biographical information of each of these three characters. What are their names, ages, marital statuses, interests, desires, secrets, anxieties, etc? Conclude with the answer to this question: What does this character want to achieve or attain the most?

Once the three profiles are ready, it's time to move on to plotting your film. Have the head writer list the following narrative plot points and fill them in as a group, based on the above example of the more popular version of "Little Red Riding Hood."

Bear in mind that you need to bring all three characters of your in at various times throughout the plot, and that each of them must be instrumental in the storytelling, but that you might choose one of the characters to be your protagonist.

It may be easier not to plot each of these points in sequence. Once you have a starting point, it can help to decide on the climax, so that the points in between are working towards an identifiable goal.

Everyone in the group should have their say, and feel free to challenge each other's logic as you go through each point, so you can come up with the best possible scenario.

Keep bringing the discussion back to the question: How does this action work to help the main characters succeed in, or fail at, getting what they want?

By the end, you will have plotted a complete feature film. If you want to take this exercise a step further, you might decide to produce a treatment for your film.

- Break into three groups. Group 1 takes the Starting Point, Inciting Incident, and the Call to Action; group 2 takes the First Turning Point, Mid Point, and the Lowest Moment; group 3 takes the Second Turning Point, Climax, and Denouement.
- Each group then needs to plot between six and ten scenes for each of their three plot points. To do this, you need to

write the slug line, character list, and a brief description outlining each scene. Be sure to include a sentence which encapsulates the point of each scene; that is, what makes each scene essential to the greater story.

- Finally, redraft your plotted scenes into simple prose paragraphs. Write in the present tense and aim to write in a style which is engaging and active in voice. Each group member might want to take a scene to convert into prose.

- When you are ready, you can put all the paragraphs in order, and then combine your group's work with the other groups in your class. Do a read-through as a whole class of your prose. This is your first draft treatment of your fully plotted feature film! Congratulations!

Exercise

The following exercise is all about "pitching" ideas. It explores the answer to that impossible question your friends keep asking you about your writing: "What's it about?"

As a writer you are probably asked this question anytime somebody finds out you're working on something new. Sometimes this question has real practical applications. If a potential producer asks you at a networking event, "What's it about?", you need to have a captivating answer prepared.

Other times, that question is almost used as an icebreaker—a way for somebody to get to know you better through your work. Although these instances may have fewer professional implications, they are actually fundamental to the reasons we have for writing in the first place. We write because, ultimately, we have something to say; we have something we want to explore in a new way; we have an impulse to share our unique perspective on an old idea with the world.

Your task is to work up four different pitches for one idea for a film or television series.

1 To begin with, you will need to come up with a list of five ideas for original films or television series. Brainstorm these as quickly as you can, describing them in a few sentences or dot points. You don't have to go into a lot of detail. Then pick your favorite idea and work with it.

2   The first thing you need to do with your favorite idea is to write a short synopsis. Describe in terms of cause and effect the way the story might work as a screenplay. You might use the plot points outlined in the last exercise to help move your reader through the story in a coherent way.

3   Once you have a synopsis, rewrite the essential story in a single paragraph. Make sure you include the main characters, what they want, and what happens to them. You might also include something about genre to give the reader a more practical sense of the final product, since different genres have distinct characteristics.

4   Once you have the one-paragraph description, boil it down to two concise sentences.

5   Finally, write a pitch of 12 words or less that encapsulates the main thrust your story in a compelling way.

Now you have a series of four clear pitches to deliver in the appropriate settings. Plus, you also have some solid plans to revisit and use any time you feel like the project itself is straying from its original concept.

Example

If I had been the writer of the screenplay for *When Harry Met Sally*, my paragraph synopsis, two-sentence pitch, and eight-word pitch might read something like this (bear in mind these are not the official synopses or log lines for *When Harry Met Sally*, and you will need to come up with your own original idea rather than writing the synopses and pitches for an existing film).

Paragraph synopsis:

Harry and Sally meet in Seattle through a mutual friend to drive across to New York City together after their college graduation. They are immediately thrown together on a twelve-hour road trip where they discover that they don't like each other very much; Harry is a messy pessimist, and Sally is a slightly obsessive-compulsive optimist. They meet again five years later, both still living in New York, both starting long-term relationships. They meet once again another five years later, this time they are both newly single. They begin to forge a close friendship based on the interplay of their fundamental personality differences, until one night they end up in bed together. Awkwardness ensues and they must find a way to either re-establish their friendship, or finally accept that they are meant to be together.

Two-sentence pitch:

Harry and Sally are two perfect opposites who are thrown together on a road trip after graduation, and proceed to forge a friendship over the decade which follows. What happens when they begin to have romantic feelings for each other after a ten-year anti-courtship?

Twelve-word pitch:

Harry and Sally are 'just good friends', until sex ruins everything.

Screenwriting technical toolbox

One of the more intimidating factors of crafting a screenplay is how to include camera angles and stage directions, and how to denote scenes that aren't straightforward action and dialogue.

There are extensive manuals on the market as well as style guides specific to particular arts bodies which can teach you all the formal techniques for denoting camera directions.

Some of the more common of these will be covered in this section to demonstrate how they function in certain types of scenes.

Writing phone conversations

The rule for where a scene technically begins and ends is that where there is a new location there is a new scene.

But what happens if you are writing a phone conversation between two people in two different locations, and we cut between both characters in their separate locations at different moments during the conversation? The short answer is that the phone conversation will occur between two continued scenes.

The film within the film

A common plot device in films is the use of the six o'clock television news. We often have a character witness some breaking news which somehow alters the course of the plot, or the revelation that what was once a private matter is now in the hands of the media, which ups the tension in the plot.

So, how do you write a scene which includes a cut to a television sequence? As with the phone conversation scene, the transition between the scene and the television sequence will become two continued scenes if the news program becomes the sole focus for a period of time.

If, on the other hand, we stay in the room with our character to see him watch the television screen in a voyeuristic way, we only need a single scene to show this.

The all-illusive text message

As you know from having undoubtedly watched new films and television programs every year for most of your life, technology plays a part in the way we disseminate information within our stories.

The example of the six o'clock news, above, is something you might have seen numerous times, but it was not always a feature of storytelling for the screen. Likewise, things like text messages, emails, and social networking interactions are now often featured in film and television.

There is no necessarily right way to include these in the script format, except to treat them the same way you would any inter-textual medium— that is, to be clear about how you want the thing presented.

Example

In this example, you can see how a single conversation can span over multiple connected scenes, how to cut to a scene which is a film within a film, and one possible way of including a text message in your action.

As usual, each scene begins with a slug line. Note the annotation for when we can hear a character's dialogue but we cannot see them on screen in the third scene of this example: (O.S.) stands for "off screen."

Also note that wherever we go straight back the scene of George in his lounge room, where no time has passed, we use the annotation: (Cont.) which means "continued."

```
1 INT                    GEORGE'S LOUNGE ROOM                NIGHT

George is on the couch watching TV.

He reaches for a beer, takes a sip. On the television we
see an image of Alice pop up in headlining news.

George spits his beer out in shock, reaches for the
remote and turns the volume up.

                                                   CUT TO:


2 INT                    NEWS ROOM ON TV                     NIGHT

The Presenter shuffles papers as the photo of Alice
minimizes into the corner of the screen.

                         PRESENTER
               News just in, the woman pictured has
               been found dead by the authorities…


3 INT            GEORGE'S LOUNGE ROOM            NIGHT(Cont.)

George stares intently at the television.

A smile creeps across his face as he listens to the news
story.

The house phone rings. George picks it up.

                         GEORGE
          Yep?

                         ALICE (O.S.)
          You watching this?

                         GEORGE
          Geez, Alice. What now?

                                                   CUT TO:


4 EXT                         STREET                         NIGHT

Alice is dressed in a trench coat, hat and dark glasses,
and huddles inside a phone booth.

                         ALICE
          Phase two is a go. You know

          what to do.
```

```
5 INT          GEORGE'S LOUNGE ROOM          NIGHT(Cont.)
```

George is nodding. He hangs up the house phone and
reaches for his mobile phone.

We see that George is composing a text message, which
reads: "I have the money, do you have the passports?" He
hits send, grabs his keys and rushes out the front door.

They key is to think visually. Forget attempting to direct the director, and leave the non-essential details to the other artists working on your film. The screenplay is not about leaving complicated instructions for how to make the film; the screenplay is about verbalizing everything the audience will view and connect together to form an understanding of the story. For example, there is no need to describe how we know that George in the above scene is writing a text message unless it is important to the story somehow. It is up to the director to interpret this action and decide the best way of including the message in the scene. We have already made it relatively straightforward by keeping the message short and simple.

The ultimate question remains: is it essential for us to see this message at all? Do we see the exchange of money for passports later in the film? If we do, what is the point in stating something is going to happen right before it actually happens? Is that not a tad boring? If we need to skip the actual exchange to show what Alice is concocting while George is off buying fake identities, or if the text is meant to confound the audience's expectations about what the exchange is really going to entail (like, George plans to use the money as a diversion, take the passports, kill the purveyor of the passports and escape with both the money and the passports, for example) then perhaps the text message is a justifiable device after all.

Finally, bear in mind that different funding bodies the world over have slightly varied style guides for screenplay, synopsis, and treatment formatting. The one thing they all have in common is that the screenwriter's name and contact details need to be on the front of every document! Do some research to find out the kinds of resources film and arts funding bodies provide for screenwriters in your locale before committing to a particular format.

6

Writing for Performance

Performance writing encompasses a range of creative and conventional skills that rely on the author's ability to imagine her composition brought to life as something beyond the words on the page.

Although screenwriting is one form of performance writing, it has its own unique set of technical conventions which are separate from most other performance writing forms. Whereas screenwriting can apply to works that are educational, instructional, documentary, or more about entertainment than about art, other forms of performance writing are intrinsically more artistic and rely on the author's ability to manipulate sound, imagery, tactile objects, and human performers in the presentation of a theme, idea, or narrative. Often performance writers are also multimedia artists, directors, poets, and visual artists. So, if your arts practice is interdisciplinary, the performance writing skills you will develop in the exercises in this chapter might come in very handy.

This chapter covers four different forms of performance writing. The section on One-act Plays is an introduction to the creative practice of playwriting and theater. The section on Monologue reveals the art of oral and visual storytelling through characterization. The Spoken Word section will help you to explore the poetics of self-writing for performance and the politics of the author as performer.

One-act plays

The immediacy of telling a story in one act to a live, responsive audience makes the art of one-act playwriting very different from all other performance writing forms. You can't have infinite settings and tens of characters and you can't tell the story primarily through action like you do in screenwriting.

The one-act play transports the audience through dialogue and monologue, striking staging, imagery, and movement. It can be nearly impossible in an age where everything is digital and interactive to achieve suspension of disbelief for the audience of a stage play—and, in fact, suspension of disbelief is not necessarily something a playwright should strive for. There is something necessarily confronting about the relationship between the characters in a play and their audience; an awareness of this will help the playwright communicate effectively to the audience through the text. Arguably, theater is meant to challenge the audience more than it is meant to merely entertain like some more contemporary performance writing styles (such as television, for instance).

The one-act play has a history as long as any other dramatic form, with its origins in Ancient Greece. Like short films and short stories, the one-act play manipulates the conventions of the Aristotelian three-act narrative structure to tell a whole story, often in under 30 minutes. Whereas narratives in three acts have a distinctive arc from the inciting incident to the climax and ending, narratives in one act have the autonomy to be experimental, and centre the storytelling on a single event or conversation.

The splendor of the one-act play is that it's a distilled exploration of theme, like poetry. The playwright can examine one idea, one thematic question, using irony, farce, melodrama, or satire, in a single setting with a small number of characters. In some ways the physical restrictions of the one-act play provide the writer with a surprising amount of freedom to experiment with the medium and come up with something truly special.

Harold Pinter's *The Dumb Waiter*,[1] Samuel Beckett's *Endgame*,[2] and Anton Chekhov's *The Marriage Proposal*[3] are three of most important one-act plays of the past 150 years. All three plays have four or fewer characters; all have a single main setting; and all experiment with non-conventional ways of interrogating a central idea mainly through dialogue.

Of course, with the aid of contemporary technology and the possibilities of incorporating multimedia within the traditional theater medium, some of the constraints historically associated with telling a dramatic story in a single act are now less stringent. But the essence of creating a problem to be solved between a few characters with one main point of conflict in a short

---

[1] Harold Pinter, *The Dumb Waiter*, (premiered 1960; London, Hampstead Theatre Club), stage play.
[2] Samuel Beckett, *Endgame*, (premiered 1957; London, Royal Court Theatre), stage play.
[3] Anton Chekhov, *The Marriage Proposal*, (premiered 1890; St Petersburg), stage play.

space of time in front of a live audience remains the foundation of contemporary one-act playwriting.

Formatting for stage

Whereas the screenplay has strict formatting rules for how action and dialogue appear on the page, playwriting is a little less formally structured. The key is to keep action and dialogue clear and separate, and to format the play in a way that best communicates the aesthetic of the story. Here is a sample format for playwriting.

> SCENE TWO
> Lights are hazy and dream-like. LEE stumbles into the house with ROSE, unconscious, bloody, burnt and dirty over his shoulder and pulling PHAZ along, sprawled over pillows on a child's cart.
>
> LEE leaves the cart and PHAZ to lay ROSE down on the couch. He kneels by her still body and wipes the dirt from her face with his sleeve. She begins to stir.
>
> ROSE lifts her hand to LEE's nose as her eyes begins to open, holds it between her fingers, and guides his face down to hers. They share a small kiss. Startled and shy, LEE tries to speak to her.
>
> LEE   Can you hear me? What is your name? Where are you from?
>
> ROSE closes her eyes again, nestling into LEE's shoulder. LEE looks very unnatural and unsure of how to position himself, but simultaneously enchanted by her. PHAZ begins to groan, attracting LEE's attention. He gets up to haul PHAZ onto the floor as PHAZ briefly regains consciousness.
>
> PHAZ   That's the biggest nose I've ever…
>
> PHAZ's head drops back with a thud. LEE stumbles out of the room for a moment then back in with dressings and bandages.[4]

Note how the characters' names are all in capitals, the action is justified and the dialogue is indented? All of these informal formatting features are meant to make the script as easy to read as possible.

If you prefer, you can use the screenwriting standard format for a stage play, as long as you make it clear which medium your script is intended for.

---

[4]Tara Mokhtari, *Reverie Wreckage*, dir. Carol Woodrow (2002; Canberra: Free Rain Theatre Company), stage play.

Exercise

This is a research task. Search the web for a one-act play script which has been produced by a theater company anywhere in the world. This could be a play by a famous contemporary or classic playwright, or a play by a lesser-known playwright which has been produced by an independent company.

The object is to find the script (the full text), and also some information about the production including any details about the company, the director, the cast, and any promotional materials and photographs.

Print out the script and read it. As you are reading, see if you can mark up possible blocks of action and dialogue. Just as in screenwriting, a scene is made up of many blocks, each of which has its own distinct tone, power balance between characters, subject matter, and physicality. Dividing your play block by block will help you to see its potential pace and dynamics.

Workshop

In your workshop group, take turns sharing the scripts you found and the details about the production of the play.

Allocate a character from your play to each of your group members and do a read-through of the full script together. You might want to take the role of narrator and read out the stage directions in between the dialogue.

As you read through each play, pay attention to the following points so you can discuss them at the end.

- Did you observe the change in tone, the power shift between characters, topics of dialogue and the physicality of stage directions between each block you previously identified? Did your group members agree with the places you marked up between blocks?
- What could you tell about each of the characters just from listening to their idiosyncratic uses of language?
- How much of the story played out through dialogue?

- How much of the story was shown through stage directions?
- Where was the climax? What happened immediately before and after it?
- How did the opening scene give clues about the climax or ending?
- Approximately how long did the read-through take? How many minutes per page?

Exercise

This one is about imagining for the stage.

A playwright needs to be able to envision the way a story will play out in front of a live audience. You have already practiced the art of thinking visually during the exercises in the screenwriting chapter, but now you will add to that skill a set of physical limitations.

- Work creatively within the confines of a single setting where all the action and dialogue takes place.
- No voice-overs or conventional narrators.
- You cannot show an explosion or a car crash or anything that would require special effects.
- You may *tell* things through dialogue more than you necessarily *show* things, but you have to keep it interesting.

Beckett's *Endgame* cleverly employs a surrealist setting to symbolise some of the essential aspects of the characters. The main character is in bed and his mother emerges from a dustbin in the room (where she lives, apparently) during her scenes. Sometimes it is possible to develop the story for a one-act play simply by starting with one strong visual on stage.

Your task is to come up with an opening sequence for the scene for a one-act play with two or three characters. The challenge is to start the composition process with one strong visual, rather than planning the story and devising the characters first. Take into account the above limitations.

It might help to close your eyes, picture an empty stage, and then imagine its possibilities. Think in terms of striking imagery (like the mother leaping out of the dustbin), and unusual presentations of everyday settings (for example, a noose dangling over a fully set dining table).

Describe your scene and setting as opening action in third person, present tense, using clear formatting.

Example

Here is the opening of the first scene of *Endgame*:

> *Bare interior.*
> *Grey Light.*
> *Left and right back, high up, two small windows, curtains drawn.*
> *Front right, a door. Hanging near door, its face to wall, a picture.*
> *Front left, touching each other, covered with an old sheet, two ashbins.*
> *Center, in an armchair on castors, covered with an old sheet, Hamm.*
> *Motionless by the door, his eyes fixed on Hamm, Clov. Very red face.*
> *Brief tableau.*
>
> *Clov goes and stands under window left. Stiff, staggering walk. He looks up at window left. He turns and looks at window right. He goes and stands under window right. He looks up at window right. He turns and looks at window left. He goes out, comes back immediately with a small step-ladder, carries it over and sets it down under window left, gets up on it, draws back curtain. He gets down, takes six steps (for example) towards window right, goes back for ladder, carries it over and sets it down under window right, gets up on it, draws back curtain. He gets down, takes three steps towards window left, goes back for ladder, carries it over and sets it down under window left, gets up on it, looks out of window. Brief laugh. He gets down, takes one step towards window right, goes back for ladder, carries it over and sets it down under window right, gets up on it, looks out of window. Brief laugh. He gets down, goes with ladder towards ashbins, halts, turns, carries back ladder and sets it down under window right, goes to ashbins, removes sheet covering them, folds it over his arm. He raises one lid, stoops and looks into bin. Brief laugh. He closes lid. Same with other bin. He goes to Hamm, removes sheet covering him, folds it over his arm. In a dressing-gown, a stiff toque on his head, a large blood-stained handkerchief over his face, a whistle hanging from his neck, a rug over his knees, thick socks on his feet, Hamm*

seems to be asleep. Clov looks him over. Brief laugh. He goes to door, halts, turns towards auditorium.[5]

Exercise

The premise of Chekhov's *The Marriage Proposal* is a simple conversation with one purpose gone horribly (and hilariously) wrong. Instead of a straightforward marriage proposal, a couple end up in a farcical fight where neither party is wholly aware of the intentions of the other. The would-be groom walks out moments before the would-be bride discovers he came there intending to propose. As the conflict unfolds on stage, the audience gets a voyeuristic view of the dynamics between the characters, their flaws and motivations.

There are many events in life that should be relatively straightforward, but have the potential to end in gross misunderstandings.

Your task is to pick one of the following scenarios and figure out how to turn it into a farcical misunderstanding where the main purpose of the conversation between two characters is somehow lost in translation.

- The bar manager tells the slightly psychopathic owner that he quits, but …
- An unmarried young woman with a conservative family must tell her father she is pregnant, except …
- A young man interviews for a nanny job for a young child with a peculiar couple of parents, and discovers …
- A patient must explain the embarrassing symptoms of a painful condition to a doctor, but …

First, expand on the scenario you choose to include the details of what goes wrong before the problem is resolved between the two characters: What is the most awkward possible dilemma you can put your protagonist through before his/her issue is acknowledged by the antagonist? Write out a half-page synopsis explaining the main turning points in the prospective one-act play.

Once you have a solid plan, write out a scene or block (part of a scene) of dialogue between your two characters from any part of the play you choose. Use all of the dialogue writing skills you developed in the Screenwriting chapter exercises.

---

[5] Samuel Beckett, *Endgame* (New York: Grove Press, 1958), p. 1.

Monologue and soliloquy

A monologue is a dramatic speech performed by one character, usually to another character. A monologue can be used as a narrative device for a character to examine her or his reflections on aspects of the play's plot or themes, for exposing the character's back story.

A soliloquy is similar to a monologue in that the character performs a speech alone, but a soliloquy exists within the context of a larger play for the specific purpose of showing the audience something of the character's private, internal life. In a soliloquy, the character divulges the thoughts, emotions, and motivations she or he would not otherwise reveal through dialogue with other characters. Think about the function of Hamlet's famous "To be or not to be" soliloquy, in which the audience becomes privy to the protagonist's innermost struggles with life and death, power and guilt, right and wrong. We bear witness to Hamlet's private suffering and come to understand his motivations, actions, and reactions in a more intimate way because of this soliloquy.

Monologues and soliloquies are sometimes featured in plays to expose a part of the narrative, back story, or character development, but they also often appear outside of the context of a larger play as independent forms of staged performance.

Quite often monologues are used by actors for auditions, not only for the obvious reason that an actor can perform a monologue alone but also because monologues often bring out the most dramatically poignant moments in a character's exposition, and so they are a good gauge of the actor's ability to faithfully portray a character at its most vulnerable.

Exercise

Pick a character you are very familiar with from an existing novel, film, or television series. Now, imagine this character transformed for a stage play.

Your task is to write a monologue for this character that reveals a significant story about his or her past.

Try to capture your character's voice, intonation, process of reasoning and reverie, their relationship to the characters they are talking about, and the significance of the story to your character's present self.

This can be up to a page in length and shouldn't take longer than 20 minutes to complete.

Example

Below is a monologue from the three-act play *A Tribute to Black*. The monologue is given by the character Mr Katz who is the animated alter ego of the protagonist's alcoholic father, Bob. During the monologue the audience finally discovers the reason Bob turned to the bottle and escaped into the fantasy world of Mr Katz.

Mr Katz   She was just being neighbourly. I might have ... well, them fags don't take me much serious-like anyways, do they? I mean they're cock-suckers, just like whores, always wantin' a bit of drama to spice things up. I dunno about them two, really – but they aren't bad, you know, for a couple of fruits. Don't matter what I tell'em long as its entertainin'. As for the truth, Delilah didn't want nothing to do with me like that really ... she was always coming 'round, Mrs Katz didn't notice nothing strange, so there was nothing the matter with it ...

Ivan   The truth.

Mr Katz   You run a hard bargain, mister. Maybe she noticed. How would I know. But I certainly noticed. Delilah – she was there at just the right times. She'd bring 'round a roast, sing this song with her awful cat-in-labour voice. It was a terrible disservice to the song's original artist. I'd sit and watch her. She'd be pottering around the kitchen, she was a little younger than I was, maybe thirty-something. I dunno. I sit at the kitchen counter, and sketch. I wasn't bad either – don't have any of the pencil sketches I used to do anymore, but I wasn't too bad. She'd sing, if you could call it that, and I'd draw her while she did this or that in the kitchen. This one night, she came into the study. Don't know what she was even doing upstairs – she never used to go upstairs. I was half-asleep, listening to the radio. She came in and didn't say a thing. I thought it was strange, but I didn't say nothing either. After a good ten minutes she shut the door, and sat on the rug. I was looking at her, thinking "God she's ugly". Too bad, she wasn't a bad sort of woman. So we were alone together, and even though I was thinking how she was ugly, I went and sat on the rug with her, she didn't look at me, I knew what she was after, though. I thought I knew … she was shaking, I put my hand on her … I don't know what happened. I was still half-asleep. The radio was going, and we were … Suddenly, she pulled away from me. She was having some kind of, panic attack … I slapped her, hard. I just wanted her to shut up, I mean to calm down. She ran off, I heard the door slam down stairs. Didn't occur to me to follow her … I just sat there. I remembered Mrs Katz right at that moment … I realised how – how beautiful she was, in comparison to Delilah. I felt, guilty. She could never find out. I knew she'd know the moment she got home she'd know. I couldn't hide it. I went downstairs, I sat at the kitchen bench and I poured myself a glass of … I don't even remember anymore. I poured one glass, then another. I thought, if I was drunk when she got home, she couldn't tell if I was acting strangely. I drank, and the guilt began to fade. I s'pose I – I never really stopped.[6]

Notice how Mr Katz tells his story in his own unique vernacular and tone? He is not entirely honest the whole way through the telling of the story and he changes tangents and convolutes memories right up until the revelation at the end. After this point his tone shifts and Mr Katz becomes Bob again in a moment of perfect clarity:

---

[6]Tara Mokhtari, *A Tribute to Black*, dir. Soren Jensen (2001; Canberra: The Nineteenth Hole Productions), stage play.

Ivan	Bob?
Mr Katz	Hey? What was that?
Ivan	Bob.
Bob	She was ... my wife was ... years before Delilah moved next door: she was gone away, far far away. And forever, because she was ... she was dead.

Ivan walks across the stage and exits

| Bob | I cheated on my dead wife. Maybe, maybe she was dead. She was still my wife. |

Bob pulls a brown paper bag with a flask in it out of his coat pocket, takes a swig and exits.[7]

During the whole monologue, Bob's dual identity comes unraveled. We come to see how vulnerable he can be despite his violent rages in the earlier scenes of the play. The monologue is written in language that is true to Mr Katz/Bob's character and it doesn't try to tell parts of the story external to his subjective experiences.

Exercise

Imagine you are going to adapt one of your short stories for the stage.

Pick a story you have written previously which has just one or two settings and a small number of characters. Read back over the story and think about the way you might represent the protagonist through dialogue, monologue, and soliloquy. How might you stage the play? Where would it begin and end? What would the first scene be?

Now think of one possible monologue or soliloquy you could include in the stage play which would function to either expand on part of the plot, expose part of the protagonist's back story, or give the audience access to the protagonist's private reflections. The challenge is to limit what your protagonist will reveal in the

---

[7] Ibid.

monologue or soliloquy to one specific aspect of the plot, theme, or characterization, rather than trying to tell the whole story through a single speech.

When you have decided what the purpose of the monologue or soliloquy is, and where in the larger play it might feature, write it out in the voice of the character who will deliver it. Be as faithful as possible to the language, the tone, and the emotions your character is likely to express.

Workshop

Have a partner read your monologue or soliloquy out to you. Listen for the inconsistencies in tone and language, make sure the emotion you intended to express comes through in an oral presentation of the text, and ask your partner to give you some feedback on how easy or difficult it was to perform the piece (make sure, especially, that you haven't given your character a series of impossible tongue-twisters and overly complex phrasings to wrap her/his mouth around!).

Spoken word

Introduced to young contemporary audiences and budding performance artists by the likes of Gil Scott Heron, and broadcasts like Def Poetry Jam, spoken word is a performance form that continues to gain traction in many countries the world over. In three or so minutes, a spoken word performer is expected to excite an audience with an engaging personal monologue. Most of the time spoken word performance happens on a competitive basis, with performers pitted against one another at the mercy of judges and crowd response. Some people find this fun. Others abhor the idea of competitive creativity. What do you think?

The central idea of spoken word is fundamentally distinct from poetry in that it seeks to communicate, in real time and basic language, to audiences who are not necessarily experienced at decoding the formal elements of poetry in order to derive meaning from the performance. Spoken word is supposed to achieve instant understanding between performer and audience. It relies on conversational styles of verbal communication, rather than on poetics, to explore themes, ideas and stories. Spoken word does, however, borrow from poetics like rhythm and rhyme for musicality's sake. It also borrows from different performative arts, including stand-up comedy, theater, and music.

At their best, spoken word performances are honest verbal representations of the artist's life, beliefs, politics, ideas, and observations. At their worst, spoken word performances can be indulgent, devoid of any aural poetics, lazily composed and, worst of all, driven by shock value. *("Oh my! That performer just said the C word! And that other one is totally unabashed about talking about all the sex she had last night!"* Yawn.)

Before you begin the following exercises, it is imperative that you take some time to watch clips of spoken word performances. Look through YouTube and TED videos and try to find performances that you especially admire.

In this section you will be taken through a series of short workshops, writing exercises and homework tasks that could lead to your class's first inaugural Spoken Word Slam. Be brave!

Exercise

The most effective spoken word performances are often described as being raw, powerful, easy to relate to, and emotive. Audiences respond better to performances that make them feel like part of the human race, understood and inspired. These performances leave a much more lasting impression than the ones which rely heavily on shock value to get a response.

Your task is to write down on a piece of paper two things about yourself that you rarely or never share with strangers. You don't have to go into great detail, just summarize each of the two things in one or two sentences.

Workshop

As a group, take turns revealing the two things you wrote down. The idea here is not to analyze each person's secrets, but simply to listen to one another.

Have you written down anything that is the same or similar to something one of your classmates has shared? Do you notice some key themes emerging in the things everyone wrote down?

Once everyone has read, have a discussion about the reasons why some of these things are difficult to expose or verbalize in everyday life. Also discuss the reasons why it is important to talk about the things that make us all vulnerable. What can humanity achieve through this kind of sharing? What are the larger possibilities of being honest about who we really are in public settings?

Exercise

Using conversational language that is easy to relate to, write about your experience with one of the topics you wrote down in the above exercise. You can write about the past, you can write about what you go through in relation to this topic every day, or you can write about your vision for the future of this topic.

Your only formal restrictions are that you must write in the first person, and you must consider that you are writing this to be told orally to an audience. Take these things into consideration:

- Poetic rhythms and the rhythms of conversational speech.
- The importance of pausing and annunciating each of your ideas.
- The concept of storytelling to demonstrate a larger issue.
- The ways we naturally relate to each other: asking rhetorical questions, using humor, frankness, vulnerability, and trying our best to tell the truth (as we know it).

Exercise

When you have a quiet moment, use a recording device (a Dictaphone or a smartphone app) and record yourself reading your piece aloud. Try to read it expressively. Emphasize the important phrases, use pauses and annunciate your words.

Leave the recording for a day or so before listening back to it. When you do listen to it, note down on the page the places you need to emphasize, slow down, speed up, go on a tangent, ask a rhetorical question, extend out a block of ideas or questions, repeat an idea or pause for dramatic tension.

Use these markings to rewrite your spoken word piece, and then re-record your new draft.

Leave the new recording for a day or two, and then listen back to it: What are the passages that require audience feedback or participation? Where is the climax of your piece and how will you build up to it? Which parts are dedicated to appealing to your audience's empathy or experience?

You can either write another draft, or begin rehearsing your piece.

Workshop

Welcome to your first Spoken Word Slam Of The Non-Competitive Variety! Perform your piece to the group. Be supportive and give each other responsive feedback during each performance: clap, click, laugh, cry, or listen quietly. Just don't throw anything.

7

Writing for Digital Media

Right from the beginning, the idea was introduced that, in some capacity, everybody writes—although not everybody is a writer. But what happens when published texts start to diverge from their origins as forms of one-way communication? What happens when readers become increasingly engaged in the process of publicly responding to, commenting on, disseminating, rating, and reviewing published texts to the extent that the original text becomes just one part of a larger collaborative discourse? This is the unfolding reality of digital media.

Published texts on digital media are now merely starting points for larger discussions or arguments, community and knowledge-sharing at the best of times—and pushing agendas, trolling, and abuse at the worst of times. The immediacy of dissemination and the potential for anonymity on the web brings out the best and worst in readers, who have new power to leave their mark on digitally published material. This brave new world is something publishers of traditional texts (like print newspapers, magazines, and journals) are forced to grapple with in order to remain relevant and profitable.

Digital media includes the following communication platforms:

- Online publications of newspapers, magazines, journals
- Blogs and vlogs
- Podcasts and live streams of radio
- Video
- Social media like Twitter and Facebook
- Chat and virtual worlds and communities
- Forums
- E-books

The single greatest simultaneous blessing and curse for early career creative writers is the fact that suddenly anybody can publish content for a potentially infinite readership thanks to the internet. On one hand, it means the opportunity to develop a readership via, say, a blog, in conjunction with social media; many dedicated bloggers have made lucrative careers for themselves by cleverly marketing their blogs, gaining sponsors, advertisers, and making industry connections this way. On the other hand, it means you are just one of millions of people trying to stand out in a crowd of constantly expanding information: do not let that dissuade you!

One, rarely discussed, benefit of engaging in blogging and social media is that it is a chance to expedite the development of your writer's voice—if you are smart about it. You know that Facebook friend you have who posts 17 status updates every day, without fail, about every annoying thing that happens to them? They are so unabashedly and innately themselves in every post that you could almost predict what they will post next and how they are going to phrase it; you can almost hear the voice in their brain dictating each update. This is an unfortunate example of an abundantly developed writer's voice. But, if you work from the same principle and post regularly (except with more deliberation and discernment) you can start to identify the elements of phrasing, tone, vernacular, and approaches to subject matter that make your writing completely unique from everyone else's.

In this chapter you will have a go at digital storytelling, planning an article for an online publication, blogging, contributing to a journalistic discussion, and thinking about e-publishing and digital literary art.

Digital storytelling

A digital story is a short clip, usually presented as a video, which incorporates narration with accompanying visuals and audio. Much of the content on YouTube can be considered digital storytelling. Digital stories include, but are not limited to, personal histories, current events, and instructional videos. They are cheap and technically simple to create as long as you have some basic computer skills.

The challenge of good digital storytelling is not figuring out how to plug in your webcam, it's framing your story in a succinct three-minute presentation without compromising your voice or your message in a script with strong narrative features.

In this section you will create a script and storyboard for a digital story about a part of your personal history. The exercises that follow ask you to start by workshopping a personal story before writing it out and story-boarding it.

Workshop

This is an improvised storytelling workshop you can do with your workshop group.

Think about the stories that you tell about your family to explain where you came from. These might be long answers to questions your friends ask you, like: How and why did your family immigrate to this country? Why is there such a big age difference between you and your siblings? Have you ever been in a life-or-death situation? What have you learned about relationships from your parents? What was it like growing up in your family? When did you find out you were adopted? What is your relationship with your siblings like? Do you have any old family myths?

Your first task is to choose one of these stories—one which you have told to somebody before—and retell it to your group mates. There is no need to preface your story with explanations or disclaimers. Just tell it like you normally would to a curious friend over coffee.

Your second task is to listen carefully to the stories your group mates tell you about their families. What images do these stories conjure in your mind as you are listening? What larger issues and themes are raised? What are the tones your group mates use to tell these stories? If you were to put music to these stories, what would it be? Do any particular songs come to mind?

After each person has told their story, discuss the points above as a group. Make a note of any interesting feedback you receive on your story.

Exercise

Write your story down as prose, making a special effort to capture the story exactly the way you would normally tell it aloud. Write the whole story out from beginning to end. For the purposes of this task, you will need to intentionally use short paragraphs rather than long ones, and you will also need to leave four or five blank lines between each paragraph.

Once you have written out the whole story, revisit it section by section. Number each paragraph and, for each one, try to think of how that part of the story might be visually and musically represented in a video. Underneath each paragraph note down the following.

1 An image to illustrate the main idea of that paragraph. This might be a photo you have, an artwork you've seen before, or a drawing or cartoon.
2 The specific emotional intent of that paragraph. Are you trying to express frustration? Fear? Relief? Pride? Confidence? Loneliness?

It's alright if you find that one image or one emotion is relevant to a few consecutive paragraphs. The challenge is to ensure that you capture the dynamic shifts in subject, time, place, and mood with descriptions of new images and emotions.

Workshop

Take turns sharing your written plan for a storyboard. Check your group mates' work for faithfulness to the original telling of the story, and give each other feedback on the types of images and emotions you have allocated to each paragraph.

Exercise

Your next task is to draw up a storyboard for your digital story based on the plan you have developed and workshopped.

1 Draw up a table with as many boxes as you have paragraphs. Number each box with each corresponding paragraph of your story.
2 Give each box a subtitle taken from the first sentence of the corresponding paragraph.
3 Using stick figures or your best God-given artistic talents, draw the image you have chosen to go with each paragraph in each of the corresponding boxes.

Example

1 In the early 1970s, my mother, father and brother moved from the Middle East to Oxford where my mother was to study.	2 My mother used to say, "health first, education second."	3 My big brother was good at everything, but the only thing I really excelled at was writing.

Your drawing skills can't possibly be any worse than mine. Give it your best try.

Once you have story-boarded your whole narrative, you have a script and a plan from which to create your digital story.

Web 2.0 and journalism as conversation

Web 2.0

The term Web 2.0 was coined to describe the development of World Wide Web content and usage from a relatively straightforward text and communication method to something encompassing multimedia, virtual communities, social media, real time interactivity—something you can use constantly all day from your mobile phone, laptop, tablet, television, car, and even your home appliances.

As writers, these are all tools available to us for research purposes as much as they are job opportunities. You could be in London writing your novel based in Manhattan using Google Maps as well as interactive images, videos, and Google Earth to plot your protagonist's journeys around the city and describe the settings. You could interview somebody via Skype for a profile article or character research and your interviewee could send you links, files, photographs to illustrate the topics you discuss. You can look at all these things as you're talking and ask for more information according to what you discover. You can use newspaper and magazine archives as well as blogs to find out where Allen Ginsberg lived and hung out in New York City, find the places on a map app on your smartphone, and plan a little Beat literary tour of the city for yourself. The possibilities are almost limitless.

Journalism as conversation

Traditional media including television news, current affairs and human interest programs, print newspapers and magazines, and radio shows are all beginning to come to terms with the digital possibilities of journalism as conversation—the idea that news and information can be disseminated in real time, using any kind of text, or the multimedia, by anybody, not just journalists. Some of the earliest footage of the past decade's major world events was captured by regular people on personal devices.

Journalists and writers use Web 2.0 for more than just uploading articles and promotional material, especially where micro-blogging and social media platforms are concerned. Now, there exists the potential for engaging in conversations about current events, news, broadcasts, public performances and panels, festivals, and sporting and arts events, both for participants and for audiences or external observers. Many television programs now include live Twitter feeds with an advertised "hashtag" that allows open and interactive audience feedback. The feedback in turn becomes part of the information disseminated. Journalists can go to media events, public speeches, or do on-the-ground reporting and Tweet or broadcast their findings in real time.

What does this mean for new writers? Well, it means you have opportunities to partake in public discussion on the things that interest you and receive instant feedback in order to learn more, build a public profile, and interact with peers and experts in your field.

Online media toolbox

Article structure

The overall structure for writing news articles for the web is generally the same as the inverted pyramid structure used in print journalism. The concept of the inverted pyramid structure is that the information should be presented in order of importance, beginning with the most essential details of the subject.

Feature articles tend to be more narrative-focused than they are concerned with presenting the information in order of importance. However, feature articles have a defined structure which most writers work within. Here is a map of all the parts of a feature article (some of these you will remember from the exercises in the chapter on Writing the Self).

- Headline: This is the title of the article. It should simultaneously encompass the essence of the topic and also attract the reader's attention.

  New Year's Eve Ball Buster

- Subhead: This is the subtitle which usually appears right under the headline as a teaser.

  The slingshot that stopped Times Square

- Lead: The first sentence of the article is the "lead" (or "lede"). In a news article, the lead includes the who, what, when, where, and why of the article. In a feature article, though, the lead is more like a hook in a short story. Very occasionally, the two styles of lead overlap:

  An eight year old school student from Soho aimed a slingshot loaded with a water bomb at the controls of the famous New Year's Eve mirror ball in Times Square causing a short circuit, moments before the midnight ball drop.

- Nut Graf: Sometimes called a "billboard paragraph", the nut graf is the paragraph in the feature article which appears after the details of the lead have been expanded upon, and explains the relevance or significance of the topic to the reader.

  The event begs the question, who are the nut jobs dragging their bored children through the crowds at Times Square on New Year's Eve, anyway?

- Body: This is where the thrust of the narration happens. The feature article body paragraphs include details, evidence, and examples to elucidate the basic information provided in the lead. The body, as a whole, demonstrates the relevance of the topic as set out in the nut graph.

- Kicker: This is the last sentence, which summarizes the article. A good kicker leaves the reader with a new appreciation for the topic and its surrounding issues.

  Whatever happened to the good old days of military school, dexampheta-mines, and offloading the kids on grandma before a wild night on the town, anyway?

Lists

Historically, lists of information comprised one part of a larger article across both digital and print media. You might include a list of events leading up to or following an important event you are writing about. Or you might provide a list of possible outcomes of an incident, or symptoms of a disorder, or people who all have something in common and arrange it somewhere within the article to give the reader an overview of information, rather than going into depth on any single point.

More recently, though, lists are featuring as stand-alone channels of entertaining data on websites like Reddit, Buzzfeed, and Upworthy that source viral stories and videos. These lists are disseminated via social media platforms and often include gifs, videos, hyperlinks, and images alongside subheads. They play off humor, irony, pop culture icons, and are meant to entertain rather than inform readers.

But it isn't just these types of websites that feature published material which is more list than article. Many special interest websites that openly take submissions from all kinds of different authors, including psychology websites, cooking websites, culture, arts, fashion, and music websites, are recognizing the importance of publishing material that readers can easily scan or read in full without losing interest. Lists are one method of achieving both of these things at once, provided they are well written. Here are some tips for writing lists for digital media.

- **Subhead each point in the clearest way possible**. (Like that.) That way your readers know immediately whether they want to read the rest of the point in detail or move on to the next point.
- Keep the list uniform. Make sure all of your points are about the same length, and use the same tone, vernacular, and grammar through the whole list. Not only does this make for better reading, it also makes your thesis more compelling.
- Use hyperlinks, but use them sparsely. If you need to link to

explanations of each of your major points, you should probably be writing a more traditional style of informative article rather than limiting the presentation of the details to dot-points.

- Keeping it simple is not synonymous with dumbing it down. Yes, you need to present the information in a way that is easy to understand without a lot of extraneous detail, but you also need to say what you really want to say! By not compromising the crux of your message in favor of writing a more generally palatable list, however controversial that message is, you are ensuring a captive readership.

Hyperlinks

Hyperlinks, and the philosophy behind them, are probably the most defining feature of writing for digital media. By linking your readers to external sources of instant background information, definitions of terms, and contextual details, you have pretty well done all the hard work for them. No more thumbing through the *Oxford English Dictionary*, no more collecting editions of *Encyclopaedia Britannica*, no schlepping to the public library to research the history of the Gaza Strip to understand the conflict in Israel and Palestine; now there are links to millions of well-researched, up-to-date articles on everything you need to know right there on the web.

The trouble is then differentiating the valuable information from the dodgy stuff. Handled with care, hyperlinks are a fabulous way of directing your readers to the specific type of information you want them to have about your general topic. Just avoid filling your article with hyperlinks—it looks messy and distracting, and it disturbs the continuity of your ideas. It is generally better to spend a sentence or two expanding on an idea than hyperlinking your ideas away to other authors, anyway.

Of course, if you write compellingly enough, your readers will wander off and do some wider reading independently and form their own opinions on your topic. This just means you've done your job as a writer of digital media: you have contributed to, and perpetuated, a dialogue.

Exercise

Find an online publication on a topic that interests you. Read through as many articles as you can, paying attention to the following points.

- Do the articles mostly use a typical feature article inverted pyramid structure? Can you identify where the headline, subhead, lead, nut graf and kicker appear in each of the articles you read?
- How do the articles incorporate lists to give the reader more information?
- Click on some of the hyperlinks in each article. What are they linking to? Do they take you to other articles from the same publication? Other articles by the same author? External pages? Wikipedia pages or dictionary definitions?
- What kind of storytelling techniques are used in each article? Do they incorporate first person accounts of experiences? Quotes and paraphrase from interviews? Intrigue and mystery? Humor? Do they play on emotion or are they generally more objective?

Make some notes on your findings and take them to class with you.

Exercise

Your task is to plan an article to submit to the online publication you researched.

First decide on a topic, and then answer the following questions.

- What is the lead? See if you can come up with a sentence or two which succinctly introduces the key details of your topic.
- What is the nut graf? Why is this topic pertinent, interesting, worth thinking about?
- What are the pieces of background or contextual information and jargon words which require some further explanation that you might hyperlink? Narrow this down to four hyperlinks you would include in the article.
- Give the article a heading and a subhead.

Once you have these four points down, you will have a starting point for research and write-up if you want to draft the whole article and submit it for publication. The kicker will come to you once you have done the rest of the work!

Personal publishing

Social media

If you have ever tweeted or posted a status update on Facebook, you have engaged in the strange craft of personal publishing. As a relatively new publishing platform, social media is still in the throes of self-realization.

Although the first Twitter posts were about what somebody was having for lunch that day, and such relatively mundane information continues to form much of the information disseminated via social media, the important role of traditional storytelling in culture is gaining traction across all the social media websites. The Twitter Fiction Festival celebrates the possibilities of storytelling in 140 characters or less. Newspapers, magazines, and blogs are finessing the art of capturing the essence of larger stories for social media, incorporating "hashtags" for context and links to full published articles. Websites like Storify allow users to collage social media posts to create narrative timelines dedicated to any topic.

In addition to all of the above, a whole new shorthand language designed to express ourselves has emerged and developed, and—whether we like it or not—is infiltrating our everyday verbal communications outside of Tweets, Instant Messaging and Facebook chat boxes. (Have you ever heard somebody say "LOL", instead of actually laughing?) This means that language is evolving, not only to allow our rapidly advancing technological needs but also because technology has shifted the way we verbally represent ourselves and our ideas. Several think tanks, publishers and publications, and research bodies like If Books all over the world are dedicating time to interrogating the implications of social media for storytelling.

On a practical level, social media is a terrific way for an early career writer to disseminate messages about their work and parts of the work itself, inspirations, and the creative process. You can create a following by finding a creative approach to posting, and you can also stay up to date and even communicate directly with favorite authors, publishers, publications, festivals, events, literary organizations. Use social media for publishing and work opportunities, and access to competitions and prizes. In a very real way, it is easier than ever before to maintain a presence in the writing and publishing world—which is an essential part of establishing yourself as a professional writer.

Blogs

Blogs are no longer reserved for student and amateur writers, although they are a terrific way to begin collecting a folio of work, receive feedback through comments and develop a following or network of writers and readers.

Authors at every career stage are keeping stand-alone blogs, and blogs as part of a profile website, as a way of disseminating news, ideas, philosophies, opinion pieces, as well as teasers and complete pieces of creative writing.

Increasingly there are technological benefits to keeping a blog of your creative writing as a student. Plug-ins like CommentPress allow your peers and other readers to comment not only on each post as a whole but also to respond to specific lines, sentences, and paragraphs. Suddenly you have an open forum for copy and structural editing in real time from whomever you allow to access your writing.

As an early career writer, there a few things to bear in mind about keeping a totally public blog.

- Pseudonyms are a blessing and a curse. Posting under a pseudonym or screen name can alleviate some of the pressure of the whole world having access to drafts of your writing. On the other hand, if you post under a screen name, the assumption is that you are not using the blog to build your profile as a professional writer; you fall into the chasm of all the amateur personal bloggers who use the platform as something of a diary.
- If you are going to use your real name, remember that everything you post will be traced back to you for an indefinite period of time. Whatever you put up on the web now will be reproduced over and over again, and it will still be out there for some nosy entertainment journalist to dig up 15 years after you've published your first best-seller. So, take care editing your work carefully and selecting writings which you are really happy with having readers comment on.

- Expanding on the idea of posting carefully selected and edited writings, consider that you can keep different blogs for different purposes. If you absolutely must vent about how your girlfriend or boyfriend broke up with you, consider keeping an anonymous personal blog in addition to a professional writing blog that has your name attached to it.
- Use social media the same way professional publications do and post subheads with links to each new blog post. Chances are you have more Facebook friends and Twitter followers than regular readers of your blog. This is a tidy way of letting your larger network know what you are writing about before they get hooked on you and sign up to receive alerts to all your latest blog posts.
- Be prepared to start discussions, no matter how confronting or unsettling they are. It can be difficult to collapse in a heap of tears at a critical comment left by someone who has found your blog. It can be very tempting to practice your moderation mouse-clicking skills and get rid of every comment that isn't complimentary. But, by signing up to keep a blog which is open to comment, you are making a loose kind of commitment to two-way communication with your readers. To shut them down whenever they say anything you don't like sort of defeats the purpose of having a blog with open comments.
- Either switch commenting off altogether (and enjoy the consequences of never receiving feedback on your work), or keep the moderation of comments to things that are seriously offensive, and spam.

E-books and vanity publishing

Digital technology has stripped the multinational publishers of their formerly exclusively held gatekeeper powers. No longer do books only get published if an author has an agent with access to one of the big four and manages to sell the manuscript.

Now, authors have options available to them. We have easy access to the technology to self-publish our first novel as a print book–although the legwork of distributing the books into bookshops is not quite as straightforward, unless we pay to use a distribution company.

We also have greater chances to be published by vanity presses, which charge the author to publish the work (instead of the other way around).

We can get on a website like Amazon and self-publish a digital edition of a novel.

And, because this technology is so accessible, it means that, if none of the vanity publishing methods appeals to us, we still have our pick of hundreds of small press publishers who might agree to take on the work of a first-time author. All of these things are new developments which were previously unavailable to the budding writer, who was forced to send out publishing proposals for new projects, year in, year out, hoping that someone up there would take notice.

But, of course, with the increasing number of undergraduate and graduate creative writing courses becoming available at universities all over the world, there have never been quite so many budding writers as there are right now. There is more access to literature, more access to publishing, and more writers than ever before; this "moreness" necessitates a return to the conventional wisdom that quality matters.

If you must self-publish, don't do it before you've had a brutally honest mentor, a professional manuscript assessor and an editor give the work a thorough appraisal. Make sure you are putting out the best incarnation of your best work before you commit it to public scrutiny. This, alongside a clever marketing plan, is your best chance of achieving success in your self-publishing venture. It may even result in a best-selling book deal (Fifty Shades of excellent luck?), a strong readership following, and access to a good agent.

Bear in mind, also, that the bigger publishers are responding to this shift in power dynamics with initiatives that give unpublished authors new opportunities. Some publishers, for instance, who historically have not accepted unsolicited manuscript submissions, are accepting emailed proposals from authors on one day of every month with the promise that everything received that day will be read. It's not great, but it beats being lost in the slush pile and never getting a fair chance.

Exercise

This is just a little research project you can do to familiarize yourself with the best and worst examples of the ways writers might use social media, blogs, and e-books or vanity publishing in their professional practice.

Search the web for one of your favorite (living) authors and evaluate their web presence. Try to use an example of somebody who has a Twitter and/or Facebook account, a website that incorporates a blog, and whose work is published digitally. Answer the following questions.

1 How often does the author post to social media, and what kinds of things does she/he post about? How many followers does she/he have? How does she/he interact with those followers?
2 What kinds of information and media are available on the website? What is the main purpose of the blog? Is there any creative work published on the blog?
3 On which websites, applications or other digital platforms are the author's e-books available to read for free or by purchase? What kinds of artwork or presentational features accompany the digital editions of the books?

Now search the web for an amateur writer who uses social media, blogging, and who might have self-published a book, and try to answer the same questions posed above for this writer.

What are your findings? What would you say are the best practice uses for personal publishing as an early career writer?

8

Critique and Exegesis

The scholarly component to university courses in Creative Writing is often the cause of much distress and abject neglect for both undergraduate and postgraduate students. For undergraduates, having to write essays about their creative writing can appear to negate almost everything they have learned about academic composition and research. For postgraduate students, often the allure of a Masters or Doctoral degree in Creative Writing is that it is the perfect excuse to intensively work on a creative project like a novel and earn a degree in the process. So, the realization that (on average) half the writing you are required to produce is in the form of scholarly papers and theses can be a bubble-burster.

To make matters more complicated, it can be difficult to understand what is being asked of you in critiquing assignments, and the policies around exegeses in postgraduate writing programmes have a knack for bewildering changeability depending on how established the degree of study is at your particular university.

Essentially, a critique is a scholarly piece of writing which explains the technical approaches you took in a particular, accompanying piece of creative writing.

An exegesis (in a creative writing discourse), similarly, is a scholarly piece of writing with a focus on textual analysis and comparison using literature which relates to your creative writing project. Usually an exegesis is longer than a critique and reads more like a dissertation. There tends to be greater emphasis on your chosen comparative text than on your own creative writing project, with a clear thesis linking the two.

The good news is, once you learn how to write a critique on your creative process, you will find that it actually helps you to better understand your creative writing in terms of:

- Your strengths and weaknesses

- The techniques you are honing
- The feasibility of your creative choices
- Where your work sits within your genre, and
- How diverse your literary inspirations are and what exactly you are learning from your readings

The following sections are divided into discussions and exercises on Critique and Exegesis respectively. The section on Critique is focused particularly for a foundational undergraduate course of study in writing, whereas the section on Exegesis is aimed at advanced undergraduate and graduate level courses which incorporate a combination of literary theory and practice-led research.

By the end of the section on Critique, you should understand what a scholarly critique of your own creative writing is supposed to be about, what features it should include, how to plan it out, and how to combine primary and secondary research in an essay on your own creative process.

By the end of the section on Exegesis, you will have developed some strategies for systematic analyses of texts, identifying your thesis based on the issues pertinent to your creative project, planning and structuring your exegesis, and justifying the correlations between your textual analyses of an existing piece of literature and your own creative writing.

Critique

Much as most writing students abhor the things, it might help in the first instance for you to think about the critique as the equivalent of an exam. As an assessable piece of writing, the critique is basically there as a way for you to demonstrate the following to your examiner or teacher.

- You have done your reading and attended lectures, and your creative writing practice is increasingly being informed by the creative writing theory you are learning.
- You understand all of the creative writing techniques you have learned in class and from readings and research.
- You understand the practical application of all of those techniques and their specific effects on a piece of writing, and you are aware of how and why you use them.
- You appreciate that you are not writing in a bubble. You read widely

and you can name the literature which inspires and informs your personal style.

- You can view your creative practice with some objectivity and apply textual analysis to your own writing and identify and articulate its intent, strengths and weaknesses.

If you can demonstrate these five points in your critique, you are on your way to an "A" grade. Once you have addressed these things, you can begin to plan your critique the same way you might plan any other scholarly essay, bearing in mind that there are a few basic ways in which critiques and essays differ.

A critique can and should be written in the first person voice, since you are writing about your own work. Usually academic papers and essays are advisedly written in the third person. What you should aim for, however, is the most objective and impersonal first person voice you can muster. Opening with a personal pronoun does not necessitate a series of private revelations about how hard it was coming up with an idea or what your mother thought of your short story. The reason for using the first person in a critique is simply that it is awkward to refer to yourself in the third person (you know what I mean). For the most part, you should be referring directly to the text and to the techniques you are analyzing, in the most objective way possible, only bringing the word "I" into play when you are explaining your intent for a particular section of writing, or justifying the reasons you used specific language.

Whereas in the five-paragraph argumentative essay format you arrange your paragraphs in a way that makes a strong point, in a critique you have a few different options for ordering your information. Since you are likely not making a distinct argument in a critique, you might elect to dedicate each of your paragraphs to the techniques you want to exemplify in your creative writing.

Finally, whereas in a regular essay you primarily site scholarly sources to back up your assertions, in a critique you can use a balance of both scholarly and creative sources to justify your creative choices.

Aside from the academic requirements of critique writing, what you are actually doing is becoming cognizant of your creative process. As we discussed in the chapter on Fiction, when you write creatively you often enter a kind of zone where you are largely spontaneous, and ensconced in expression of the images and ideas you're dealing with. The more creative writing studies you undertake, the more you are likely to unconsciously include the techniques you have learned and practiced as often as you consciously implement them. It can be very helpful to consolidate the application of your newly acquired skills by observing them through analysis after you write the final draft of a creative piece. The more awareness you have of your progress, the more rewarding a course in creative writing can feel.

The exercises in this section are all linked and will help you to practice each step in drafting a Critique on a piece of creative writing you have worked on in a previous chapter.

Planning and structure

The first thing to do when you have a critique to write is to break it down into logical paragraphs and allocate an appropriate portion of your word limit to each one. Like any other type of essay, your critique needs an introductory paragraph, body paragraphs, and a conclusion. How you divide your body paragraphs is largely your call, but there are a few ways you can make sure you have organized your information in a way that serves the particular needs of your critique.

First, you might base your critique's structure on the criteria set out on your assessment instruction outline (if you have one). If your instructor has listed the specific points on which your project will be assessed, you can arrange your paragraphs so that each one speaks to a different point of the assessment criteria. For example, your assessment instructions for a short story might specify the following: *Students will be assessed on the effective use of figurative and literal language, coherent narrative structure, originality of voice, and adherence to the set theme of alienation.* Then your job in the critique is to speak to each of those points, elaborating on your use of the techniques learned in order to meet those criteria.

If, on the other hand, you don't have such specific criteria with which to organize your critique, you might opt to dedicate each paragraph to one of the broader issues pertaining to the drafting of your story. For example, one paragraph might be on the exposition of theme, another on characterization and dialogue, and a third paragraph on imagery and sensory description. How you order these will depend on what is the most logical flow to a discussion on your particular piece of writing. For example, if you have written a story which is clearly character-driven, then it might help to talk about characterization first so that you can explain how the other techniques you employed worked to emphasize different aspects of your character.

Exercise

All the exercises in this section ask you to take steps toward writing a critique on one of the pieces you wrote in either: the Self-writing, Short Fiction, Poetry, or Screenwriting chapters of this course book. So, your first task is to pick a piece of creative writing to work on. Pick something that is completed to at least a second draft stage.

Once you have chosen your piece of creative writing, it is time to start planning the structure of your critique.

The critique you will aim to write should have a word limit of 1,000 words.

Your first task is to read back over your piece of creative writing and try to identify what the three major features of your piece are. Write them down as subheadings.

Then reread your piece and note down every possible technique you used during the composition and drafting stages—whether consciously or unconsciously—and list each one as a keyword that fits beneath one of the subheadings.

Finally, map out your whole critique in terms of paragraphs. You will have an introduction, then your body paragraphs will be determined by your three subheadings and their corresponding keywords, and finally a conclusion. Break the paragraphs down by word length, depending on the importance and depth of information in each, so you have a total of 1,000 words.

Example

I am going to plan a critique for my sonnet which features as an example in the poetry chapter, "Stupid Sonnet II."

Stupid Sonnet II

Her granite-black streets soaked

mist abound at every gutter

floating above sidewalks, boots and cloaks,

coffee brews and voices mutter.

Gothic shadows wake from dreams

of European romances and Rioja wine,

oak-tree hems and tram-track seams,

regular rhythms and sporadic rhyme.

Lime and lemongrass emanate from little Bourke lanes,

beats and riffs pulse underground

through dark hours the warmth remains

she holds my hand and walks me 'round.

She holds my heart, recites poetry,

and inspires mine – Melbourne, my obsidian city.[1]

Here are the three main features of the poem:

Contemporary sonnet form, theme of place, sound devices.

Here is a list of all the techniques I have used in that poem:

Irregular meter, Shakespearean sonnet rhyme scheme, alliteration, assonance, consonance, end-stop, enjambment, caesura, quatrains, rhyming couplet, imagery, personification, metaphor.

Now here is how I would organize my paragraphs with all of that in mind:

- Introduction (150 words)
- Contemporary sonnet form: (250 words)

  Shakespearean rhyme scheme, irregular meter, quatrains, rhyming couplet
- Theme of place: (250 words)

  imagery, personification, metaphor
- Sound devices: (250 words)

  alliteration, assonance, consonance, end-stop, enjambments, caesura
- Conclusion (100 words)

---

[1] Tara Mokhtari, *Anxiety Soup* (Melbourne: Finlay Lloyd Press, 2013), p. 6.

Introduction paragraphs

In the simplified essay model of "say what you're going to say, say it, then say what you just said," the introduction is the part at the beginning where you "say what you're going to say." Ideally, an introduction in a critique should provide similar information to a regular essay introduction—minus the generalities often posed in opening sentences of essays. The reason for this is that critiques are all about textual analysis of technique, and technique is characteristically very specific subject matter; inevitably, you will sound like you are stating the obvious if you attempt to open with a broad statement about applying technique to writing. Here are a few (bad) examples.

Short stories use many different creative writing techniques.

Creative writing techniques are important to the composition of a short story.

Several creative writing techniques were applied in the composition of this short story.

You examiner is well aware of these facts—they are the whole basis for your course of study. Opening like this is the equivalent of opening a history essay by saying:

History is important to establishing an understanding of our past.

You would never include such a haphazard sentence at the beginning of a history essay, nor should you attempt to at the beginning of critique. Instead, you should open with a specific introduction to your creative work, since that is really the topic of your critique.

After your opening sentence, the rest of the introduction can follow a typical essay introduction structure. Here are the points to include in a suggested logical order:

1 Introduction to your particular creative piece and its central theme and subject.
2 The overall scope of the critique based on the focuses of your creative piece.
3 A map of your body paragraph topics and their relevance to the scope of discussion.
4 An indication of one or two main conclusive points you want to demonstrate through your analysis.

Exercise

Your task is to use the points above to draft an introduction to your critique.

The first point should guide your opening sentence. The second point requires you to explicate your intentions for the creative piece and its genre. The third point is a summary of the major topics you will present in the body of the critique as you set them out in the last exercise on planning and structure. Finally you need to show the significance of this discussion and allude to the outcome of the critique.

Remember that a critique is not an argumentative essay: it is analysis for the sake of illuminating the features of a creative piece and an evaluation of their effect on the communication of ideas. This also means that you may not have a standard thesis statement, as such, to articulate.

Example

Here is how I would speak to each of the above points in my critique on "Stupid Sonnet II".

Introduction:

This critique seeks to interrogate the formal devices applied in the accompanying poem "Stupid Sonnet II" for their effect on the evocation of sensory imagery in the presentation of themes surrounding metropolitan life.

Scope:

"Stupid Sonnet II" loosely takes the poetic form of a contemporary Shakespearean sonnet, devoid of iambic pentameter but incorporating the classical rhyme scheme. The intention behind this manipulation of classical form is to evoke a present-day metropolis which is comprised of a mixture of new and old architecture, and simultaneously communicates the speaker's emotional attachment to the subject.

Map:

In order to demonstrate the efficacy of devices applied in the composition of

"Stupid Sonnet II", this critique will begin with an examination of the rhyme and metric constraints of the Shakespearean sonnet and the degree to which they are manipulated in this poem. Following a discussion on form, a close reading of the poem for thematic conventions and finally its employment of sound devices, drawing upon comparative and contrasting examples from Shakespeare as well as one modern sonneteer, will demonstrate the intended communication of meaning in "Stupid Sonnet II."

Conclusion Allusion:

In critically evaluating "Stupid Sonnet II" for its use of poetic devices, I will attempt to elucidate some of the technical and artistic relevancies of the modified sonnet to poetic explorations of place in contemporary settings, revealing both the potential strengths and weaknesses of adapting free verse conventions to classical form.

Body paragraphs

The goal of body paragraphs in a critique, like those in an essay, is to coherently and comprehensively develop the scope of your focal discussion and provide evidence in lieu of the conclusion. It is important that body paragraphs should have a logical flow in order for your discussion to develop in a rational way. It is also as important in a critique as it is in a regular essay to provide evidence to support each of your main points. In the case of critique writing, the evidence you provide is there to justify your creative choices.

Here is a potential outline for the structure of a body paragraph in a critique.

1 A topic sentence which clearly states the main point of the paragraph.
2 Analysis of the techniques pertaining to the main point of the paragraph in relation to appropriate evidence.
3 A summary of what your analysis shows.
4 A transitional phrase which leads onto the following paragraph.

Exercise

For this exercise you will plan each of the body paragraphs of your critique. You have already done part of the work when you planned the overall structure in the first exercise of this chapter. Now you can add detail to the framework you set out earlier.

Using the points above, write a topic sentence, create dot points for each of the techniques you will analyze, and compose a concluding transitional phrase for each of the body paragraphs of your critique.

At this stage, you don't need to worry about the actual analysis and the evidence you will use to support your creative choices. The main thing is to have opening and concluding sentences, and to know how each body paragraph is going to contribute to the discussion scope and focus set forth in the introduction you have drafted.

Example

Here is my body paragraph plan for a Critique on "Stupid Sonnet II":

Topic sentence:

> "Stupid Sonnet II" can be classified as contemporary Shakespearean sonnet because of its manipulation of sonnet conventions to suit a contemporary vernacular.

Key points:

- Shakespearean rhyme scheme

- Irregular meter

- Quatrains and rhyming couplet

Transition:

> My intention for the non-conventional sonnet was to match the poem's form with its major thematic goal.

Topic sentence:

> The juxtaposition of new and old in a contemporary metropolitan setting and the feelings of affection that that evokes in the speaker encapsulate the main intended theme of "Stupid Sonnet II."

Key points:

- Imagery

- Personification

- Metaphor

Transition:

> While sensory imagery and metaphor drive the central theme of the poem, the formal techniques I employed evoke the subject of the city itself, which is essential to the communication of meaning in "Stupid Sonnet II."

Topic sentence:

> Sound devices borrowed from forms other than the sonnet were employed in the spirit of free verse poetry in an effort to evoke the nuances of the city of Melbourne, which inspired this poetic treatment of attachment to a city.

Key points:

- alliteration

- assonance

- consonance

- end-stop and enjambment

- caesura

Transition:

> Each of the devices analyzed here emphasizes details which are meant to affect the intellectual and emotional thrust of the poem.

Referencing scholarly texts

Just like in an essay for any other subject, you need to include references in your critique to back up your choices of creative writing techniques to convey meaning and emotion in your creative piece. This section will show you how to use scholarly references to justify your creative choices, and the following section will explain how you can also reference creative texts which use the same techniques to similar effect.

The point of referencing scholarly texts in a critique is that this is usually the only academic document you are assessed on in a creative writing course. As such, the critique is your only opportunity to demonstrate your applied knowledge of key terms and theories pertaining to each genre you are studying. It is important at a university level that you should be able to not only use the techniques you learn about, but also to articulate how you have used them in a scholarly context. This is especially important preparation for students who might be interested in pursuing postgraduate studies where the expectation is that you will contribute something new to the creative writing pedagogy.

For an undergraduate critique of less than 2,500 words, you should aim for between 5 and 15 references in total: half of those scholarly, and half creative. A more prescriptive way to look at it is that you should aim to have at least one scholarly reference and one creative reference in each of your body paragraphs. So, for a 1,000-word critique, you will likely have three body paragraphs, which means three scholarly references and three creative references. This is only a general guide, and you should consult your assessment instructions and your instructor for more specific information. Note that these suggested numbers are a little less than those recommended for research essays. This is because the concentration of a critique is textual analysis through close reading and reflection, and the evidence you provide is in place to validate and contextualize your analyses.

Make sure you are only referencing credible, authoritative sources—that means articles by authors who you are sure know more about creative writing than you do. Look for experts in the field who are published, rather than websites without attributions, or personal interest blogs. One sure-fire way to know your source is credible: you found it in (heaven forefend) a book!

For the next two exercises you will need access to the required and recommended readings for your creative writing class. You may want to either go to the library or plan to come to class prepared.

Library Exercise

This is a directed approach to researching your critique based on all the preparation you have already done in previous exercises.

At this point you have your full essay plan. You have an introduction and three body paragraphs with clear topics, content, and all in a logical order.

Your task now is to find three scholarly sources to include in your critique from your readings for this course, from an academic database, or from books in your library. Each source should deal with the topic specific to each of your body paragraphs.

Once you have found the three sources, borrow or copy them and take them home with you.

Exercise

This is a reading exercise.

Read over each of your three sources and highlight two quotes in each that relate specifically to your creative piece and which you could include in your critique, either verbatim or paraphrased.

Add the quotes you have highlighted to your body paragraph plan and reference each of them.

Finally, write one or two sentences to show how you will respond to the quote according to your own analysis. Remember: never orphan your quotes. If you're going to use a quote, always take the time to explain its relevance.

Example

Here is how I might use a scholarly reference in one of my body paragraphs:

Topic sentence:

"Stupid Sonnet II" can be classified as contemporary Shakespearean sonnet because of its manipulation of sonnet conventions to suit a contemporary vernacular.

Source:

David Caplan, *Questions of Possibility: Contemporary Poetry and Poetic Form* (Oxford: Oxford University Press, 2005)

Quote:

> *"The most common way to reinvigorate an old form is to replace outworn conventions with more contemporary language." (73)*

Response:

I attempted to reinvigorate the sonnet form in "Stupid Sonnet II" to achieve an old-meets-new aesthetic which reflects the subject of the poem: the city of Melbourne, Australia. As well as using contemporary vernacular, as Caplan recommends, I also replaced the Shakespearean iambic pentameter with a rhythm closer to that of everyday Australian-English utterance.

Quote:

> *"If the poet seeks freedom from 'description & rhyme', why not write free verse as so many poets who share these assumptions have done?" (79)*

Response:

Despite Caplan's advice in favor of free verse, the creative choice to retain the Shakespearean rhyme scheme, the three quatrains and concluding rhyming couplet is made with the intention of evoking the cultural and artistic aspects of the city's heritage. A poem written wholly in free verse might fail to adequately convey the sense of history which is present in "Stupid Sonnet II."

Referencing creative texts

Whereas scholarly references are used to demonstrate your knowledge of theory and technique, referencing creative texts is an important way of comparing and contrasting your application of certain techniques with the work of authors whose writing (in some small way) influences your own.

Some students have mixed feelings about admitting they have been influenced by other writers; there is that niggling apprehension that it might seem as though you have stolen someone else's ideas or that your voice is unoriginal because it draws some of its strength from existing literature. These are understandable concerns, of course, but think of the alternative: if you fail to openly reference the writers who influence you, your examiner might mistakenly garner from reading your creative piece that you are hoping to write the next *Eat, Pray, Love,* and grade you accordingly, when what you were going for was actually closer to a modern day *The Second*

Sex (which your instructor totally would have intuited had you mentioned it somewhere in your critique).

The fact is that no writer is completely devoid of literary inspirations. You might have the most unique voice since Walt Whitman wrote *Leaves of Grass*, but even Whitman drew inspiration from other poets as well as the King James Version of the Bible for his long-line style. And Allen Ginsberg drew inspiration from Whitman. And I drew inspiration from Ginsberg when I wrote my own novel, *Lion!* So acknowledging the literature which has taught you something about your own craft is far from an admission of guilt. Actually, you are demonstrating your awareness of the techniques you implement in your own work as they effect the communication of meaning in a range of existing literature. This shows that you are well read, and capable of critically evaluating creative writing theory as it relates to more than just your own writing. This is also important practice for students who are hoping to undertake postgraduate studies later on which require you write exegetically on the work of another author in relation to your own creative practice.

Here are tips for referencing creative works in a critique:

- Use creative sources to exemplify the effects you were trying to achieve by using similar techniques in your own writing.
- Quote directly from the text to demonstrate the author's use of the techniques you wish to analyze in your own creative piece.
- As with scholarly referencing, don't orphan your quotes, spend some time explaining their relevance.
- You can both compare and also contrast your creative references with your own writing, you don't just have to show how they are similar.

Library Exercise

This is a creative text-referencing exercise.

Start by revisiting the plan for your critique. Brainstorm (from things you have read in the past) existing literature in the genre in which your creative piece is written, which is comparable to your own creative piece in the ways you've detailed throughout your body paragraph summaries. Try to think of one existing text for each body paragraph topic.

Once you have a list of three comparable texts, go out and source each of them so you can reread the parts you feel might have inspired your writing in some specific way.

Exercise

… And another reading exercise.

Go over the texts you collected in the above exercises. They should all be things you have read before, so you don't necessarily have to read them in their entirety. Just scan them for the parts which relate to the discussion set forth in your critique.

Your task is to locate and note down three quotes, one for each of your critique's body paragraphs, which you could use to justify or exemplify the creative choices you made in the composition of your creative piece.

Make sure you reference the sources properly. Then write down the quotes alongside each respective body paragraph plan. Also write one or two sentences after each quote explaining its relevance to your analysis.

Example

Here is how I might plan to include a creative reference in one of my body paragraphs:

Topic sentence:

> "Stupid Sonnet II" can be classified as contemporary Shakespearean sonnet because of its manipulation of sonnet conventions to suit a contemporary vernacular.

Source:

> Vikram Seth, *The Golden Gate* (London: Faber and Faber, 1999)

Quote:

> *"That, when he was a child, the mystery / Of San Francisco's restless history / Kindled in him an answering spark, / It strikes him now as, through the park"* (5)

Response:

> The efficacy of manipulating classical sonnet formality to convey a modern city setting is demonstrated in Seth's use of contemporary

English language in his interpretation of the Onegin sonnet to describe 1980s San Francisco. However, Seth's description of place is contrastingly less concentrated than my attempt at evoking the city of Melbourne through an altered sonnet form in "Stupid Sonnet II," and his choice of the Onegin sonnet is more particularly effective in driving the narrative throughout his verse novel.

Analyzing your creative work

You already have a detailed framework (including research) within which to analyze your creative piece for all of the techniques you listed under each body paragraph topic sentence. You know how each technique feeds into each of the main topics of the critique. You also have a scholarly context for each of your main topics, and you have a collection of existing pieces of literature which offer points of comparison or contrast.

Here are some basic rules for analyzing the techniques you have used in your creative piece.

- Use key terminology discussed in class and in readings to describe the techniques you used—don't simplify them or give them different names!
- Identify exactly where you used each technique by referring directly to specific paragraphs or sentences in your creative piece.
- Articulate your reason for using each technique based on your intent for the creative piece as a whole.
- Critically evaluate the outcome of your creative choices where appropriate.

Example

Here is how I would analyze and speak to one of the keywords I noted down in my first body paragraph:

The rhyming couplet after the three quatrains in "Stupid Sonnet II" ("*She holds my heart, recites poetry, / and inspires mine – Melbourne, my obsidian city*") is intended to convey the crux of the poem in the same way concluding couplets in traditional sonnet forms usually do. Arguably, though, my extensive use of caesura, coupled with the irregular meter, have the effect of softening or obscuring the emphasis which was intended for these lines.

Exercise

You can go ahead and write up the remainder of the body paragraphs of your critique incorporating analysis of the techniques you used. Speak to each of the dot pointed keywords, use the detailed plan you have drafted, and include the references you have sourced and researched.

Conclusions

The conclusion of a critique is your opportunity to synthesize the analyses in each of your body paragraphs and show how they work together to build a fully formed discussion of the scope and focus of the creative piece as established in your introduction. Like the conclusion in any other type of essay, you are not required to give any totally new information or cite any new sources. Rather, you should use the conclusion to show the significance of your findings through analysis and research.

The conclusion is also an appropriate place for a more general evaluation of your creative piece. Here you might explain how the different parts of your creative piece inform the intended meaning of the piece as a whole and whether or not you feel the completed draft effectively achieves what you set out to do. Whereas the body paragraphs are wholly dedicated to textual analysis and research, the conclusion can indicate something about the creative process you used to compose and develop the text.

Here is a suggested structure for a single paragraph critique conclusion:

1 Refer back to the scope and focus set out in your introduction.
2 Reflect on the points of analysis in your body and show how they relate to each other and to the focus of your creative piece.
3 Evaluate the overall communication of your intended meaning.
4 Conclude by stating the significance of your findings.

Exercise

Use the above points to write up your critique's conclusion.

Example

Here is a brief possible breakdown for the conclusion of my "Stupid Sonnet II" critique:

Scope and focus:

> The choice to largely abandon free verse techniques and instead to modernize the sonnet form in an effort to communicate contemporary themes is perhaps an unconventional one, but it is not without precedent.

Reflection on points of analysis:

> My analysis of the adherence to most of the formal constraints of a sonnet and the treatment of the major thematic goal through metaphor show the relevance of applying classical technique to contemporary subjects, and the sound devices and irregular meter in "Stupid Sonnet II" demonstrate the possibilities for elements of free verse to function as an adjunct to formality.

Evaluation:

> The major weakness of "Stupid Sonnet II" is the way in which the free verse elements obscure the emphasis on the intended poetic climax in the concluding rhyming couplet. The lines are, perhaps, over-punctuated and the meter too staccato to give weight to what should be the poem's ultimate crux.

Significance:

> A greater adherence to the metric considerations of a Shakespearean sonnet might strengthen this poem; however, the contrasting classical and modern poetics remain an apt aesthetic for the conveyance of the new and old imagery and its emotional significance to the speaker of "Stupid Sonnet II."

Critique writing toolbox

The following are few general tips on appropriate critique composition style and some examples of the kind of language you should be aiming for.

Bear in mind your university's particular style guide for essay writing, in conjunction with the following examples. For instance, many universities discourage the explication of intent in the introductory paragraph of even an undergraduate essay, so choose your approach carefully.

First, here is some revision of the basics:

- Use academic vernacular and syntax the same way you would when writing an essay.
- Use the vocabulary you have learned in class to describe the creative choices you made
- Use scholarly references as evidence to support your creative choices
- Use creative references to compare and contrast your work, using direct quotes and citing them both within the text and in a bibliography
- Bear in mind the whole point of writing a critique, that is: to show that you're actively aware of the way your piece of creative writing fits into the world of creative writing!

Now, some examples

You might start like this:

> This critique seeks to analyze the use of creative writing techniques implemented in the drafting of my self-writing piece entitled "Bum," which explores confessional style themes of anatomical expansiveness.

Or like this:

> This critique will demonstrate and justify the creative writing techniques I used in the accompanying short story, "About a Bum," a fairytale style narrative of finding love in modern day New York City.

Or, if you attend an institution with an essay style guide that discourages explications of intent, you might instead say something along the lines of:

> "The Bum" is a poem in free verse which interrogates the central theme of the personification of anatomy. The intention for this poem is to convey a complex of grief and relief evoked by the experience of flatulence. Sound devices employed in the composition and subsequent editing of this poem, including assonance, emphasize the physicality described within the first and last stanzas …

But you surely won't start like this:

> In my story "About a Bum" I used a range of techniques. I found it really hard to write, but I'm pretty happy with the final draft.

But if you must talk a bit about your personal process, you might say:

> I encountered several challenges in drafting the short story, "About a Bum," which I will outline in this critique; and I will subsequently demonstrate the creative writing techniques I used to overcome those challenges.

When you're introducing a new paragraph, you might explain that:

> My short story opens with a moment of dramatic tension which is intended to provoke curiosity in the reader's mind. Mokhtari (2012, p. 3) flags the importance of opening with a hook to entice the reader to read on.

You might then go on to say:

> Davide Angelo, in his story, "Double tap" (2012, p. 1), uses a similar technique in his opening sentence. I wanted to emulate his attention to fine, intimate details in a description of reacting to a very common experience.

Exegesis

What is it?

What? Indeed! An exegesis is a critical written analysis of a text. Like many modes of interpretive textual analysis, the exegesis has its roots in the study of religious texts, but it is now used in many disciplines including literary criticism, fine arts, and creative writing.

What's its function in creative writing pedagogy?

In creative writing the purpose of an exegesis is to critically interrogate a literary text that contains themes and compositional conventions which are connected with an accompanying original creative work.

A strong exegesis will elaborate on the themes and creative writing techniques and structures you have implemented in your creative work in a scholarly framework, to demonstrate that you have mastered their applications beyond just the ways they consciously or unconsciously inform your creative process.

How is it different from a critique or an essay in English literature?

An exegesis differs from a critique in that its focus is on an existing work of literature as it relates to your accompanying creative piece—whereas a critique focuses on your creative piece and draws from multiple works of literature and scholarship to exemplify its points of analysis.

Whereas English literature essays ask you to compare two or more works of literature based on a designated thesis, the exegesis is usually about 80 percent critical analysis of one work of literature and 20 percent your own creative piece as it relates to that work of literature.

In terms of structure and planning, an exegesis has more in common with the essay than with the critique. An exegetical introduction establishes the main topics for analysis, but also needs to clearly state the relationship between the creative and the scholarly components of the project. The approach to research for an exegesis is also more like researching for an essay or a thesis. You are required to read widely and support your assertions with evidence, examples, and precedents.

The topics for analysis in an exegesis can extend beyond a strictly technical examination, and include contextual information about the text to support proposed interpretations. The crux of exegetical writing, though, comes from the process of analyzing a literary text for its structure, conventions, and meaning. In this way, exegesis has strong ties with hermeneutics and New Criticism.

Exegesis research methods

Where to start?

The first thing you need is a research topic which encapsulates how you intend to analyze your chosen text. You should be able to sum this up in one sentence. Inevitably you will embark on an exegetical project based on the advice you receive from your professor or supervisor. Many students enter into courses and degrees in creative writing with a creative project in mind; for those students the trick is to develop a research topic which complements the creative work they want to do. For those students who don't already have a creative project they want to pursue, getting started is often a case of marrying their interests in reading and writing.

How specific your topic is depends on the degree level you are pursuing. Commonly (albeit, depressingly) the analogy of digging a hole is how students are taught to think about identifying their exegetical research projects: how broad should it be and how deep should I go? An exegesis for an undergraduate degree will have a broader and consequently shallower research topic—simply because in an undergrad course you are expected to demonstrate a more general range of knowledge, in a smaller word limit. At the opposite end of the scale, an exegesis as part of a PhD programme needs to have a narrow research focus with deeper analysis—you are expected to know everything about one specific topic and actually contribute to existing knowledge. Honors and Masters level exegeses sit somewhere in the middle.

Here are some examples of research topics for creative writing exegeses at different academic levels:

Undergraduate level:

> What are the crucial devices employed by authors in the memoir writing genre?

Honors or 4th Year Undergraduate level:

> What are the functions of multiple narrators in "And the Hippos Were Boiled in Their Tanks" and other modern fiction?

> How do archetypes manifest in contemporary television drama series since "The Sopranos"?

PhD level:

> What are the poetic devices employed to examine themes of "death" in the characteristically childlike poetry of Stevie Smith?

Literature reviews including creative and scholarly literature

Once you have brainstormed the topic for your exegesis and identified the author and the text you want to study, you are ready to embark on some background research.

The first phase of research for an exegesis, which usually coincides with beginning to prepare a thesis proposal, is the almighty literature review. A literature review is a survey of all the most important existing literature on your general topic, and, in the case of a creative writing exegesis, a literature review can also cover the creative literature connected with your specific subject; this might include other works by your chosen author, and relevant works by comparable authors which deal with similar themes to your topic. Here are some steps you can take in preparing a literature review for your exegesis topic.

- Collate a detailed bibliography based on advice from your lecturer or supervisor and with some help from a librarian who specializes in writing and literature subjects. Search for books and articles using a good library database, the web, bibliographies in key-texts journals, and list all the most relevant texts you find.
- Source the texts in your bibliography and read them. This is the time-consuming part, so it is important to annotate your bibliography with summaries of each of your sources. For each source, note down the angle of the book or article, its main findings, whether its analysis corroborates or contradicts your own thesis, and any other information pertinent to your exegesis topic. Don't forget to include page numbers so you can find the passages you need later.
- Write up the literature review following the same structural and analysis principles as essay writing. Detail the scope of your literature review in the introduction and then dedicate each of your body paragraphs to a synthesis and analysis of how your sources treat the main topics of your proposed exegesis.

Once you have a completed literature review, you can submit it alongside your thesis proposal to prove the relevance and context for your exegesis. You will then be able to use all the research for your literature review in the exegesis itself.

Identifying your exegetical thesis

So far, you have selected a text you want to analyze, narrowed down your analysis in terms of a research topic, and conducted a literature review. You are now ready to identify your thesis, which should elucidate the way you intend on incorporating the scholarly and the creative components into one coherent, assessable project.

In a creative writing exegesis, the challenge is finding a substantial connection between your creative work and the work of your author of interest. For example, it isn't sufficient to link your exegesis subject with your creative project merely on the grounds that they share the same genre;

the two accompanying parts of your thesis need to also relate in terms of their core thematic, formal, or structural values in a way that will add context and credibility to your creative project.

Examples of effective thesis statements in corresponding exegesis introductions

The following example thesis statements are based on the example topics in the previous section.

Conventions of Memoir Composition:

> This exegesis will examine the features of memoir composition in Oliver Sacks's "Uncle Tungsten" and compare them to the devices employed in my own short self-writing piece, "The Science Teacher."

The First Person Voice in Split-Narrative Short Fiction:

> The use of two narrators in "And the Hippos Were Boiled in Their Tanks" (despite its being the result of co-authorship) represents two unique perspectives on the lead-up to one dramatic climax; an effect I intended to achieve by employing a split-narrative in my own novella, "Shipwreck".

The Antihero Protagonist in Contemporary Television Drama Screenwriting:

> The problems of character development of the antihero protagonist in contemporary television dramas such as "The Sopranos" are the impetus for my choice of centring the accompanying pilot screenplay, "Mania," on the journey of an escaped prisoner with borderline personality disorder.

Representations of Death in the Poetry of Stevie Smith[2]

> This PhD seeks to address why so little has been written about representations of death in Stevie Smith's poetry. Through my research I identify the poetics of these representations through my exegetical study and through the creative project's verse novel.[3]

---

[2] Tara Mokhtari, *Representations of Death in the Poetry of Stevie Smith* (Melbourne: Royal Melbourne Institute of Technology University, 2011).
[3] Ibid., p. 8.

Hermeneutics and close reading as primary research

What is hermeneutics?

Hermeneutics, simply put, is the study of the interpretation of texts. Historically, hermeneutics has its roots in the interpretation of biblical texts—the art of which came into prominence during the rise of the Protestant ideal that an individual could have a personal relationship with the Bible based on a subjective interpretation of its stories. Prior to Protestantism, during the Middle Ages, the accepted ideology of biblical interpretation was based on the importance of meaning and the difficulty of finding meaning. Later, principles of hermeneutics were applied to interpretations of legal texts and the constitution.

Eventually, during the Romantic movement of the eighteenth century, literature revolted against the scientific rationalism of the Enlightenment period in favor of concepts such as the "author as genius," the idea of secular scripture and the new importance of literature for its capacity to provide emotional and spiritual fulfilment in the same way religion did in the Middle Ages. At this time, hermeneutics became pertinent to the understanding of literary texts.

Hans-Georg Gadamer, in his book *Truth and Method* (1975), describes the relationship between reader, text, and author in terms of prejudices (or preconceptions) which limit the reader's ability to fully understand a text according to the author's intentions. Gadamer's theory of the "merging of horizons" demonstrates the limited possibility for a reader's "horizons" (or subjective concepts of reality) to merge comprehensively with the author's "horizons" in order to achieve an objective interpretation of the text. Another key theorist of hermeneutics, Martin Heidegger (1927), describes what he calls the "hermeneutic circle," a paradoxical cycle of interpretation where, in order to understand the whole text, the reader must understand its individual parts, but in order to understand the individual parts of a text the reader must understand the whole.

There are many other theorists and theories of hermeneutics, including Historicism which values understanding a text according to the author's intentions, and Wolfgang Iser's *The Act of Reading* (1978) which emphasizes that meaning is formed by the relationship between the reader and the text alone.

Of the schools of thought which have influenced the study of meaning in literature in the past century, New Criticism and its method of "close reading" is perhaps historically the most influential in its applications to academic study. Theorists of the New Criticism esteemed the text and its structure above its author and reader. Deep analysis of the conventions and formal devices present in the text such as character, setting, meter, and sound devices alongside evaluations of figurative and literal language and theme are used in close readings in order to establish meaning which is as objective as possible. It is this basis for studying literature and its capacity for inspiring lively debate that made Literature classes fun again!

Even where other theories of hermeneutics which value the reader's prejudices and the author's intent are applied to the analysis of a text, in the context of Creative Writing scholarship, the analysis of writing techniques is vital. As such, although New Critical theory is not as prominent as it once was in literary studies, it still has crucial presence in Creative Writing studies.

How to perform a "close reading" for an exegesis

A "close reading" usually involves simultaneously analyzing a text for its structure, formal components, thematic concerns, and linguistic conventions in an effort to construe a unified meaning. This is the kind of exercise you might have done in Literature classes in order to have a critical discussion about how all the elements of the short story, novel, poem, or other piece of literature work together to convey meaning. However, in the case of close readings as primary research for an exegesis in Creative Writing scholarship, a more directive approach can be taken in an effort to critically analyze the connections between your chosen creative work and the piece of literature you are comparing it with. You might, for instance, decide to analyze your chosen piece of literature for the specific conventions that inspired your own creative work.

The following are a series of steps you might take towards a close reading of your chosen text.

1 Step one is, shockingly, to read the full text. Yes. Close reading requires ... reading! Write down everything you know about the text from your initial reading.

For example: What form does the text take? What genre? What are the names and descriptions of the characters? Where is it set? What kind of dialogue is included? What is the narrative point of view? What are the major themes?

2 Once you have noted down everything you already know about the text, do a second reading. This time, go through the text line by line, paragraph by paragraph, and, as you read, annotate it in the margin for its formal and linguistic devices.

Some things to look for might include: The use of metaphor, analogy, irony, parody, and other figurative language conventions. Its poetics, rhyme, rhythm, sound devices, imagery. Any narrative devices present including a protagonist, plot, climax, foreshadowing, denouement, scenes, transitions, and internal and external monologue and dialogue.

Go through the whole text, annotating every technique you can identify.

3 Time for a third reading! This time look for the relationships between all of the techniques you have identified in your first and second readings. At this stage it might help to do a full read-through and record your findings at the end.

Here are some connections you might make between your identified techniques: How do the uses of figurative language conventions convey different aspects of the major themes? How do the characterization techniques and plot devices work together? Is there greater emphasis on characterization or plot, and how do we know this? How do the poetics within the text work to convey emotions and ideas?

Once you have performed a close reading of your literary text, you have a foundation from which to compare and contrast the text with your creative writing. At this stage you are ready to merge the primary research results of your close reading with the secondary research you compiled while you prepared your literature review. The secondary research you conducted into existing scholarship on the text and on comparative texts, biographical sources about the author to contextualize the key points you want to make about the text and its influences on your own creative practice.

This is where the write-up process really begins!

Exegesis planning and structure

The structure of an exegesis in Creative Writing should be planned in a way that each part, subheading, or chapter speaks to one of the key aspects of the thesis you have proposed. Some Creative Writing exegeses intersperse discussion on the relevance of the creative project to the chosen literary text throughout each part or chapter, while others focus on the literary text and dedicate one part or chapter to engaging a critical interrogation of the accompanying creative work in relation to the existing literary text. The structure you plan will depend on the requirements of your degree and your supervisor's advice, but below you will find examples of plans for both possible structures.

Example

Here is a plan for an exegesis which incorporates discussion and analysis of the creative project within each part.

Title:

Representations of Death in the Poetry of Stevie Smith

Introduction:

Representations of Death in the Poetry of Stevie Smith and the Accompanying Verse Novel, *Killing the Jay*

Chapter 1:

Death of the Self: Stevie versus Jay

Suicide, Internal Death, and Fantasy

Chapter 2:

The Sexual Death: The Female Left for Dead

Smith's Heroines and Jay's Post-Divorce Escapism

Chapter 3:

Death of the World: Poet as Armed Spectator

The Politics in the Poetics of Death

Conclusion:

Embracing Poetic Deaths: Smith and *Killing the Jay*

Note that Smith's poems are examined alongside the creative project, *Killing the Jay*, in each chapter. Although in each chapter research into Smith's poems would be given more weight, an analysis of the connections between Smith and the creative project would feature in some significant way.

Example

The following is an example of a plan for an actual exegesis which can be read online at this URL: http://researchbank.rmit.edu.au/eserv/rmit:10301/Mokhtari.pdf

The structure of this exegesis focuses on Smith's poems throughout the body and concludes with an interrogation of the relevance of the creative project, *Killing the Jay*.

Title:

Representations of Death in the Poetry of Stevie Smith

Introduction:

Representations of Death in the Poetry of Stevie Smith

Chapter 1:

Death of the Self: Suicide, Internal Death and Fantasy

Chapter 2:

The Sexual Death: The Female left for Dead

Chapter 3:

Death of the World: Poet as Armed Spectator

Chapter 4:

The Death Pact: How Stevie Smith influenced *Killing the Jay*

Conclusion:

Summary of Findings

The introduction includes references to the creative project. The first three chapters in this exegesis are solely dedicated to research on Smith's poems, and the fourth chapter is largely dedicated to an analysis of the creative project. The conclusion consolidates the findings in the first three chapters and connects them with the fourth chapter.

Linking creative and scholarly writing

Some final tips

- It might help to start the process by doing some reflective writing on your biggest literary influences, who they are, which works are your favorite and why, the techniques you might have learned from them. Then you can begin to identify a text to research that you are genuinely passionate about.
- Look for significant similarities between the literary text (or texts) you choose to focus on and your creative project. "Significant" means similarities that transcend the superficial. It is not enough that they are both poems. It's not even enough that they are both free verse poems, or that they are both about death. Look for specifics: line lengths, stanzas, meters, narrative conventions, poetics, and treatments of theme. The stronger your argument for why, based on your creative project, you are the right student to be interrogating your chosen literary text, the better the outcome of your exegesis.
- Remember that the focus for the exegesis is on an existing literary text and its relevance to your creative project—not the other way around.
- Don't fear a change of thesis if the one you have come up with isn't working for you. It is totally normal for the original thesis to undergo a few metamorphoses before your exegesis is written up and ready to submit. It's much better to be adaptable than to kill yourself trying to stick it out with the wrong thesis.
- Although it might feel tiresome writing up a scholarly exegesis when all you really want to do is write meaty stories, scripts, or poems, it's like broccoli for your writing skill set. Yes, broccoli. Sure, the steak (or the spicy fried tofu) is your main course, but the boring broccoli is good for you. It keeps your critical thinking sharp. It helps with concentration and verbal clarity. It will even help you to digest that juicy steak and absorb its nutrients. You will find that practicing

your scholarly writing actually improves your creative writing in unexpected ways. You might even find that you quite like broccoli.

- Be aware of your supervisors' role in your research (if you are at honors or postgraduate level). It is their job to make sure the thesis you come up with and the way you approach it is strong enough to pass an external examination process. Inevitably that will occasionally feel like they are intentionally making your life difficult. Relax. That is what it is supposed to feel like. You will thank them for wielding that whip, on graduation day.

Glossary of Terms

Absurdist: A text which plays with the philosophy of the tension that exists between the human desire for meaning and the inherent meaninglessness of life.

Action: The prose in a script which describes the physical actions to be shown onscreen in a scene.

Affirmation: The third paragraph in a five-paragraph argumentative essay which presents the evidence in favor of the thesis stated in the introduction. It precedes the negation paragraph and immediately follows the narration paragraph.

Alliteration: The repetition of sound at the beginning or in the stressed syllables of multiple words in close proximity. For example: *The salubrious citizens opposed her self-assured sensuality.*

Analogy: The communication of the likeness of one scenario with a manifestly familiar counterpart scenario. For example: *Colin had trouble saving cash. After he broke a hundred dollar note it was like trying to shovel sand with a fork.* A more clichéd example: *The mathematics teacher had a voice like nails down a chalkboard.*

Anecdote: A brief story with one single intended crux. All the information provided works towards the twist at the end of the anecdote. Unlike other stories which depend on characterization, plot, theme, and setting, an anecdote is told only for the purpose of making a specific point.

Antagonist: The character in a literary text who most directly opposes the protagonist, either actively, as in a villain, or passively, as an existential competitor. Sometimes the antagonist's role is very subtle; he or she could simply be a character who demonstrates the qualities that the protagonist wishes to embody. Other times the antagonist's role is to aggressively roadblock the protagonist's efforts at overcoming his or her fatal flaw.

Argumentative Essay: An essay that makes an argument in favor of one side of an issue. An argumentative essay is structured like any other essay, with an introduction with a thesis statement that articulates the essay's central argument, a body, and a conclusion. Some of the evidence provided in an argumentative essay is supportive of the thesis statement. Other evidence which counters the argument is provided to give the author tangible opportunities for rebuttal.

Aristotelian Structure: Describes the functions of the beginning, middle, and end of a dramatic narrative according to Aristotle's *Poetics*.

Attribution: The formal, written acknowledgment of the source of a quote or paraphrase in a scholarly, nonfiction, or creative text.

Autobiography: All or part of the author's own life story which is written with the intention of representing true accounts.

Ballad: A narrative poem with distinctly musical qualities.

Beat: A section of a scene in a screenplay which is subtly distinguished by a sustained level of tension, a balance of power being held by one character, a mood, or a tone. Sometimes this is determined by a change in the tone or topic of dialogue, sometimes it is marked by a shift in action or setting, other times the introduction of a new character within a scene punctuates a beat.

Billboard Paragraph: See Nut Graf.

Block: A unified section of a scene in a screen or stage play that maintains one distinct mood, tone, power balance between characters, or topic of conversation in dialogue.

Blocking: The job of directing the action in a scene of a film or play.

Blog: An informal web publication (and sometimes a discussion forum) consisting of multiple posted entries of text and/or multimedia content.

Body: The combined paragraphs between the introduction and the conclusion in an essay, critique, exegesis, or article which present the main information and narrative thread of the subject matter.

Canto: One unified section of a longer poem.

Cathartic Writing: Writing which serves a therapeutic purpose for the author. Cathartic writing is written for the sake of self-expression or venting emotion. Cathartic writing is not necessarily written to be read.

Cause and Effect: The philosophy of causality. Causality is about the necessarily dependent relationship between an outcome and the factor which initiated it. In literature it can be thought of a sequence of dependent events in a plot which challenge the protagonist. Sometimes in order for the protagonist to succeed in the end, she must wilfully intercept the cause and effect sequence and take some kind of definitive action.

Characterization: The conventions for developing and exposing a character's inner workings, motivations, relationships, and history in a work of fiction.

Climax: The plot point in a story in which everything comes to a head.

Close Reading: The act of analyzing the individual parts of a text in an effort to understand the text as a whole. This might mean going through a poem line by line and identifying the poetic techniques used and the meanings conveyed through those techniques.

Conceptualization: The process of bringing an idea into fruition, or the planning stage which precedes writing.

Conclusion: The last paragraph in an essay, critique, exegesis, or article which amalgamates the information in the body to respond to or reiterate the point of the text as it was stated in the introduction.

Concrete Poetry: Poetry that takes a physical shape on the page which conveys an integral part of the poem's meaning; came into prominence in Europe in the 1950s.

Confessional: Poetry and literature which deals with the poet's own deeply personal and internal life.

Conflict: A problem that arises in a work of fiction to drive the plot and force the characters to act.

Couplet: A stanza or other unified set of two lines in poetry.

Craft: In creative writing, the artistic skill required to compose literature.

Creative Nonfiction: A literary genre in which true stories are written using creative writing techniques.

Critique: A text which critically analyzes a piece of creative writing or other artefact.

Denouement: The plot point at the very end of a story which shows the protagonist's life return to normal after the climax.

Dialogue: The speech and conversation exchanged between characters.

Digital Poetry: Poetry which is composed with a strong presentational, usually multimedia, component. Digital poetry might be thought of as the technologically advanced grandchild of concrete (or shape) poetry.

Discursive Symbolism: A language-based, linear and logical way of communicating which is limited by syntax and grammar.

E-book: A book published on a digital platform that can be downloaded to an electronic device such as a PC, laptop, smartphone, tablet, e-reader, Kindle, iPad, or iPhone.

End Stop: In poetry, when a line break occurs at the end of a natural phrase. (For example: *Lime and lemongrass emanate from Little Bourke lanes / beats and riffs pulse underground / through dark hours the warmth remains / she holds my hand and walks me 'round.*)

Enjambment: In poetry, when a line break occurs in the middle of a natural phrase. (For example: *his name is a breath // of fresh air.*)

Epic: A long narrative poem.

Exegesis: A critical analysis of a text, its meanings, and the literary conventions and creative writing techniques it employs. In the context of Creative Writing scholarship, an exegesis is usually a longer form of critique, with an articulated thesis and points of comparison and contrast.

Exposition: The mode of fiction writing whose purpose is to give back story or introduce settings or characters. The art of good exposition requires the author to know how much detail is really essential and at what point to stop explaining the past and enter the characters' present dilemmas.

Fable: A short story with a moral lesson revealed at the end, often intended for children.

Fairytale: A magical or fantastical children's story.

Feature Article: Generally, any article in a publication that is not deemed hard news.

Fictionalization: The process of taking real life events or people and imposing imagination onto them to create a work of fiction.

Figurative Language: The use of devices like metaphor, irony, and subtext to manipulate meaning. For example: *The cat is the master of her domain and we are just the minions who wait on her.*

First Person Voice: Narrative written from the point of view of the speaker or protagonist of the text. For example: *I put my sneakers on and walked down the street where I saw my naked reflection in the barber shop window.*

Focus: The key topic or point of a text.

Foreshadowing: A literary technique of giving a subtle hint or an allusion at the start of a story of what the outcome of a particular plot line will be. Foreshadowing can help the reader or audience to feel more satisfied at the end of the story because something is resolved that was set up in the beginning.

Form: In poetry, the categorization of a poem according to prescribed stanzaic, metric, and other technical rules.

Form: The genre of poetry as delineated by formal constraints including meter, rhyme scheme, and stanza lengths. For example: the sonnet is a form characterized by its iambic pentameter, a b a b rhyme scheme, and three quatrains followed by a concluding rhyming couplet.

Formality: Of or pertaining to poetic form.

Free Verse: From the French *Verse Libre*; poetry which is not restricted by classical form. Line lengths, stanzas, rhythm, rhyme, and other sound devices are used at the creative discretion of the poet rather than to adhere to a prescribed structure.

Free Writing: See Stream of Consciousness.

Genre: A basis for differentiating texts based on their subject matter, style, and approaches to theme, plot, and characterisation. For example: romance, mystery, drama, comedy, creative nonfiction, autobiography.

Ghazal: A form of Persian lyric poetry consisting of five or more couplets, usually with themes of mysticism and love.

Haiku: A poem of Japanese origins consisting of three lines totaling 17 syllables, often on themes of nature.

Headline: The title of an article.

Hermeneutic Circle: Martin Heidegger's concept of the challenge of interpretation of texts being the relationship between the whole text and its individual parts. Essentially, to understand the whole, one must understand the parts; paradoxically, to understand the parts of a text, one must understand the whole.

Hermeneutics: The theory of the interpretation of texts based on the relationship between the author, the text itself, and the reader. Hermeneutics has its origins in the interpretation of Biblical texts, but is now applied to a range of disciplines including literature and law.

Hook: A narrative device at the beginning of a work of fiction or nonfiction which entices the reader to read on.

Human Interest: Text that pertains to human desires and emotions, including the need to engage socially and to feel understood and not alone in our personal experiences.

Hyperlink: A live, working link within a text published online to another website or article published online.

Iambic Pentameter: A poetic meter with a regular five stressed syllables in each line.

Identical Rhyme: In poetry, the repetition of both the stressed vowel sound and the consonant sounds of two words. For example: *sum* and *wholesome*.

Improvisation: Impromptu creative processes, usually involving two artists, actors, or writers reacting to each other spontaneously.

Intention: The author's objective for the meaning communicated by his or her own text.

Internal Rhyme: Rhyming in poetry which occurs within the line rather than at the end of the line. For example: *The yellowing lime was a sign of the time spent at sea.*

Lead: The introductory paragraph in a news or feature article. In a news article, the lead gives the essential information of the story: who, what, when, where. In a feature article, the lead hooks the reader's interest and the essentials are detailed later in the nut graf (or billboard paragraph).

Lede: See Lead.

Literal Language: The use of language which does not deviate from each word's actual meaning. (For example: *The cat scratches up the furniture, malts fur all over our clothes, and only pays us attention when she is hungry.*)

Literary Theory: The philosophies that exist for the interpretation of literature.

Literature: The art of writing.

Literature Review: A text which elucidates the key findings and relevance of all the key texts on a designated topic. In creative writing scholarship, a literature review is often one of the earliest stages of proposing a research topic. A literature review demonstrates the viability and appropriateness of your thesis or exegesis topic to your examiners while serving as the starting point for your proposed research.

Log Line: A one- or two-sentence synopsis which encapsulates the major theme of a screenplay. The log line is useful at all stages of the writing process, from clarifying the intention for the script to pitching the script to funding bodies and producers, and finally as potential copy for the promotion of the produced film.

Manifesto: A document which explicates the philosophical and practical artistic beliefs and intentions of its author or authors.

Map: A plan which outlines the major plot points of narrative or the intended trajectory of a nonfiction text. Maps are a great way of making sure your macro-structure is sound and logical (or appropriately illogical) before you get too deep into composing the work.

Map (Fantasy Fiction Genre): A visual representation of the fictional or imagined places where the protagonist's journey takes place in a work of fantasy fiction. Often this is a hand-drawn map which features at the beginning of a fantasy novel for the reader's reference.

Memoir: A literary representation of all or part of the author's own life story.

Metaphor: The communication of meaning by likening one concept to another more dramatic or more tangible concept. For example: instead of literally describing the feeling of depression, explaining instead that one *is being followed everywhere by looming dark rainclouds.*

Meter: A regular rhythm comprised of a designated number of stresses in each line of a poem.

Micro-Story: Also called "flash fiction." A very short story usually contained in one paragraph or less, which appeals to the reader's imaginativeness. Micro-stories have gained prominence through social media platforms, many of which have character restrictions for public posts.

Modernism: The period from the late nineteenth century to the mid-twentieth century. In art and literature modernism marked a rejection of realism, a move away from the attitudes of the Enlightenment, and a denial of traditional religiosity. Modernism embraced the abstract and the avant-garde, adaptations, experimentalism, and tearing down the old to make way for the pragmatic new in terms of industry, society, architecture, and technology.

Monologue: A speech delivered solo by a character in a film or play.

Monomyth: Joseph Campbell's "Hero's Journey," which details a series of plot points which are commonly found in stories with origins all over the world.

Narration: The story-telling in a literary text, film, or television program.

Narrative Arc: The trajectory of a story from the first scene or chapter, through to the climax and the eventual conclusion.

Narrative Point of View: The perspective from which a story is told. For example: first person, second person, third person.

Narrative Structure: The way a sequence of events is ordered and presented in a story.

Negation: The fourth paragraph in a five-paragraph argumentative essay which presents and refutes the evidence against the thesis stated in the Introduction. It precedes the Conclusion and immediately follows the Affirmation paragraph.

New Criticism: The dominant approach to literary theory in the mid-twentieth century initiated by the key works of John Crowe Ransom and I. A. Richards. New Criticism valued the autonomous text above author intention and encouraged the close reading approach in the analysis of the text. This approach significantly aided in making classroom literature studies interesting and challenging for students, inspiring lively discussion and debate on the possible meaning of different parts of a poem or story.

Novel: A long narrative written in prose, usually divided into chapters, with a protagonist and a plot. Generally a novel is somewhere between 60,000 and 100,000 words in length.

Nut Graf / Nut Graph: The paragraph in a feature article which defines the news value of the story and gives the essential information. The nut graf is usually found towards the end of the first quarter of the article, often somewhere between the fifth and tenth paragraphs. It is also known as the nut graph or the billboard paragraph.

One-act Play: A shorter stage play written and presented in a single act.

Oral Poetry: Poetry which is composed and delivered orally instead of being written in the first instance.

Outline: Something between a synopsis and a treatment, the outline is a piece of prose which explains the turning points in the unfolding of a plot for a screenplay.

Patois: Dialects of language that are considered non-standard but which have their own consistent syntactical and grammatical systems.

Performance Art: Any art form with a presentational or performance element. For example: installation, video art, spoken word.

Performance Poetry: Poetry which is written to be recited in front of an audience. Performance poetry is composed with performance values in mind, such as character, intonation, and aurality.

Personal Essay: An essay with a clear introduction, body, and conclusion, which interrogates its subject through the reflections of its author.

Petrarchan Sonnet: The Italian sonnet form which consists of a rhyming octave which introduces the subject or dilemma, and a sestet which resolves the subject.

Pitch: A brief compelling summary of a screenplay or literary or media text which presents the premise of the story, its genre, and its main theme to a prospective producer or publisher. The goal is to sell the story as convincingly as possible. Ideally, a pitch is drafted in a way that it only takes a minute or two to deliver orally.

Plot: The sequence of events and conflicts which affect the protagonist and the other characters in a narrative. The plot can be thought of as a kind of external manifestation of theme.

Practice-led Research: Research that is based on empirical creative practice.

Presentational Symbolism: An intuitive and instant, usually visually derived, way of communicating.

Primary Research: Research comprising primary sources derived from empirical methods such as observation, interviews, questionnaires.

Prose: Texts which follow the dynamics and structure of speech rather than poetry.

Protagonist: The main character (or characters) in a novel, film, play, or other literary text. The protagonist is at the centre of the plot, and the plot is in place specifically to force the protagonist into action. The protagonist also goes through a journey of self-discovery or self-improvement as a result of the plot, and it is his or her internal conundrum which engages the audience.

Quatrains: A stanza or other unified set of four lines in poetry.

Reflective Writing: A genre of self-writing in which the author records his understandings, thoughts, feelings, tangential responses, associations, and values on a particular topic in order to fully explore its personal or intellectual significance.

Refrain: In poetry, a line or phrase which is repeated throughout the poem.

Rhetoric Parallelism: Two or more successive sentences or phrases which use repetition to emphasize meaning. For example: the quote attributed to Julius Caesar, *"I came, I saw, I conquered."*

Rhyming Couplet: A couplet in which the last words in each of the two lines rhyme with each other.

Scope: The breadth of a particular subject which is relevant to and forms the discussion within the text. You might think of scope in an essay as the limits you set for what is and is not essential to cover in your approach to the essay question in order to avoid getting off topic (or going over the word count).

Second Person Voice: Narrative written from the point of view of the reader of the text. For example: *You put your sneakers on and walked down the street where you saw your naked reflection in the barber shop window.*

Secondary Research: Research which is derived from existing studies on a subject.

Sestina: A poem consisting of six stanzas of six lines each and a concluding tercet (or triplet) with a set algorithm for the repetition of words at the end of each line.

Setting: The description of place in a story.

Shakespearean Sonnet: A sonnet which has the usual three quatrains and concluding rhyming couplet and is written in iambic pentameter and follows the rhyme scheme: a b a b c d c d e f e f g g.

Slug Line: The heading at the top of every new scene in a screenplay which denotes whether the scene is shot internally *(INT.)* or externally *(EXT.)*, the location, whether the scene is shot in daylight *(DAY)* or at night *(NIGHT)*, and sometimes whether the scene is continued from an earlier established scene *(CONT'D)*.

Soliloquy: A kind of monologue in which a character speaks his or her thoughts aloud. A soliloquy is different from a typical monologue, which is intentionally communicated to another character or the audience, because there is an assumption of voyeurism—that the audience and/or other characters are witness to the character's private reflections.

Solipsistic Writing: Writing, usually in the first person voice, that is characterized by its representation of the subjective inner world of the speaker (or author). Solipsistic writing is sometimes criticized for its inherent exclusion of the reader's understanding from the limits of the text.

Sound Device: Technique in poetry which manipulates the aural quality of words and phrases in order to complement the communication of meaning and emotion.

Speculative: Text that is given to conjecture, abstract reasoning, imagination, and contemplation rather than fact.

Spenserian Sonnet: A variation on the English sonnet consisting of three quatrains and a concluding couplet with the unique rhyme scheme: abab bcbc cdcd ee.

Spoken Word: A (usually) solo performance delivered on stage of a piece of writing written from the author's point of view which appeals to the audience's emotions and empathy. Spoken word borrows from conventions of stand-up comedy, dramatic monologue, music, and poetry.

Stanza: Can be thought of as a paragraph in poetry. A stanza is a unified set of lines which are separated by a physical space on the page. Sometimes a stanza is determined by subject matter, and other times stanzas are in place for formal reasons (for example, to create a pause in the rhythm of a poem, or to move on to a varied rhyme scheme).

Storyboard: Illustrated graphic scene-by-scene representations of a screenplay developed in the imagination phase of filming.

Stream of Consciousness: Writing constantly whatever comes to mind without censoring oneself for a timed period.

Stressed Syllable: The syllables in a phrase which are naturally emphasized when spoken in everyday utterance.

Subhead: The secondary title appearing below the heading which elucidates the emphasis of the article. A subhead can also be the title of one section of a larger text.

Subtext: The nonverbal cues which undertone the explicit meaning in a literary text.

Subvert the Dominant Paradigm: Lawrence Ferlinghetti's philosophy of what good poetry does.

Symbol: A word or object in literature which figuratively denotes something more complex or essential to the meaning and tone of the text. A symbol needs to be generally recognizable to the reader in order to contribute to a deeper understanding of the text. For example: flowers are used as symbols in Shakespeare's *Hamlet* to denote Ophelia's psychological states, water is regarded as a symbol of clarity and purity, and a rollercoaster might be a symbol of extreme emotional highs and lows.

Synopsis: A page-long summary of the plot of a novel, screenplay, or other literary text written in engaging prose.

Syntax: The principles that govern the rules of grammar, linguistics, and the construction of sentences and phrases.

Tercet: Also known as a triplet, a tercet is a stanza of three lines in poetry.

Tertiary Research: Research derived from sources which collate information from secondary research, such as encyclopedias.

Thematic Question: The theme expounded in terms of a question which the characterization and plot seek to answer. For example: *Do single women in their thirties have a chance at finding true love in contemporary New York City?*

Theme: The central idea in a story which the characterization and plot development seek to examine. Themes can be described in both general terms (for example, *romantic love*) and in specific terms (for example, *finding romantic love in a big city*).

Thesis: The general point made in an essay, exegesis, or critique.

Thesis: The proposed premise of an argument or central point of discussion. The object of a dissertation is to rationally prove the validity of the thesis proposed in the introduction.

Thesis Statement: The proposed premise of an argument or central point of discussion posed in one clearly articulated sentence in the introduction of an essay, critique, or other scholarly document.

Third Person Voice: Narrative written from the point of view of a ubiquitous narrator who is external to the story. For example: *Barak put his sneakers on and walked down the street where he was shocked to discover his naked reflection in the barber shop window.*

Three-act Play: A longer play written and presented in three acts with a discernible rising action, climax, falling action, and denouement.

Tone: The overall dynamic mood or manner which characterizes a narrative.

Topic Sentence: A sentence which summarizes the central idea of the paragraph it introduces.

Transitions: In paragraphs, transitions are the phrases which lead from one point to the next. Transitions usually occur at the end of one paragraph to simultaneously conclude that paragraph and introduce the beginning of the next paragraph.

Treatment: A piece of prose which is a scene-by-scene first draft of a screenplay. The treatment is longer and more detailed than both the synopsis and the outline.

Verbal Communication: The use of language in its various forms to convey meaning.

Verbatim: Quoting a source word for word.

Villanelle: A poetic form consisting of five tercets and a concluding quatrain and a rhyme scheme, aba aba aba aba aba abaa. A villanelle also contains two repeated refrains, the first of which is introduced in the first line of the first stanza, and the second in the third line of the first stanza.

Voice: The unique complex characteristics of language use that helps to distinguish one author from another.

Writers' Block: The much-talked-about mythological state of being irrationally unable to write.

Works Cited

Books

Aristotle, *Poetics,* H. S. Butcher (trans.), Adelaide: ebooks@adelaide, 2012 [accessed July 12, 2013].

Beckett, Samuel, *Endgame* (New York: Grove Press, 1958), p. 1.

Caplan, David, *Questions of Possibility: Contemporary Poetry and Poetic Form,* Oxford: Oxford University Press, 2005

Dickens, Charles, *Great Expectations* (London: Penguin Books, 2012).

Dylan, Bob, *Chronicles: Volume One* (New York: Simon & Schuster, 2004), p. 7.

Ferlinghetti, Lawrence, *These Are My Rivers: New & Selected Poems 1955-1993* (New York: New Directions, 1994), p. 13.

Gadamer, Hans-Georg, *Truth and Method,* London: Bloomsbury Academic, 2013

Goodwin, K. L., *The Influence Of Ezra Pound* (Oxford: Oxford University Press, 1966), p. 3.

Heidegger, Martin, *Being and Time,* translated by Joan Stambaugh. Albany: State University of New York Press, 2010

Iser, Wolfgang, *The Act of Reading,* Baltimore: Johns Hopkins University Press, 1978

Kant, Immanuel, *Critique of Pure Reason (Unabridged edition),* Norman Kemp Smith (trans.) (New York: St Martin's Press, 1965), p. 41.

Kiedis, Anthony and Sloman, Larry, *Scar Tissue* (London: Time Warner Books, 2004), p. 57.

Langer, Susan, *Philosophy in a New Key: A study in the symbolism of Reason, Rite, and Art,* 3rd edn (Cambridge: Harvard University Press, 1957).

Lee, Harper, *To Kill a Mockingbird,* London: Mandarin Paperbacks, 1989

Marks, Dara, *Inside Story: The Power of the Transformational Arc* (London: A & C Black Publishers), 2009, p. 29

Mokhtari, Tara, *Lion!* (manuscript) (New York: 2013), p. 1.

Orwell, George, *Keep the Aspidistra Flying* (Florida: Harcourt Inc, 1956).

Orwell, George, Hobley Davison, Peter, and Ang, Ian, *Smothered Under Journalism: 1946* (London: Secker & Warburg, 1998), p. 316.

Plath, Sylvia, *The Bell Jar,* London: Faber and Faber, 2013

Plato, *The Republic*, Benjamin Jowlett (trans.), Adelaide: ebooks@adelaide, 2012 [accessed July 12, 2013].

Seth, Vikram, *The Golden Gate*, London: Faber and Faber, 1999

Trollinger, Vernon, *Haunted Iowa City* (Charleston: Haunted America, 2011), p. 80.

Villarosa, Clara (ed.), *The Words of African-American Heroes* (New York: Newmarket Press, 2011), p. 5.

Woolf, Virginia, *To The Lighthouse* (London: Urban Romantics, 2012), p. 98.

Short stories

Carlos Williams, William, "The Use of Force," in *The Doctor Series* (New York: New Directions, 1984), pp. 56–60.

Chekhov, Anton, "The Slander," in *The Horse Stealer and Other Stories* (New York: The MacMillan Company, 1921), pp. 221–8.

De Maupassant, Guy, "Confessing," in *The Hairpin and other Stories* (Whitefish: Kessinger Publishing, 2004), pp. 51–7.

Poems

Bukowski, Charles, "So you want to be a writer," in *Sifting through the madness for the Word, the line, the way* (New York: HarperCollins, 2009), p. 3.

Mokhtari, Tara, *Anxiety Soup* (Braidwood: Finlay Lloyd, 2013), p. 31.

— *Dear Allen Ginsberg* (manuscript) (New York: 2013).

Shakespeare, William, "130," in *Seven Centuries of Poetry in English*, 5th edn, John Leonard (ed.) (Oxford: Oxford University Press, 2003), p. 501.

Smith, Stevie, "Black March," in *Selected Poems*, James MacGibbon (ed.) (Middlesex: Penguin Books, 1978), p. 277.

Articles and chapters

Didion, Joan, "Why I Write," Bridgewater.edu, http://people.bridgewater. edu/~atrupe/ENG310/Didion.pdf, [accessed June 7, 2013].

Flood, Alison, "Philip Roth tells young writer 'don't do this to yourself'," in *The Guardian online edition* (UK: 16 November 2012) [accessed July 1, 2013].

Gladwell, Malcolm, "Complexity and the Ten-Thousand-Hour Rule," in *The New Yorker* online edition (New York: August 21, 2013), http://www. newyorker.com/online/blogs/sportingscene/2013/08/psychology-ten-thousand-hour-rule-complexity.html, [accessed December 21, 2013].

Hutchinson, George, "Harlem Renaissance," brittanica.com, http://www. britannica.com/EBchecked/topic/255397/Harlem-Renaissance/272827/ Poetry [accessed September 12, 2013].

Jack, Ian, "Memoirs are made of this – and that," in *The Guardian online edition*, (AU: February 8, 2003) [accessed 31 August 2013].

Orwell, George, "Why I Write," orwell.ru, http://orwell.ru/library/essays/wiw/ english/e_wiw> [accessed September 7, 2013].

Portuges, Paul, "The Poetics of Vision," in *On the Poetry of Allen Ginsberg*, Lewis Hyde (ed.) (Ann Arbor: University Of Michigan Press, 1984), p. 132.

Pound, Ezra, "A Retrospect," english.Illinois.edu, http://www.english.uiuc.edu/ maps/poets/m_r/pound/retrospect.htm [accessed September 9, 2013].

Todorov, Tzvetan, "Literary Genres," in *Twentieth-Century Literary Theory: An Introductory Anthology*, Vassilis Lambropoulos and David Neal Miller (eds) (Albany: State University of New York Press, 1987), p. 195.

Film and television

David, Larry and Seinfeld, Jerry, *The Seinfeld Chronicles – Pilot*, dir. Art Wolff (1989; Los Angeles: Giggling Goose Productions, Shapiro/West Productions, Castle Rock Entertainment, 1989), television.

Ephron, Nora, *When Harry Met Sally*, dir. Rob Reiner (1989; Los Angeles; Castle Rock Entertainment, Nelson Entertainment, 1989), film.

Heckerling, Amy, *Clueless*, dir. Amy Heckerling (1995; Los Angeles: Paramount Pictures, 1995), film.

Kogen, Jay and Wolodarsky, Wallace, "Last Exit to Springfield" *The Simpsons* (1993; Los Angeles: 20th Century Fox, 1993), television.

Lawton, J. F., *Pretty Woman*, dir. Garry Marshall (1990; Los Angeles: Touchstone Pictures/Silver Screen Partners IV), film.

Nolan, Christopher, *Inception*, dir. Christopher Nolan (2010; Los Angeles; Warner Bros, Legendary Pictures, Syncopy, 2010), DVD.

Starr, Darren, *Sex and the City*, dir. Susan Seidelman (1998; New York City; Darren Starr Productions, HBO, Rysher Entertainment, 1998), television.

Plays

Beckett, Samuel, *Endgame*, (1957; London: Royal Court Theatre), stage play.

Chekhov, Anton, *The Marriage Proposal* (1890; St Petersburg, Moscow), stage play.

Mokhtari, Tara, *A Tribute to Black*, dir. Soren Jensen (2001; Canberra: The Nineteenth Hole Productions), stage play.

—*Reverie Wreckage*, dir. Carol Woodrow (2002; Canberra: Free Rain Theatre Company), stage play.

Pinter, Harold, *The Dumb Waiter* (1960; London: Hampstead Theatre Club), stage play.

Theses

Mokhtari, Tara, *Representations of Death in the Poetry of Stevie Smith* (thesis) (Melbourne: Royal Melbourne Institute of Technology University, 2011).

Radio transcripts

Cox, Tony and Aamodt, Sandra, *Brain Maturity Extends Well Beyond Teen Years* (transcript: NPR), http://www.npr.org/templates/story/story.php?storyId=141164708 [accessed December 21, 2013].

Index